The Leonard Reed Story:
Brains as Well as Feet

by Bill Reed
Foreword by James Gavin

BearManor
Media

Albany, Georgia

PHOTO CREDITS: All photos are from the author's personal collection.

Published in the USA by
BearManor Media
P.O. Box 71426
Albany, GA 31708
www.BearManorMedia.com

ISBN: 1-59393-815-2

Printed in the United States of America

The Leonard Reed Story: Brains as Well as Feet

by Bill Reed

Foreword by James Gavin

Table of Contents

Acknowledgments

THE VENERATED LITERARY AGENT, JULIAN BACH, WHOSE INITIAL enthusiasm propelled the writing of this book. Author James Gavin, who read this manuscript quite some time ago and who, from time to time, urged me to "do something with it." (Thanks for the Foreword, too, James.) My good friend and constant traveling companion, David Ehrenstein, who looked over my shoulder and offered invaluable suggestions while I was writing the book. BearManor Media publisher, Ben Ohmart, whose initial enthusiasm for this book was so fast that it engendered whiplash. David W. Menefee, my editor, whose sensitivity to this material moved me to near-tears on more than one occasion. And all of my many "teachers," who instructed me in the history of both Black and White show biz. These include—just for starters—Fayard Nicholas, Frances Nealy (to whom this book is dedicated), Herb Jeffies, Ernestine Lucas (of The Whitman Sisters family), Frances E. Williams, Barbara Reed, Kurt Reichenbach, and, of course, Leonard.

Dedicated to the memory of Frances Nealy

Foreword
by James Gavin

WITH NEARLY ALL THE EYEWITNESSES TO A GRAND ERA OF 1920S AND 1930s Black show business now gone, the stories live on only second-hand, through printed and recorded interviews. Now, out of a mist of forgotten history, leaps one of that period's shrewdest, saltiest participants. Leonard Reed, who died in 2004 at the age of 97, was not a household word. A onetime tap-dancer and Vaudevillian, Reed had segued into the role of impresario; he was probably best-known as a longtime manager of the Apollo Theatre.

In 1985, pop-music historian Bill Reed (no relation) approached him with a tape recorder and some questions. Leonard saw the microphone as a spotlight and he performed. Out tumbled the story that fills this exciting book—one that deserves a place alongside Chris Albertson's *Bessie*, Ethel Waters's *His Eye Is on the Sparrow*, and Bobby Short's *Black and White*

Baby. Like them, *The Leonard Reed Story: Brains as Well as Feet*, is set in an age when Black entertainers literally risked their lives to do what they loved to do. Reed saw it all: the tent shows down South; the brazen, beleaguered women of the Blues; the gangsters, thugs, and speakeasies; the Chitlin' Circuit; the carefree sexual hijinks. To add to the glitter, Bill Reed's book has an eye-popping array of star cameos and portraits of obscure but delightful characters, who are worth remembering.

Leonard Reed was eye-catching in his own right—an over-the-top natty dresser, slick, and light-skinned enough "to pass." Certainly he knew the racial prejudice inside his own community, as well as in the world beyond. But hard as it was for an African-American of his day to survive, Reed had an unstoppable flair for fun and thrived on mayhem. Were the participants in his stories alive, they would no doubt recall some things differently. Reed was, after all, an entertainer, and he knew how to spin a seductive (and self-aggrandizing) tale.

But whatever the exaggerations may be, he's now getting the last word, and the spirit of his life and times comes through with indisputable vividness. Bill Reed has woven in his own valuable historical narrative. As you turn the pages, you'll feel as though you were there.

[James Gavin's books include *Stormy Weather: The Life of Lena Horne* and *Is That All There Is?: The Strange Life of Peggy Lee*.]

Introduction

Leonard Reed was born in 1907. In his adolescence, he was swept up into the romantic world of live performing: carnivals, minstrel shows, medicine shows, Vaudeville, and the legitimate theater. When he entered show business in 1915, traveling tent shows and carnivals were still in full sway. Reed soon gravitated to more sophisticated realms, but his career was based almost exclusively on "live" performance. It is somehow fitting that when Reed managed the Apollo Theater in Harlem during the 1950s—perhaps the last theater in the United States to present stage shows on a regular basis—he was also presiding over Vaudeville's final rites.

The Apollo struggled on for a few more years as a live showcase after Reed left in 1960, but he rolled on. When this book was completed in 1990 when Reed was eighty-three, he was celebrating more than seventy years in show business as a dancer, producer, comic, songwriter, choreographer, librettist, and manager.

Until the 1950s, with the rare exception of such entertainers as Bill "Bojangles" Robinson and Duke Ellington, the world of Black show business was almost entirely segregated from that of White show business. Fair, with delicate features, Reed managed to troupe and tap his way through both worlds as the situations demanded. If work was available as a barker with a traveling carnival and it was expedient to do so, he "passed" for White. If the action was with an all-Black revue in Chicago as, for example, those he worked with as a choreographer and dancer in the 1920s, then you'd find him there, as well.

I met Leonard in the summer of 1985 while looking for people to talk about Dinah Washington, about whom I was thinking of writing a book. My friend, dancer Fayard Nicholas, suggested, "Call Leonard Reed. He worked with her early in her career." I set up an appointment to talk with him.

Reed was then operating out of quarters in a ten-story Hollywood office building owned by Scientologists, one occupied mostly by fringe entertainment industry types, including two-bit talent agencies, scuffling record promoters, and exploitation movie producers . . . all just a scream away from downtown Rape at High Noon (musician Van Dyke Parks' terminology). I can still recall the two bumper sticker-style signs over his desk. One read: "He who ends the day with the most unreturned phone calls wins"; the other: "PLAN AHEAd," with the "d" running off the right end of the signage due to the unplanned-for lack of space.

The man still had class. Impeccably groomed in a manner typical of show business veterans, Reed finished working with his last student for the day, and began to tell me about Dinah Washington: how he'd given the singer one of her first professional jobs at Chicago's Regal Theater in the late 1930s; how he was "the first one to teach her, the first one to say, 'Here's what you do, here's how to walk on stage, here's how to walk off.'" Possessing just enough Black blood to have made things terribly difficult for someone born in racist America at nearly the turn of the century, the very light-skinned Reed had to shoulder the burden of being a member of both races. "However," he joked, with more than a trace of irony and bitterness, "I always knew what I was in Mississippi."

After my first meeting with Reed, I sensed that here was a kind of "Don Juan and the Show Business Way of Knowledge." I wanted to hear as much of his own story as he was willing to tell.

Reed perhaps sensed this; for leaving office that first afternoon, he called after me, "Do you have a place to hangout?" (He might just as well have added "kid.")

"No," I said.

"Well, you do now!" he shouted as the elevator doors sprang closed.

The next time I went to his office, it wasn't so much to talk of Dinah Washington but about Reed and this show business in which he had been such a major player. As the weeks wore on, I was hit with stories that jumped all over the chronological map and spanned the globe. One moment he was in Paris in the 1950s performing on the same stage as Edith Piaf; the next he'd leapt back in time to 1920, galloping across the Oklahoma landscape in a medicine show wagon pulled by wild horses just like in the movies, with Reed performing from the back of the wagon with his partner, Crackaloo, while a Fieldsian character by the name of Doc Clark conned the locals out of their last few pennies by selling them a patent medicine of turpentine and sugar. Another day, he quantum-leaped forward three decades in time to the Apollo Theater in the 1950s. For months, through all of it, there was never a thought of getting it down on paper, just a desire on my part to hear recalled first-hand what it was like producing shows at the Cotton Club; working for Al Capone at the Grand Terrace in Chicago; and, of course, acting for many years as a theatrical straight man, golfing partner, and *aide-de-camp* to Joe Louis. Reed's last major show biz outing was working with producer David Merrick on a production of the Gershwin's *Oh, Kay!* in 1990.

In 1992, I was co-curator of an exhibit at the California Afro-American Museum about Black Hollywood in the 1940s. Part of the show was devoted to Reed's activities as a producer-choreographer on

Central Avenue, Los Angeles' fabled entertainment strip. In the course of working on "Hollywood Days/Harlem Nights," I interviewed a number of old-timers, African-American entertainment professionals and "civilians" alike. Invariably I was told that Reed was a "very famous man in his time" who had performed "everywhere." However, he was thought by many I spoke with to be no longer among the living, which wasn't so surprising when you consider he had managed to outlive nearly every one of his contemporaries. Moreover, premature reports of his death had already begun to circulate nearly a half-century earlier due to a serious auto accident. (Reed eventually died in 2004.)

Starting in 1985, I began tape recording an oral history of Reed. This consisted of many dozens of hours of conversations which I have now (at last) cobbled into narrative for a memoir.

Lo these many years later, here is *The Leonard Reed Story: Brains As Well As Feet*. I hope when you've finished reading it, you'll think it was worth the wait.

PART ONE

A Helluva Life

CHAPTER ONE
Where the Wind Comes Sweepin' . . . .

YOU DIDN'T HAVE TO TRY TOO HARD TO GET LEONARD REED TO SUPPLY you with details about his past. As for the actual year he was born, "Your guess is as good as mine," he once told me. "It was January 7, somewhere between 1906 to 1909." He didn't know for sure because birth records for Blacks and Indians weren't generally kept back then. "I usually stick with 1907," he laughed, "because that seems old enough for anybody."

Reed was born on an Indian reservation in Lightning Creek, Oklahoma in either Oklahoma, or what was once Oklahoma territory . . . depending on the year of his birth. If 1907 is correct, then Reed came into the world before Oklahoma was even granted statehood, and right after Native Americans were finally granted U.S. citizenship in 1906. He was born at nearly the turn of the century in a teepee: "Most people find that hard to believe, but I don't just make these things up."

1

The frame house that Reed's mother lived in with her own mother and grandmother was a half-mile from a Cherokee reservation. A few weeks before she was due to give birth, she visited her great grandmother (a full Choctaw, who had married a part-Black part-Cherokee), when she went into early labor. The upshot was that Reed was delivered by a tribal midwife, while all around the fur and animal skin teepee, Indians announced his birth by circling the dwelling, he was later told, in a frenzy of ceremonial dancing. "You can tell just by looking at me that my dad was White," said Reed. Although he possessed a photo of his father, he never met the man, and had only a single memory of his mother from shortly after her death, when he was two. "They put nickels on her eyes to close them, and I remember her face from trying, like any child would, to reach down into the coffin and grab at the bright shiny coins."

"The first time I became aware that my life was destined to be complicated by my Black ancestry was around 1920," recalled Reed. "I was thirteen or fourteen and working in a carnival in Enid, Oklahoma. All the Black comedians were on stage, and the Black girls were up there, too, singing and dancing. And just then, this White woman—one of those people in every town, who came around to see if the show was 'moral'—snatched me right off the stage. She thought I was White! She said, 'Get down from there with them niggers! Don't ever let me catch you up there again with 'em 'cause I'll spank you till you can't sit down.' So, I went and put on enough cork to pass for Black, and that's how I got back on stage."

The Oklahoma social worker's reaction was typical of a time when racial integration on the American stage was still a touchy issue. Minstrel shows sometimes featured both races, but always in segregated scenes, and the great African-American comic, Bert Williams, had begun appearing in the *Ziegfeld Follies* starting in 1911. Some Broadway musicals and revues featured fully integrated casts, notably *The Southerners* in 1904, but in provincial America, the color line between Blacks and Whites behind the footlights was still strictly observed. In 1920, with the exception of

Williams, the stars of Vaudeville and the Broadway stage (Eve Tanguay, Ed Wynn, Irene Franklin, Leon Errol, et al) were all White.

Given Reed's fair complexion and wavy hair, the Oklahoma do-gooder's assumption and shock are understandable. The mere fact that eight-year-old Reed was on stage at all was bad enough; this was the period when association with show business brought with it the kind of second-class citizenship normally reserved for Blacks. Signs in boarding houses across the country still proclaimed "No Actors or Animals Allowed." Nearly every major city contained representatives of the Geary Society, an organization formed to protect minors from the evils of working on stage. Posted notices warning Blacks to remain segregated were common, especially throughout Southern and Midwestern White America. Whites crossing over into Black territory was equally taboo ... especially when it came to young White boys cutting up on stage with a bunch of ragtag Negro entertainers. However, public notices directed against racial interaction never meant much to Reed as a boy; he just considered himself to be somewhat above it all.

On his mother's side, a great-great-grandmother and great-grandfather were Choctaw and Negro. Reed's grandmother on his mother's side was Indian and his grandfather was half-Black and half-Creek, thus making his mother a four-way mix of Black, Creek, Choctaw, and Cherokee. Choctaws had been slave owners, and his paternal great-great-grandparents were descended from unions between slaves and their masters. The Oklahoma of Reed's boyhood was still wide open wild west territory. For him, entertainment meant doing things like hoisting himself up into trees and knocking possums off their branches.

He recalled, "Possum and sweet potatoes, that's what we usually had on Thanksgiving and the other holidays. It's something you did in the dead of night as a two-person operation. The possum hangs on the limb sleeping, and one of you creeps out and shoves him off, while your partner stands below with a gunny sack and catches him."

Lightning Creek, where Reed was born, was adjacent to the village of Hayden, but neither site exists any longer on the Oklahoma map. Both were near Nowata, now a populous area fifty miles north of Tulsa. Lightning Creek, Hayden, and all the other little dots on the map had come into being because of a trading post that was established a short while after the Cherokees sold land in the area to Delaware Indians of Kansas in the mid-nineteenth century. Soon the town of Noweta, as its name was originally spelled, grew up around the post. When the railroad was built through the area in 1895, two company surveyors are said to have named it Noweta at the suggestion of a Cherokee woman who said that the word meant "We welcome you to come." Later, the spelling was changed to Nowata because of a post office error.

Reed retains the memory of his mother at her funeral when he was two, but he never met his father, a White peddler, who sold blankets and whiskey to the Indians. Major Reed had not been married to Leonard's mother, Sarah Landrum, when the boy was born, which might have been overlooked by the Indian community, since sexual relations between Native Americans and Blacks, Chinese and Whites, were a fairly common occurrence at the time. The real problem was that Major Reed was unable to wed Leonard's mother because he was already married to Sarah's sister, Helen.

When both women became pregnant by Major Reed, he was run off by tribal elders and forbidden to return to the territory. Helen went with him, and the couple settled in California. Had it not been for the existence of the Black press, Reed would probably never have met any of the half-brothers and half-sisters she subsequently had by Major Reed. Daily newspapers, such as the *Chicago Defender* and the *Pittsburgh Courier*, were read regularly, not just locally but nationally by hundreds of thousands of Black Americans. Reed's social and professional activities in the 1930s were charted by these and other periodicals on an almost daily basis, and it was through reading these stories in the Black press that

Sarah Landrum, mother of Leonard Reed.

siblings, of whose existence he'd only been vaguely aware up until then, were able to get in touch with Reed for the first time.

In 1992, Reed's half-sister, Hermie Reed (now Crowder), was cheerfully philosophical about Reed's writing about what some might consider their somewhat shocking family background:

"We're just about the only ones left, I guess, so it doesn't matter now who knows about all of it. Besides, these kind of mixed up situations were, unfortunately, fairly common with Blacks back then. Everything Leonard says about my father also being his father is true. One thing I don't believe I ever told Leonard is that one time as a little girl living in California in the early 1920s, a friend of mine came back from a basketball tournament in Kansas and said he'd seen a fellow who I'm sure must have been Leonard, who looked just like me and did I have any brothers living in Kansas City? I told him 'no,' but then later on I asked my mother about it. She just waved me away, but when I was in my teens she told me all the truth about my father having children by her sister as well. Till the day he died, my older brother Harvey denied Leonard was related to us. However, Harvey was very strange, kept to himself, and was thought of as an odd duck by just about everyone who knew him."

Children of mixed parentage, such as Reed and his kin, tended to be only partially accepted by Indians, who were generally unwilling to identify with Blacks, and such offspring found themselves shunned by Whites, as well. Many sections of the country even had their own epithets for such racial outcasts. In South Carolina, they were called "Brass Ankles" in New York; "Jackson Whites in New Jersey; "Melungeons" in Tennessee; "Red Bones" in Louisiana. Reed's early years were so migratory and multicultural that he had little sense of racial identity, or even the concept of race. Those taking care of him were also of a variety of backgrounds, and for a while, Reed was entirely unaware of the concept of race and merely surmised that everyone in the world simply possessed their own unique skin tone.

After his mother's death, Reed lived in Hayden with his Indian grandmother for two years. She became too old to take care of him, however, and he was soon launched on a ten-year odyssey of being passed from one household to the next. At first, the households were in the general vicinity of the reservation. There were the Montgomerys, distant relatives of his grandfather, who were Black. After that came the Statlers, White and unrelated. Both families lived in Nowata. In addition, there were probably several other caregivers, whom Reed has since forgotten.

Passed from family to family, Reed finally began to be aware of racial differences. Whites who took care of him treated him as White, but he overheard racist remarks about himself and others and grew confused, especially after he would then be shunted off to live with Blacks and saw first-hand how badly they were treated by Whites. This was especially true when Reed went to live with mixed-race husband and wife, Bob and Ella Taylor, who would become his foster parents for nearly five years.

Reed was subject to continual beatings inflicted by Bob Taylor, which caused him to run away from home almost every time the opportunity presented itself. The Taylors moved around the Midwest on a fairly regular basis, seldom remaining in one place for any length of time, and the nomadic lifestyle only served to boost the frequency of these attempts to escape from his sadistic foster parent.

The lore of passing runs deep in Black culture. In singer Bobby Short's autobiography, *Black and White Baby*, he writes of a friend light enough to pass: "He was what colored folks called a 'Mey-rye-nee.' The word is Negro slang, and I'm spelling it phonetically because I've never seen it written down, but old-timers explain it as a derivation of 'Merino,' a breed of sheep with thick curly coats. Another long-gone expression that my brother Bill used to use was: 'Three-quarters Kelt with molly-gloss hair,' which meant a colored person with fair skin and light hair. 'Kelt' was Negro slang for a White person, and the 'Molly' in molly-gloss has some sort of Scotch-Irish connotation."

Throughout his life, Reed would have to struggle with the "problem" of being a very light-skinned Black. However, even as a six-year-old, he was discovering that this seeming conundrum also had an advantage. He would go to the White section of nearby Hayden where Bob Taylor or any other Black man would not be able to pursue him. When he reached the forbidden zone, he would then "meet a little White boy and play with him. He'd ask where I lived; I'd tell him my mother and father were dead."

By the time Reed got to the fanciful part about how he came from Coffeeville, Kansas with "a guy in a wagon," he had his new friend eating out of his hand. "Well, c'mon and stay with us. I'll tell my mother and father." Blacks didn't dare go over into White sections to try and find Reed. It sometimes took Bob Taylor weeks and weeks to catch up with him. When it finally happened, it was usually because of Reed's carelessness. On several occasions, his downfall proved to be going down to watch the trains come in on Sunday. It's something that everybody did. Whites on one side of the tracks, Blacks on the other. More than once, Reed forgot and stood on the Black side, and that's how they caught him.

"Even my beginnings in the field in 1915 were somewhat impressive," Reed told me early on in our friendship. "My first job on stage was with none other than the man who practically invented modern show business, the great Billy McClain." Twenty years before Reed went to work for him, comic-entrepreneur Billy McClain had produced the phenomenally successful outdoor musical, *Black America*. Performed throughout the summer of 1895 at Brooklyn's Ambrose Park (the earlier site of Buffalo Bill's Wild West Show), the extravaganza featured a cast of over 500 African-American entertainers, including ex-slaves, and veterans from both the U.S. Ninth Cavalry and from the many dozens of *Uncle Tom's Cabin* troupes prevalent at the time. They were then turned loose to do their thing in the park, which had been transformed into an "authentic" Southern plantation, replete with a working cotton gin, poultry, livestock, and log cabins (used also as living quarters for the company). Audiences—mostly White—came from miles around (many by ferry from Manhattan) to spend the day walking through the environmental set and then to see a show performed by the cast in a huge outdoor amphitheater. This extravagant, now forgotten, forerunner of everything from David Belasco's *The Girl of the Golden West* on down to the latter-day *Tamara* played to tens of thousands in the summer of 1895, and had as its music director none other than Victor Herbert.

By 1915, however, the showman was reduced to operating on a much smaller scale with a twenty-member cast performing a traditional revue in a tent in Kansas City (he was also the owner of the somewhat notorious Yellow Front Cafe there). Here's how Reed's association with this fascinating footnote to African-American show business came about: In 1918, nearly six years after foster parents Bob and Ella Taylor had taken Reed in, and despite constant attempts to run away from them because of Bob Taylor's corporal sadism, the boy was still with the couple. After WWI began in 1914, the three had moved from Nowata to Pittsburg, Kansas. After yet another relocation back to Nowata in 1917, just prior to the end of the war, their wanderings took them to Kansas City, Missouri, where area cattlemen and farmers with money to burn retreated after traditionally long seasons of hard work. This thriving crossroads was also where Jazz made one of its first stops on its way up the river from New Orleans, coincidentally at just about the time that Bob and Ella Taylor, with ten-year-old Leonard Reed, also reached there. A few years later, Reed got swept up in Kansas City nightlife, but for a ten-year-old boy, this was still a time for going to school and helping Bob Taylor earn a living assisting him with odd jobs in a wealthy district of the town known as the Country Club (although it was not an actual club).

Kansas City was a good town for traveling shows, and when Reed was finished helping out Taylor, he moonlighted as a soda-pop boy for the attractions that came through town. The money wasn't all that great, but at least he got to see a free show. Because Reed was small for his age, he could only carry six or seven bottles at a time, but he made up for his slight stature with a good strong barker's voice. "Popcorn! Peanuts,

Candy, Soda Pop," he'd shout out loud enough to be easily heard above the din of most crowds. This aggressiveness paid off in something more than extra profits when, in the summer of 1917, he actually got a chance to work at *Billy McClain's Yellow Front* tent show. He'd only been working as a vendor for a day or two when his over-the-top style caught McClain's attention. He gave Reed a bit part in the show.

The routine went something like this:

A comic in McClain's show by the name of Buzzin' Harris came on stage, did a little bit of shtick, and then was followed on by a woman pushing a baby carriage. Per the custom of the times, both Harris and his foil, both dark-skinned to begin with, were made even darker by the application of burnt cork (the idea was to lend them the same look as White minstrel players, who also corked up).

The woman then accuses Harris of being the father of the child. He insists, however, "It's not my baby. This can't be my baby. It's gotta be the saxophone player's baby." They'd shine a spot on this musician, who happened to be very light-skinned. Harris would then say, "This is not my baby. Take a look."

And up White-appearing Reed would pop out of the baby carriage. Blackout.

CHAPTER TWO

A Last Minute Reprieve

"Every night on stage with Billy McClain's revue, I'd put my bucket of soda down just before the bit started, go backstage, and get in the baby carriage.

"McClain's tent show was a permanent setup, and I got to do several other bits whenever they needed kids. Kansas City 1918 was also a time for pranks. The other boys and I called ourselves the 'Flashlight Gang' because we used to go to the ten-cent store and steal flashlights. We'd hide under the house and flash the lights, and that was a signal for the others to come running. There were two Sunday morning hustles we had. In those days, they used to put milk bottle empties out on the front porch and leave money in them for the milk man. We had a real smooth way of putting our hand over the bottle and quickly turning it up so the money would fall out, but you couldn't hear it. An hour or so later, the milk man would leave the milk, and we'd snatch a bottle to go with the bread we'd already stolen from the local bakery. Then we'd filch newspapers and stand in front of the churches, and when they let out, we'd sell folks newspapers.

"To thwart us, the *Kansas City Star* soon switched to a 'Home Edition' meant specifically for delivery to homes. So, for a while, I decided to get my papers legally and sell them in front of K.C's Biltmore Hotel. However, even when I went straight, Bob Taylor continued to beat me. Today, he would be put away for child abuse for what he did. He was Black and because I was so light-skinned, he used me as an outlet for his hostilities toward Whites. 'Get just like you came into the world,' he'd command. I'd take off all my clothes. Then he'd put my head between his legs, hold my hands up behind me, and beat the tar out of me with a razor strap.

"The beatings were usually for doing things like going to the park when I was told not to, coming in late, or if the teacher said I wasn't paying attention. Not that I was exactly an angel. We'd do things like go to the dime store and slide rings on our fingers and then put our hands in our mouths, then take them out and leave the store with the rings in our mouths. That sort of thing.

"However, the harshness of the punishment seldom fit the crime. Admittedly, a few times found me pushing things a bit. Like my gang going out of our neighborhood and stealing bicycles and reassembling them when we got back so you couldn't tell they were stolen. Could put a bike together as good as any a mechanic could pull a car together so you'd never recognize it in a million years.

"We had started to hang around the baseball park, and when a sport drove up in a big car to go to the game, we'd offer to look after it for a nominal fee: 'Watch your car, mister?' It was nothing more than a kind of protection racket, and sometimes we'd drive the car around town until

12

Reed with caretakers, Bob and Ella Taylor

the game was over. Then one day, we made the mistake of driving all
the way to Kansas City. There was a traffic jam on the Missouri River,
and the drawbridge stayed up for a long, long while, and we couldn't get
back by the time the game was over, so we had to keep the car. We put
it in my friend Preston Kelly's old barn. Then when the sun would go
down, we'd get it and ride around to girls' houses and show off. This went

13

"BILLIE" M'CLAIN.

Showman Billy McClain

on for weeks until, one night, the law pulled us over. That got me sent off to Beck's Boys Home. I feared the worst there, but the life at Beck's consisted mostly of playing baseball and basketball and swimming all afternoon after a morning of tending the corn, okra, and tomatoes in the vegetable garden. They even gave me the chance at Beck's to put into practice what I'd learned and observed from watching Billy McClain's and other people's revues where I'd been a soda pop boy. The home was going to stage a show, and I was to be the producer. Gathering up a bunch of old rags for costumes, pulling together a bunch of chairs and tables for sets, and copying some of the routines I'd seen, the show was a big hit.

"The few months spent at Beck's gave the welts that Taylor inflicted a chance to heal over for the first time. That, plus all the good times we had at the home, made me almost want to not leave; and as the end of my term drew hear, I became more determined than ever to place some distance between Bob Taylor and myself.

"Putting on that stage show at Beck's had given me the idea of cooking up a sort of act with my buddy, Orlando Robeson, who was later with the vocal group, The Ink Spots. When school let out for the summer of 1919, we ran off and hitched up with the carnival circuit. The bit went like this: the emcee would call me 'Jim Jeffries,' and then he'd summon Orlando out of the crowd and call him 'Jack Johnson,' and we'd improvise an imaginary bout between the two of them. In 1910, Johnson was the first Black World Heavyweight Boxing Champion when he beat James L. Jeffries, and almost a decade later, White America had still not gotten over it; it was a Black against White thing. We'd get to see the carnival free for doing this. People would throw money in the ring, and part of the fun for the crowd was the both of us trying to pick it up with the gloves on. As one of us stooped to pick up the money, the other would beat him up, and that's what they laughed about. Orlando would hold up his hand and I'd hit him. He'd roll over, and I'd pick up money. Then he'd hit me, and I'd roll over. We had it down to a science, and roamed all over the Midwest that summer. We never traveled with the carnival when it pulled up stakes; we just hopped a freight train to catch up with it, or to move on to another outfit.

"The next summer, Orlando and I took off again, and this time we were joined by our other buddies, Lemuel Edwards and Bob Weston. We were hoboing on the Rock Island Line. My having had enough of Taylor's beatings, we all decided, for one reason or another, to head for California. Maybe I'd even stay away for good.

"However, we didn't get very far before running into trouble in Lawrence, Kansas, exactly twenty-seven miles from home. Dumb as we were, we stashed ourselves in the cattle car, and the railroad dicks came through the yard with the lanterns and one of them saw us. He stood at the end of the car. There was an opening about three by three feet, and he said, "Out this way." As we came out, he whacked us across the butt. I ran across the tracks and fell into a moving turntable used for turning train engines around and was scared to death. I thought I was dead. "As it turned out, it was only two or three feet deep. The two of us went all the way around and headed back in the direction we came from. We were going to get back on the train. However, the railroad dicks caught up with all four of us.

"The two Black boys, Lemuel and Bob, took a bad beating, but Orlando, who looked Mexican, and I got off easy; we were run off and warned not to get caught again. As soon as the train pulled out, we were back in business. Hopped right back on the train, which was carrying a furnace with a label that said it was being sent to Denver, Colorado.

"'Hey,' Orlando said to me, 'we can stay on this and go all the way to Colorado.' We crawled inside a car and hid. However, in Topeka, Orlando was smoking a cigarette, which drew attention to us. The dicks kept banging on the door that was locked from the inside, and finally they had to take off the door to get us out. We ended up at a detention home, where the windows had bars not much wider than pencils. On the second day there, we were able to take slats out of the bed, wedge them in between the bars, and bend them back and forth until there was enough room to escape. It was about two or three in the morning, and after running a little distance, we slept in a stack of wheat. In the morning, we woke up with bites all over us where the field mice had nibbled on us all night.

"We hopped aboard the next westbound train, still hoping to go to California, and rode for sixty or seventy miles till we got to Hutchinson, Kansas. Starving, we hopped off, looked around, and saw a sign for a carnival. However, there was a more immediate problem. It had been nearly twenty-four hours since we'd eaten. Walking down a railroad track, we come to a handcar, where some Mexicans working a quarter-mile on down the line had stowed their lunches. Orlando and I snatched up an armload of lunch and took off running, but almost immediately the workers spotted us. We ran, then dropped the pails, which were slowing us down, spotted a barn, ducked into it, and tried to get lost in a haystack. However, the railroad cops, who were now also in on the chase, caught us by jamming pitchforks into the hay, and for the second time in twenty-four hours we found ourselves in jail.

"Orlando and I cooked up a tall tale. We told them our mothers and fathers were dead and we were trying to get to California to find our relatives. They ordered us to sit there while they sent messages, and so we sat there for at least an hour and a half. We weren't locked up or anything and could roam around freely, even out into the street. Guess they thought we were too scared to escape.

"Outside was where we were when I suddenly turned to Orlando and said, 'What in the hell are we doing? Let's get out of here.' And we did. It was as easy as that. This time we didn't even bother to run; we just walked away. I'm still an escaped jailbird from Topeka, Kansas.

"We soon met up with a carnival, joined it, and boxed in every town they went to. We'd had such a rough time of it freelancing that we remained with the troupe rather than riding the rails on our own. We traveled all over Oklahoma: Harrington, Atcheson, Texoma, Enid, all those little towns. By then, Orlando and I had given up on the California dream. However, when summer came to an end, it was kind of tough getting back into the swing of things in Kansas City. Too keyed up to sit

Reed with adoptive brother Hartwell Cook

behind a school desk, I played hooky the first few days of the fall term in school. Besides, I just couldn't face up to what Bob Taylor had to dish out. Instead of going home, I made straight for my friend Lemuel's house.

Lemuel was a little older than us (he was a junior and we were freshmen), and, best of all, he knew ways of getting gin.

"We were in Lem's house drinking and trading off girls, when we made the mistake of getting too high and noisy. The people next door called the truant officer, and that's when we got arrested.

"The following Tuesday found me hauled into court before a notorious hanging judge. I'd been warned beforehand that whenever this Judge Porterfield took off his glasses and tapped his nose it meant an automatic four years in Booneville prison. I was the last one to come up before him. All the others of the gang got probation because their folks came to court with them, and I told him to just go ahead and send me away. With no intention of going back and living with the Taylors, I told Porterfield that I had no family and was an orphan. Well, sure enough, the glasses came off, the finger started tapping the nose, and he barked out something to me that contained the word 'Booneville' and I got sent back to the detention home to wait. The following Tuesday, they came to get me, but I wasn't hauled off to Booneville. Once again before Judge Porterfield., this time not only were the Taylors there, but also my high school principal, Mr. Hugh Cook.

Gesturing toward the Taylors, Porterfield looked down at me and asked why I'd lied about having no parents. Even then I must have had a flair for the dramatic. I hadn't planned it in advance, but approaching the bench, I whipped off my shirt so that the judge and my school principal could see firsthand the bruises and welts that Bob Taylor had given me. Even though he hadn't had the chance to beat me for a couple of months—I was off with the carnivals—it was still so bad that a gasp filled the courtroom, and all eyes turned toward Taylor and his wife.

"Right there on the spot, my school principal, Hugh Cook, stepped forward and told the judge that if I was set free he would be responsible for me. He also warned Taylor about what he'd do to him if he ever laid a hand on me again. In what turned out to be the turning point in my life,

Porterfield bound me over to Cook's custody. I went off to live with him, his wife and his two sons, Hartwell and Hugh, Jr.

"It was a close call. I still think about what might have become of me were it not for taking off my shirt and showing the judge the results of Bob Taylor's beatings. It was almost like a fairy tale. Overnight, I became a member of one of the most prominent Black families in America. Both of Hugh Cook's parents were graduates of Oberlin College. His father, John Hartwell Cook, after getting his law degree from Howard University in 1871, became a professor and first dean of the law department at the school. John Cook was also the first practicing Black lawyer in Washington, D.C. One of Hugh Cook's brothers was the famous Broadway composer, Will Marion Cook.

"My new dad called me 'Beau' and would say things to me like, 'Beau, now this is your opportunity to become something. An education is very important and, here you're going to get one. However, if you miss one day of school, if you leave and go away and stay, you don't come back. You can't leave here and come back the day after tomorrow and say you still live here. Because once you leave, you don't live here anymore. You're on probation for four years. If you miss one day living here, you go to Booneville.'

"And that was that! It was now or never. Definitely didn't want to go to Booneville. Besides, Cook was nice to me, the man's wife was nice to me, and their son Hugh and I fit like brothers (the Cooks' other son, Harty, was away at college). Living with the Cooks was highly regimented . . . a new experience for me. Had to get up at a certain time, make my bed, and arrive at school, all on schedule. I could ride with Mr. Cook to school if I'd gotten all the chores done, or else walk. It was five miles to school, and a lot of times I wasn't ready on time and had to walk, or hop a truck or wagon. I had to get to school on time, because being the principal's son, you couldn't afford to walk in late.

Living with the Cooks, I began to channel all that anger, bitterness, and energy into other directions. Cook's son played saxophone in the school band and he wanted me to be in it, too. I took up clarinet, but wasn't very good. I'd hit a bad note, and look back at the kid behind me to make it look like he'd done it. 'If you look back one more time,' he'd threaten me, 'I'm gonna break your goddamn head with this clarinet.' I didn't look over my shoulder any more. I learned well enough to play the music of the time. Staying in the band one more year, after that I really didn't play much anymore, for by then I'd really begun to catch the dancing bug. A fellow named Herp Wilson, who used to play the piano at house parties and little affairs, taught me how to play the Blues. When he took a rest break I'd play. Not very good at piano either, still I played well enough for people to dance to.

"Pretty good at picking up the latest dance steps, one weekend I decided to enter a Charleston contest at the Orpheum Theater. Even though Blacks weren't allowed to enter, I did it anyhow. Except for the ushers, the theater didn't even allow any "coloreds" on the main floor of the theater; they had to go upstairs to the balcony to see the show. The preliminaries of the contest were Monday through Saturday, with the finals on Sunday. I won first prize on Monday, $15. The big prize the next Sunday was $50, which was a tot of money back then. Not wanting them to come and see me, I didn't tell anyone at school about winning the first go-round. I wanted to win that money and was banking on none of my Black schoolmates getting wind of what was going on! "Unfortunately, a couple of Black ushers told some of my friends from school, and come Sunday, the balcony was filled with my classmates. To make matters worse, one of the ushers even told the owner about my being Black. He didn't stop me from dancing, though, because he didn't think there was a chance of my winning. The theater balcony turned out to be full of Blacks from Lincoln High after all, and it was an advantage after all. I danced. Did that Charleston and the entire theater, led by the balcony, went wild. Afterward, the owner called us all backstage, and he had this black box full of money. He opened it, but paid everybody off but me."

"'You wait. Wait right here,' he said."

"He went away for a minute, presumably to get the police, and while he was gone I just grabbed all the money and put it in my pocket and ran out or the stage door at the side just as the crowd was letting out. The owner spotted me and started running after me.

"'Catch that nigger,' he yelled."

"I just echoed his call, 'Catch that nigger, catch that nigger!'"

"'Where? Where?' the people coming out of the theater all wondered, as I flew past them."

"I pointed ahead of me at an imaginary person. 'There! There! He's got the money! He went that way!'"

"You never saw such a commotion. They were all chasing this 'nigger' and they just ran right past me.

"So, as you can see, as much as some things had changed living with H. O. Cook and his family, that's how much other things remained the same.

"Aside from music and dancing, there were also sports. Very dumb until basketball season came, then I was very smart. I couldn't play if my grades weren't above average, but thought I could fool my old man. Lying on the floor appearing to do my homework, I was really sound asleep.

"Then he'd say, 'Beau.'"

"I'd pick my head up and try and fake it. 'Now, lemme see . . . .'"

"'You're not fooling me. You're the one that's gonna have to pass,' he'd say."

"It was a sin to get kept back a year in school. The reason I did so well at Lincoln High had little to do with actual scholarship. Five years old when I first began my education, it was at a at a one-room school house in Hayden, Oklahoma. Six grades and one teacher in a single room. A pretty common situation for rural areas at the time, but not nearly as backward as some people today might think. Here you were in the first grade, and you'd be soaking up what the teacher was instructing six-graders in math or reading a row or two away. A few minutes later, cocking your ear behind you, you could pick up on a fourth grade-level geography lesson in progress, and so on. Was actually able skip a couple of grades by the time the Cooks gave me shelter. No, learning was never a problem for me; showing up at school in the first place was the real obstacle. Dad Cook inspired me to kick that one out of the way, too."

Lincoln High School. Kansas City, Mo

The belief in the need for education was probably never greater among Blacks than it was in the U.S. around the time Leonard Reed was taken in by Cook and his family. Lincoln High, where Hugh Cook was principal, was Kansas City's best secondary school for Blacks and was typical of its time of many places of learning throughout the U. S. attended by young African-Americans. The quality of the art and music faculties at Lincoln provides some idea of the overall level of instruction to found at the school: Aaron Douglas, soon to become a nationally known painter, was the school's mechanical drawing instructor; the music director, William L. Dawson, would eventually bring international renown to the chorus of Tuskegee Institute. Along with Major N. Clark

Smith, and several other gifted music instructors at Lincoln, Dawson helped sew the seeds for a generation of Kansas City jazz legends.

The atmosphere at such Black institutions as Lincoln was charged with faith in the transcendental powers of higher learning. "Nearly all that was acquired, mental or moral, was destined to be fitted into a particular system of which race was the center," wrote diplomat-composer-educator and NAACP co-founder James Weldon Johnson in his autobiography, *Along This Way*. Behind this emphasis on education, suggests Johnson, lay the sense of service to the Black community needed to produce brave and worthy men and women who would ultimately become saviors to those Blacks still cast outside society's circle.

Not only did Reed adapt fairly well to the strictures of this formal learning process under Cook's guidance, he also found himself curious about the basic differences between his school and the institutions in Kansas City that served the White community. Unlike most young Blacks, he didn't have to be satisfied with abstract answers; he could find out first-hand. He went to summer session at a nearby White school under a fictitious name, as much to keep his grades up as to just see "what it was like there."

Reed recalled, "At Lincoln, we had been taught about Paul Laurence Dunbar, Booker T. Washington, George Washington Carver, slavery, and Black history in general. At both Lincoln and colored Northwest High, the students were taught about George Washington and Lincoln and basic American history, but at the White school, the only Black history they had was about Crispus Attucks, a Black man and the first of five men killed at the Boston Tea Party in 1770."

Hugh Cook's brother, composer Will Marion Cook, was crucial in the evolution of Jazz, and directly paved the way for the-likes of Ellington and Gershwin, but until Reed went to New York for the first time in 1927, he had no sense of just how well-known and widely-regarded Cook was. It pleased him, when I first interviewed him, that he had lived long enough to see a revival of interest in Will Marion Cook, who is now felt by some scholars to be if not, in fact, "the" inventor of big-band Jazz, certainly "an" inventor.

The histories of many African-American families contain tales of relatives light-skinned enough to pass for White in the deeply racist America of the 1930s and 1940s. They cut ties with their entire family, moved to a new locale, perhaps changed their name, and more or less fell off the edge of the earth. It was often the case that those left behind instinctively knew what had happened and didn't even bother to try and trace their missing relative(s). Both Blacks and Whites over the years asked Reed why (some convenient "passing" episodes notwithstanding) he chose not to take this expeditious route. He explained, "It's because the first people—White or Black—who ever truly loved me and who took care of me, the Cooks, were Black. If it had been a White family, I could just as easily have passed over into that world and never looked back."

CHAPTER THREE
A Narrow Escape

"My teenage years in Kansas City with the Cook family were unbelievably sweet. One year I even managed to still sneak off with the carnivals: Dad Cook had rented me a room at the YMCA for the summer and got me a job selling newspapers. Then, he and his wife went off to spend the season at the popular Black resort, Idyllwild, Michigan, However, their train was barely out of the station before Orlando and I hit the road. They never did find out.

"I even managed to turn into a passable student in high school. So after graduating, plans were set in motion to send me to Cook's alma mater: at age sixteen (my managing to skip a couple of grades) I was packed off to Ithaca, New York, for pre-registration at Cornell University. Ithaca, New York, in '23 was beautiful . . . and different. The rolling green hills and the New England-style architecture weren't at all like the Midwest of my childhood. It also felt much less up-to-date than Kansas City. Arriving there, I felt like a pretty cocky young pup and started touting my dancing ability around campus, pushing just hard enough, it turned out, to propel myself back in show business.

"There was a show in town, *Lasses White's Minstrels*, playing at the Lyceum Theatre. Like 'Molasses,' only it's 'Lasses'. They had a dancer in the show and featured a Charleston contest.

"One of my new friends at Cornell issued a challenge. 'You've been tellin' us how good you are. Let's see you go down there to the contest and win.'"

"'If they got one,' I shot back, 'I'll win it!'"

"All the time in Ithaca, all I'd seen were Whites, and at the Charleston contest the minstrel folks thought I was White. Anyway, I won, and I was so good that right there on the spot was offered a job. After writing to my father and explaining to him what happened, off I went.

"After staying with the White show for only a couple of months, for the next year I worked all kinds of carnivals and shows throughout the Midwest. When you were with a show and you came into a town, you'd meet up with the outfit that preceded you, just as they were getting ready to leave town. You'd ask them, 'How are you doing? Are you getting paid?' And they'd say, 'Oh, yeah, we're getting paid over here,' and if you weren't getting paid where you were, you tried to get on that other show. When you did, you'd find out, likely as not, they weren't getting paid over there either. If you were smart, you'd sometimes end up switching shows three or four times a month. Also you found yourself forming an act with a new partner because a show wasn't looking for a single but a double.

"Then there was the medicine show, where I performed on the back of a wagon with horses hitched to it. The guy who ran it, 'Doctor' Howard Clark, was making a fortune selling some terrible stuff mixed with turpentine. The dose was four drops on a teaspoon of sugar. Clark carried all his medicine bottles with him, and we all traveled in a wagon.

You'd stop, let down the gate, put a brace under it, and stand on the end gate and dance and sing. Doc would play some great down-home guitar while a fellow called 'Crackaloo'—my dancing partner—and I banged away with tambourines and shouted.

"Then Doc Clark started his spiel. 'Now don't be impatient, there's a few more bottles, and you can have yours.'"

"We'd jingle a few coins in our pockets as if we were making change and yell, 'Thank you, sir.'"

"We hadn't even actually sold a bottle, but this would get them excited, and we'd wind up selling a couple of dozen depending on the crowd. This medicine was supposed to be a cure-all for everything: aches, pains, corns, and bunions on your feet, headaches, any kind of disease you had. It was hopped up with alcohol in addition to the turpentine and made you drunk. We were run out of nearly every town we rode into.'"

All of this in 1923 was a far cry from Reed taking over the production reins of *Tall Tan and Terrific* at the Cotton Club fourteen years later, but it was, for him, a learning experience drawn from the rich tradition of Vaudeville companies, medicine shows, minstrel shows, Wild West shows, circuses, and carnivals that traveled throughout America in the first three decades of the century. Traditions and pastimes that kept America entertained and amused with a motley of acts running the gamut from *commedia dell'arte*-inspired comedy to freak shows, magicians, and musical comedy, sometimes all under one roof or tent top.

With the background of his Billy McClain beginnings and the learning experience of repeating the Jim Jeffries-Jack Johnson act countless times over the course of two adolescent summers, Reed ditched Cornell University and became increasingly serious about the business of entertainment. Because of his light skin and his previous carnie experience, sixteen-year-old Reed not only pulled down jobs as a Charleston dancer, he was also able to secure work as a barker for several moderate-sized carnivals. Usually he worked outside the Jig Top, which was the part of the carnival that featured Blacks. The name "Jig Top" came from the word "jig," at one time a widely used offensive slang term to denote a member of the Black race. Along with the Jig Top, such operations also usually featured the likes of a Mat Show boxing and wrestling, often, a magic show, and invariably some sort of skin show or "hoochie coochie" presentation. Carnivals of the size Reed usually worked in the early 1920s were known in the trade as "gillies" or "mud shows," and in addition to the side shows, such as the Jig Top, also traveled with two or three rides, such as a Ferris wheel and/or a "whip" ride and a merry-go-round.

When Reed ballyhooed the Jig Top, it was important that the crowd think that he was every bit as White as they were, for the idea of a Black man shouting at Whites to "gather round" or to "hurry hurry, hurry" would have been considered unthinkable.

Reed would do his barking out on the bally (i.e. midway) with the four girls and the two Black comics. Dancing and singing with tambourines something like "Come Along Little Children." Just a little . . . to attract attention. Then, the six of them would then go on back inside and wait while tickets were sold, and if it still hadn't filled up, most of the troupe would go back on the bally again to attract more attention until they got the size of audience they needed to proceed profitably with the show. The situation varied from region to region, but generally some accommodations were made for traditionally segregated Blacks, who represented too large a profit potential to be entirely disenfranchised, to come inside the tents to view the various presentations. A common method used for dealing with Blacks, in areas where race mingling was frowned upon, was The Rope. Stretched down the middle of the tent, a rope was a common form of audience segregation, especially in the South, not only at carnivals but in dance halls, theaters, and other paid public gatherings well into the late 1950s. Performing with a rope bisecting the audience was a tricky business. If you worked the White side of the rope too much, your Black constituency would be offended; give too much attention to the Black side, and Whites could become unruly to the point of violence. Especially, for Black Rhythm and Blues artists of 1950s, mastering The Rope was an art form in and of itself.

One had been separated you from a couple of bits as the price of admission, and as for what you saw once Reed had managed to cajole you inside the tent, much of it looked like the sort of thing that the Burlesque show popularized a few years later. Bawdy blackout sketch comedy was the linchpin of the Jig Top: a burglar breaks into a house while the husband is away and takes advantage of the wife. Then the husband walks in and the wife tells him someone broke in. "Did he steal anything?" asks the husband. The wife answers, "Yes, but I thought it was you who snuck in." Blackout!

The audience went wild.

Presentations of the shows were almost nonstop. Just as one was finishing up, the sound of Reed's voice from outside touting the next go-round could be heard.

"Ladies and gentlemen, gather up closer. I've got a colossal collection of cannibalistic curiosities on the inside. I tell you what I 'm gonna do, pay one quarter of a dollar, twenty-five cents . . . ."

That's what they told Reed to say—"Cannibalistic curiosities on the inside." Seventy years later, he flinched when he recalled the phrase.

Attitudes of Whites towards Blacks during this era were highly variable. On the one hand, Summer 1919 saw bloody White-precipitated race riots in Chicago, Omaha, Longview, Texas, Phillips County Arkansas, Washington, D.C., and other communities. The frenzy in the capital continued for three days, during which time Blacks were pursued through the streets, dragged from street cars, beaten, and even killed.

In happy contrast to the racial conflagration, however, the American recording industry was just beginning to open up to "colored artists." Ex-slave George Washington Johnson, a.k.a. "The Whistling Coon," was in 1891 the second male singer (of any race) to ever be recorded. The initial recording of any consequence by an African-American was Mamie Smith's "Crazy Blues" (1920). The song became the first record release to sell in excess of a million copies. "Crazy Blues" was a hit with both races. After the success of Smith, with whom Reed worked on the stage of the Lafayette Theatre in New York a few years after her 1920 windfall, literally hundreds of Black female Urban Blues singers were quickly signed up by recording companies to capitalize on the Smith success.

In 1919, just prior to the success of "Crazy Blues," Congress had ushered in prohibition with the passing of the Volstead Act. That year, somewhere in the Midwest, if Reed had been in the habit of drinking, he could have used a shot or two after the Fourth of July with a carnival, where he recalled that he and his company of Jig Toppers performed a grand total of forty-eight shows from nine-thirty in the morning and continuing on until well past midnight!

CHAPTER FOUR
A Sentimental Journey

"AFTER MORE THAN A YEAR ON THE ROAD, AND CLOSING OUT A WEEK in Dayton, Ohio, the urge finally came over me to head back home. I hadn't seen Dad Cook since leaving Kansas City for Cornell, and only written him a couple of times. If he wrote back, the letters never caught up with me, so I had no idea of what my reception would be like back in Kansas City. All I knew was that, for the first time in my life, I was homesick. Hopping a freight in Dayton, I headed for Chicago, and out of Chicago, right back to Kansas.

"Arriving home, unlike the usual movie cliché of parents dead set against their children going into show business, it was obvious Dad Cook couldn't have been prouder of me than if I'd graduated from Cornell *magna cum laude*. He was so excited and proud, in fact, that he had me come to a school assembly and speak and perform as a distinguished graduate of Lincoln High. Standing before his students and doing a few jokes and my dance, looking toward the rear of the auditorium there he was standing and smiling.

"After that I strolled right on down to the Lincoln Theater, where only a few years earlier I'd started in show business selling soda pop and candy. The Lincoln was also my first exposure to real Jazz.

"When people think of Kansas City and Jazz, a name that usually comes to mind is Count Basie, but Basie was a Johnny-come-lately as far as Kansas City Jazz is concerned. When I was in high school, it was Benny Moten, George E. Lee, and John and Mary Lou Williams, who were the big local stars at theaters like the Eblon and the Lincoln, and clubs such as Piney Brown's, the Panama, and the Novelty Club. Not old enough to get into these places, I still managed the trick of hanging around the entrances, listening to the music that poured out, especially those around the intersection of 12th and Vine, and 18th and Paseo. Leaving home with my long pants turned up like short pants, when I got out the door and around the corner, pulled them down and, voila, long pants!

"By the time I came off the road that first time and returned to Kansas City, 12th and Vine and the Jazz scene were coming to a rapid boil. These included twenty-four-hours-a-day joints like the Yellow Front Cafe, owned by Billy McClain, which actually shook when you danced and was located quite close (too close) to the Phillis Wheatley Memorial Hospital. Then there was the Sunset Club, where singer Big Joe Turner would soon make a name for himself.

"Jazz musicians from all over the country were heading for Kansas City. Count Basie, Andy Kirk, Lester Young, Big Joe Turner, and Charlie Parker were just a few of the dozens of great players who came out of K.C.'s legendary all-night jam sessions.

"Racketeering and prostitution, under the control of the Tom Pendergast political machine, were also going full blast. Prohibition had only made it that much wilder, and by the time it all came crashing down around Pendergast in the mid-1930s, there were thirty-odd nightclubs in the area that featured Jazz.

"Some of the other Jazz spots were the Cherry Blossom, the Subway, Lucille's Band Box, the Hey-Hay Club, and the Boulevard Lounge. Kansas City was also a good town for tenderfoot tap dancers, like myself. The only dancer I ever saw that I thought was better than the great Bill 'Bojangles' Robinson was King Rastus Brown. [King Rastus Brown's name still crops up from time-to-time in Bob Hope biographies as a teacher of the comedian while the latter was still living in Ohio.] Saw him first in Kansas City. He was fairly big in his time, but today no one remembers him. Just like Robinson, Brown was not a tapper, but a flat-footed dancer who relied upon heavy soles rather than tap for his sound.

Earliest publicity photo of Reed, 1927

"I'm not the only person who remembers Brown as a great dancer. The comedian, Pigmeat Markham, told me once that he first saw Brown in Cincinnati, and that, at first, King danced all over the stage, then kept on dancing right on up the aisle of the theater, on across the street to a bar, where they had a drink waiting for him. Most of the audience followed him into the street, cheered him when he came out with a drink in his hand, then followed him as he danced right on back inside the theater. He tapped his way down the aisle, and back onto the stage. The audience went crazy as he finished his drink and tossed the glass into the wings, still dancing. He was the best I ever saw, but he was a juicer.

Even when he was half-drunk, he was better than anyone else. He never got a chance for the big-time because he stayed on the bottle.

"During my hiatus from the road, I became a backstage regular at the Lincoln Theater, and although never having studied with King Rastus Brown, started picking up steps from dancer Johnny Nit, another great tap dancer, like King Rastus, now all but forgotten. Nit was nearly ten years older than I; and it was the perfect setup for a teacher-student relationship.

"However, I guess it really is true what they say about show business getting into your blood. I was just getting comfortably settled into Kansas City, and hanging out at the Lincoln one day with Johnny Nit when I got wind of a big Charleston contest to be held in Oklahoma City two days hence. You'd soon find me on a midnight bus out of town, Oklahoma bound . . . off and running again. Arrived in Oklahoma City to join a mass of dozens of contestants who'd come came from all over the Midwest; Texas, Louisiana, Mississippi, Florida, and elsewhere to vie for the quasi-official title of Southwest Charleston Champ.

"I was *some kind* of Charleston dancer, because I'd been doing what was basically the Charleston back in high school before they even had a name for it. Winning easily, I was invited to join the carnival sponsoring the contest. The name of the carnival escapes me. We're talking [in 1920] seventy years ago. The one thing I do recall is that it had a lot of chorus girls. That's the main reason I went on it. My job was to come out, do the Charleston, then take on all local challengers to my title in every town the carnival rolled into.

"Dancing from Oklahoma to Chicago, all the way to Biloxi, Mississippi to the Gulf of Mexico and onward to the Atlantic Ocean. By the time we reached the eastern seaboard, I'd also learned to do the Tap Charleston. It's just what it sounds like: some of the big, broad movements of the Charleston rolled into a tap routine.

"Every town we hit had a champion Charleston dancer with whom I competed. There'd be contests Monday through Thursday or Friday, and then the winners would challenge me on Saturday. Getting a chance to see all my competition and knowing what I was up against, I always won. It also helped a little to have the band on your side.

"During this time, found me starting up an act with a fellow who was so dark they called him Inky. We were known as 'Pen and Ink' and played a number of carnivals, most every one of which featured the Charleston that season. I revived the Jim Jeffries/Jack Johnson bit for us to do in addition to my dancing (here I was not yet twenty years of age and already I had *old* material in my act!). Then I'd do the Charleston and Inky would tap dance barefoot, slapping his feet so hard that you could see the dust fly.

"If the city was big enough so that no one would recognize me, I'd not only be the Charleston Champ in our show, sometimes I'd go over to another part of town and win local contests just to earn a few bucks. Coming right up out of the audience, pretending to be a citizen of the place. No one ever caught on.

"Sometimes we'd hit a big city like Atlanta or Charleston with the carnival, and there'd be not one but two other Charleston contests going on in town at the same time. If the timing was tight, I'd pay someone to let me go on first. That would usually give me time to run around the corner, or down the block, and get into another contest while the first one was still going on. Like I say, I was *some kind* of Charleston dancer.

Reed's decision to run off with the Lasses White Minstrels instead of attending Cornell for four years wasn't entirely impractical. By 1923, motion pictures had evolved from a state of novelty, and Vaudeville and other forms of "live" entertainment still constituted a booming industry. To the list of theaters providing entertainment, you could also now add many of the 5,000 speakeasies that had sprung up as a result of prohibition. So it was an active if not always stable profession with which Reed allied himself.

The "killer" routine that had brought about his hiring by *White's Minstrels* was based on the Charleston, the dancing fad just coming into vogue in 1923. Now, a year-and-a-half later with this same set of steps, Reed rode the original dance sensation that was sweeping the nation to the crest of a major entertainment wave. The Charleston became a phenomenon that has come to stand as a major symbol for the Roaring Twenties, yet which many social observers claim that it was performed in the South as early as 1903 and is thought by most experts on the subject to be of African origin. (Reed claims to have known how to do the dance long before Whites ever took it up.) Whatever its ethnic source, it's a fact that the wild, abandoned dance reached epidemic proportions among both Blacks and Whites during the early part of the 1920s. It should also be noted that it was the common practice of many White dancers to "black up" with cork whenever they performed.

Described in *Webster's Seventh* as "a lively ballroom dance in which the knees are twisted in and out and the heels are swung sharply outward on each step," the dithyrambic phenomenon reached a large public for the first time in the 1923 Broadway hit *Runnin' Wild*, an all-Black show intended almost exclusively for White consumption with music by James P. Johnson, lyrics by Cecil Mack, and orchestrations by Will Marion Cook. New York critics were rapturous over the production. "Such a demonstration of beating out complex rhythms," wrote one reviewer, "has never before been seen on a stage in New York." The song, "Charleston," introduced by Elisabeth Welch, however, was not a standout in the New

York run. By the time *Runnin' Wild* opened in Philadelphia the following year, however, the number was the main reason for continuing popularity of the thinly-plotted show. In a 1959 interview, James P. Johnson said he'd first witnessed the dance while playing piano at the Jungles Casino in New York in 1918. A little more than a decade later, Leonard Reed and almost every other U.S. youth set on making it in show business were, in the words of the song, doin' it.

Joan Crawford danced her way to movie stardom with the Charleston in *Our Dancing Daughters* (1928), a story about the dance craze and its effect on a nation of would-be flappers. In 1933, Ginger Rogers utilized another dance sensation, the faux "Carioca," invented for the movie *Flying Down to Rio* as her ticket to almost instantaneous movie stardom. However, she was still Virginia McMath when, a few years earlier as a sixteen-year-old, she used the Charleston as her springboard out of Independence, Missouri.

She wasn't alone. Charleston contests represented a possible way out of America's backwaters and into the chrome and smoked glass glamour of the Roaring Twenties for thousands of White youths from upper-lower and lower-middle social classes.

The reason for the popularity was a simple one: here, for the first time, was a dance, athletic in character, thus, not considered too effeminate for men to cultivate. Males might have balked at the waltz a century earlier, but with the Charleston, little prodding was called for.

Understandably, Reed's recollections of his year spent as a professional Charleston dancer summon up those montage sequences, included to convey ceaseless migration, in Warner Bros. musicals of the 1930s. Imagine the legend "1924"spiraling toward your point of view, followed by shots of Reed doing the Charleston across a map of the U.S., while dozens of town names slide left to right, right to left across the screen.

Spending his next year after winning the division championship dancing in various carnivals and Vaudeville shows, Reed comes off sounding like a kind of "steel drivin' John Henry," whose specialty happened to be the laying down steps. Alas, even superheroes have their Achilles' heels, and after nearly a year of such long journeys, and although still a teenager, his health began to precipitously decline. In his essay on carnivals, "Masters of the Midway," A. J. Liebling writes of something called doughnut tumors or "abdominal lumps, which, carnies say, appear upon the bodies of show people who have subsisted for months at a time on nothing but coffee and doughnuts." At the age of sixteen, Reed was burned out from his year on the road and badly in need of a rest. Next stop . . . Tulsa.

The last time Reed had been there was 1921. Then, he'd just arrived almost at the exact instant a KKK-fanned full-scale race riot had broken out over a Black youth's alleged rape of a young White girl. One thing led to another and, soon, Tulsa and especially its African-American financial district, known far and wide as the "Black Wall Street," were embroiled in a full-scale race riot. The conflagration lasted several days duration, resulting in the deaths of 180 African-Americans and forty-eight Whites, and $4,000,000 worth of property damage to thirty-six blocks in the Black section of Tulsa, known as "Little Africa."

CHAPTER FIVE
"...that Woman's NOT Your Sister"

"My first warning of the '21 riots was smoke on the horizon, and the next thing you knew hysterical Whites were running up to warn me (a White man, they thought) that rampaging coloreds were headed in my direction and to 'run for your life.' Suddenly, I was being chased by marauding Blacks who were out for my (presumed) White blood. The sickest and saddest part of it all was that the teenaged Black boy and White girl who started the whole thing were lovers and had run away to a neighboring state to get married and were man-and-wife practically before the smoke from the riots had even cleared. Being back in Tulsa once again, even though it was now more than three years later, was not something I especially looked forward to.

"The first night there, we'd just finished up our show at a very nice medium-sized theater called the Princess, when backstage I saw coming in my direction a very attractive, light-skinned woman. She turned out to be Zell Roan, the owner of the theater who, though a successful businesswoman, didn't appear to be a great deal older than myself. She was not only pretty . . . she was, right off, very motherly.

"'How old are you?'" she asked after we'd chatted for a minute or two about the show.

"'Nineteen,'" I said, adding a couple of years.

"'You're lying. How come you're not in school?'"

I told her the truth, that I'd graduated but, my not looking much older than fifteen or sixteen, she wasn't buying any of it.

"'I'm going to keep you here with me as my little brother, and when school starts you're going to go back. Besides,' and she meant it when she said that I had no business being in the show 'with all those vile women.'"

"Taking her up on the offer was a smart move. It gave me my first serious education in what went on behind the scenes in show business. Zell was the one who taught me how to check tickets and watch for theft, and she sent me backstage to learn everything that went on there. I found out about light cues, stage lingo, the works. Learned what a proscenium was; what a tormentor was (it held up the proscenium and prevented the audience from seeing into the wings); downstage from upstage; and what the battens and lines were (in those days they had moveable wings and when the curtain fell you pulled the wings in).

"However, when winter came, Zell never mentioned my going back to school, and I didn't say anything either. I made friends with a guy named Pencil, who said to me one day, 'I know that woman's not your sister. I've known her a long time. That woman's in love with you.'"

"'No, no, she's my sister.'"

"He didn't even hear me. I was a fool for not taking advantage of the situation, he said, and came up with a plan: tell Zell that I liked to shoot pool and ask her to give me some money so I could play. 'Then you save that pool money 'til you have a hundred dollars,' Pencil said, 'and then take it back and say, 'Look what I won!' Then she'll give you more money.'"

"Pencil was right. Not only did she stake me to pool when I asked her for money, she said, 'Go get anything you want.' She began buying me things. Took me downtown and bought me suits and shoes."

"Then she said, 'You ought to have a car, everybody else has cars.'"

"So she bought me a car. It was called a Blue Goose, made by Willys-St. Clair. It had a goose on the front of it. Finally, I took the pool money savings and, like Pencil told me, represented it to Zell as my 'winnings.'"

"'Oh, good! I can use that!' she said, and snatched away every goddamn nickel of it."

The ex-wife of a Chicago doctor, Zell Roan had received a large divorce settlement, moved to Tulsa, and bought a theater two years before meeting Reed. Her Princess Theater was part of a loose federation known as the Theatre Owners Booking Association (T O.B.A.), a chain of Vaudeville houses that catered to an exclusively Black clientele, located throughout the Southern, Midwestern, and Southwestern states; principally Oklahoma, Missouri, Texas, Louisiana, Florida, Alabama, and Georgia. Eventually, the circuit grew to encompass theaters along the eastern seaboard and the Great *Lakes.*

Theatre Owners Booking Association letterhead

Theater Owners Booking Association (T.O.B.A.) was the Vaudeville circuit for Black entertainers during the 1920s and 1930s. "Time" was the word often used to refer to Vaudeville in general, and the Black vernacular for the T.O.B.A. circuit was called "Toby Time." In *Way*

Down South, a thinly fictionalized memoir of doing "Toby Time," actor Clarence Muse (with co-author David Arlen) explained why, somewhat less-than-affectionately, the initials T.O.B.A. also stood for "Tough on Black Actors" (or Asses). This was because no matter how careful they were, the actor who played "time" usually ended up at the close of the season as broke as when they started, having left unpaid board, lodging, and laundry bills in most of the towns along the route.

Organized in Chattanooga in 1920, the T.O.B.A. offered theater owners—for a yearly fee of $300—exclusive franchises to stage shows in the cities where their theaters were located, i.e., showmen (and women) banded together to organize a booking agency dedicated to maximizing the efficiency and profitability of the touring shows that played in their Black theaters. Essentially, "Toby Time" was a Black variant of successful booking franchises such as the Keith, Orpheum, and Pantages circuits. In the peak years of the 1920s, there were more than eighty T.O.B.A. Theaters; however, Reed said that nearly all of them were owned by Whites, with the few Black owners being mostly women. Roan, along with Ella B, Moore in Dallas, was among the most successful owners on the circuit. Charles Turpin, the T. O. B.A. vice president, was also Black, and since he also happened to be the owner of the Booker T. Washington Theater in St. Louis, it was considered extremely important that you impress him with the quality and drawing power of your show while playing there.

Traveling T.O.B.A. revues that passed through the Princess Theater, where Reed was learning his trade, were headed by or featured such once-popular Black performers as Detroit Red, Willy Too Sweet, Boots Hope, Baby Seals, and Daybreak Nelson. In *Way Down South*, Clarence Muse describes another of these artists, String Beans Price, as being ". . . the most famous colored comedian in America among [Black] theatergoers, a tall gangling comic sporting a diamond tooth which he was able to unscrew and remove from his mouth, this funny fella could sit on a tiny stool in the center of the stage with one leg flung over the top of the grand piano [and sing] and inspire more hilarity than a whole revue of average comedians."

Reed agreed with Muse's opinion of Price's effectiveness with an audience. Unquestionably, there were dozens of others just as potent as String Beans, and who, like him, did not share Bill Robinson's or Bert Williams' rare capacity to cross over into the big-time.

Sunshine Sammy and His Pals, starring Ernie Morrison, who died in 1989, is one revue that played the Princess in Tulsa when Reed was working there that might not be entirely lost on several generations of TV kids weaned on endless reruns of the *Little Rascals*, the *East Side Kids*, and the *Dead End Kids* comedy series. Ernie "Sunshine Sammy" Morrison was in the first *Our Gang* (a.k.a. *The Little Rascals*) short subject ever produced, *One Terrible Day* (1922). By 1924, after he had appeared in twenty-eight entries of the classic series, his father accepted a lucrative three-year offer for his ten-year-old son to appear in Vaudeville.

Reed recalled, "He came out wearing a gray tuxedo and derby trimmed in blue, strutting and singing, 'I'm Sunshine Sammy, the life of the gang, Sunshine Sammy the kid with a bang.' I was amazed because it was the first time I'd ever seen a tux any other color than black."

Other "names" Reed came into contact during his stint at the Princess were comic Gallie De Gaston, comedy teams Brown and Brown, Butterbeans and Susie, and singers Ida Cox and Bessie Smith. Reed insists that, contrary to current popular notion, Bessie Smith was not nearly as popular in her time as two other Blues divas, Mamie Smith and Clara Smith, the latter who also played the Princess.

In his book, *Jazz Style in Kansas City and the Southwest*, scholar and record producer Ross Russell asserts that, "In the opinion of those who knew T.O.B.A. [some of its stars were] better than the one or two, like Bert Williams and 'Bojangles' Robinson, that were able to break into show business."

While most would question the total accuracy of such a statement and be curious as to the identity of Russell's sources (better than Bert

Williams and Bill "Bojangles" Robinson?), still there is little question that the players on Toby Time were every bit the equal of their opposite numbers on the mainstream Vaudeville "wheels."

Unlike Russell's remarks about the relative merits of the great Bert and Bojangles, there is little to contest in his observation that "Certainly, and in numerous respects, Toby Time was Uncle-Tom-ish, undesirably rooted in plantation attitudes, not to mention imitative of culture and even Negro stereotypes. In other respects it was reflective of a vital culture, endowed with wit; a spirit of social criticism, both of mores and its own; an awareness of separatism and implied protest against it; and, above all, a very high quality of musical elements."

Reed also remembers a show, *Step 'n Fetchit*, that came through Tulsa and played the other Black theater in town, the Dixie. The revue starred the comedy team of Lincoln Perry and Ed Lee. A few years later, Reed saw a film featuring one of the first major Black film stars, Stepin Fetchit, whom he recognized at once as Lincoln Perry (who had held on to the title of his old T.O.B.A. show for his new stage and screen name after splitting up the act with Ed Lee).

Tap dance style evolved by leaps and bounds on Toby Time, and the T.O.B.A. was also an invaluable crucible for the unique artistry of Black singers, musicians, and comics of the post WWI period. New words, phrases, comedy routines, and dance styles created by Black America in T.O.B.A theaters from shortly after the end of the WWI until the advent of the Depression were eventually assimilated into and remain a permanent part of the mainstream of American entertainment. The T.O.B.A. was an early casualty of the Depression as a result of Blacks being among the first to be affected by the economic crunch, and also of talking pictures that put a damper on the demand for "live" entertainment.

American comedy would also have evolved much differently were it not for the contributions of T.O.B.A. mainstays, such as Dusty Fletcher and Pigmeat ("Here Comes the Judge") Markham. The comedian was the most important part of the Toby Time show; if he or she was a hit, the production was also likely to be a hit. Unarguably the four most influential (and at the time beloved) of the African- American comics were Fletcher, Markham, the lesser known (today) John Mason, and Jackie "Moms" Mabley. Eventually, the three male comics would be brought to Los Angeles in 1944 by Reed when he was producing stock at the Lincoln Theater.

Reed did not work with Mabley until the 1950s at the Apollo Theater, but he did manage to catch her act in earlier years and remembers her as not being especially funny and struggling along for recognition until she hit upon the idea of doing her usual risqué material, but with a minor twist: she performed the same act with her false teeth removed, and she became an instantaneous hit with Black audiences throughout the country. Before dying in 1975, this eccentric performer even achieved a measure of success with White audiences.

In his autobiography, *Black and White Baby*, singer Bobby Short describes a typical routine of Mabley's fellow performer, Pigmeat Markham, who Short, as a child performer, had the chance to observe while sharing a bill with the oversized, raspy-voiced voiced comic during in the mid-1930s. Mabley would eventually become something of a Black *and* White household "name" due to her out of left field 1969 "cover" version of Dion's recording, "Abraham, Martin and John," and her numerous TV appearances on such hit shows as *The Smothers Brothers Comedy Hour*.

"He [Markham] did his 'In School' skit that week, everyone done up in children's clothes, sitting at rows of desks, and Pigmeat with long blond curls. One little girl gets up and says, 'I'm late this morning, teacher, because Momma had a new baby.'"

"'Hasn't Sally's father been out of town for the past year and a half?'"

"'Yes, he has,' says Sally, 'but he writes to Momma every single week.'"

"Then Pigmeat in his big blond wig says, 'Hmmmm … What kin' of fountain pen is dat?'"

In 1947, Dusty Fletcher would have his fifteen minutes of fame when his novelty recording of "Open the Door, Richard" hit the Billboard Magazine Top Ten chart. In 1944 Reed brought together Markham, Dusty Fletcher, and John Mason on the stage of Los Angeles' Lincoln Theater. It was, he says, "no big deal at the time, they weren't even that well known on the west coast." Given the latter-day respect accorded these comedic gods, however, the booking was, in retrospect, not without its Olympian overtones.

Comics "Pigmeat" Markham (left) and George Wiltshire, circa 1949.

CHAPTER SIX
Stripped for Action

"I HAD IT MADE WORKING FOR ZELL ROAN IN TULSA: ON-THE-JOB training, a Blue Goose car, and a warm place to sleep. After five or six months, there was absolutely nothing sexual going on between us, until one cold October night. As usual, she was in the bedroom and I was in the living room on the Duofold daybed; about two o'clock in the morning, she called in to me.

"'Leonard, are you cold?'"

"'A little bit,' I said."

"'Well, I am, too. Why don't you come in here?'"

"'Okay,' I answered."

"Got into bed and turned my back to her. She turned and cuddled up to me and nearly scared me to death. The woman literally pulled me on top of her. Damned if she wasn't treating me just the way I'd treated all the little girls in school! I decide to really show off, because what Pencil had said was true. Zell really did love me. Grinding over and around, making a figure eight and up and down thinking I'm really hot stuff, the best stud this woman ever had when, the next thing you know, she throws me off and sits up yelling, 'Hold it!'"

"Maybe Zell wasn't up to all the sexual excitement I had in my bag of tricks?"

"'For god's sake, don't try to be a fancy fucker,' she grumbled. 'You're not doing anything. You're moving and moving. No sooner do you hit the spot than you're off of it. I am going to teach you how to do this.'"

"Back then, sex was something that was never discussed. You did it, but you didn't talk about. Nonetheless, Zell proceeded to give me my first good lesson in sex. 'Do this . . . Don't do that . . . Now hold it . . . if you move, I'll kill you . . ..'"

"I'll never forget that phrase 'fancy fucker.' I felt so little . . . so small. Here I'd had all these pretty little girls from the age of eight, and now this woman's telling me I don't know what I'm doing. Learning fast, though. For the next month or so, everything went smooth as silk until . . . I started wanting to show off what Zell had taught me.

"Teresa Bowen was a little girl in the Princess box office that I was crazy about, and even though Zell kept telling me to leave the girl alone, I just couldn't keep away and started meeting Teresa on the sly. There was a place called Berry's Farm in town. Berry was the biggest Negro deal in Tulsa. He had his own airplane, a bus line, a hotel, and he had this big dance pavilion in this park.

"In places like the South, there was always one Negro who had everything, because the Whites would let him have it so long as he kept the other Negroes in line. If there was a politician who needed the Black vote delivered, he could rely on the likes of a Berry. He took good care of all the other Negroes, gave him work and money, he was good to them and provided. He was 'The Big Nigger.' *That* was Berry's Farm.

"One night, Hot Lips Page's band was playing there, so I got dressed up fit to kill and sneaked around the corner, picked up Teresa, and took her to Berry's Farm. Unfortunately, Zell found out about it, walked in, and spotted us dancing."

"'I want to talk to you outside,' she snapped. 'Outside!'"

Following her out to my Blue Goose car, when I turned around, she had this gun right in my face.

"'I'm gonna blow your fuckin' brains out.'"

"'Oh, Zell, don't do it. I won't do whatever it is I did again.' I was stupid enough to still he playing dumb."

"'I have asked you time and time again not to fool around with these young girls.'"

"She went through the whole ritual. I really thought she was going to blow me away. She let me think about it for a minute or two. Finally, she said, 'I'm *not* going to kill you. Just take off the clothes.'"

"'What!?'"

"'Take off the suit I bought you. Take off the clothes.'"

"I removed the coat and the tie and the shirt."

"'The pants, too,' she ordered."

"'Oh, god!'"

"She made me strip stark naked: shoes, socks, underwear, everything. Zell would have even taken the Blue Goose except she'd come in another car, but she made sure the keys were in my pockets as she walked off with my clothes and left me standing there. You could still hear the dance music playing way off in the background as a guy came out. I called to him for help.

"'What the hell's going on?' he asked."

"I more or less explained to him . . . jealous woman, gun at my head, and so on, but instead of helping me, the s.o.b. called over to five or six others. These people called over a few more people, and suddenly there I was standing there stark-naked with a crowd standing around laughing at me. Taking off running through the woods, ending up at a strange house, I found an old paper sack to put in front of me and knocked on the door. Some folks answered, and got from me the goddamnest story you ever heard. These 'strangers' had made me take off my clothes, and they were going to kill me, beat me up.

"'Were these men colored?' they asked, assuming that I was every bit as they were."

"'No, they weren't' I answered, undoubtedly preventing the formation of an on-the-spot lynching committee racing off through the woods after my imaginary attackers. A few more words were exchanged, then, taking pity on me, the man of the house gave me some old clothes to put on. It was nearly dawn when I finally slid into bed beside Zell."

"After we'd finished making love, I said to her, 'Give me another chance. I wasn't doing anything. Just out dancing. I promise I'll make it up to you.'"

"Alas, even my excellence in the sack that night wasn't enough to cool her anger down all that much. 'All right, but if I ever catch you again . . . .'"

"For a long time after Zell, I went out for older women in a big way. It became my thing. It also seems like my preference was older *married* women. Maybe it was the risk and adventure involved. The wife of a fellow, who owned a cab company in Chicago when I worked the Grand Terrace in 1932, would check up on the drivers for her husband, and between my shows at the Terrace. she'd take me to the Lake Shore Hotel (she'd have a room reserved there), and even on the way we'd have sex in the back of a taxi owned by her old man. If we had been caught, there's little doubt he would have had me killed.

"Starting in the mid-1920s, it's doubtful that very few men were fucking any more than I was. Once, I was even, serially, having sex with most of the chorus girls in a show I was producing in Baltimore in the early 1930s. In the course of which, I made the mistake of showing preferential treatment for one over the other eleven, and in protest, all twelve of the dancers walked out on the show. The moral? It was a bad idea to be fucking almost your entire chorus line if you wanted to go on with the show.

"An incident of *failing* to get the girl also taught me a lesson. In the 1940s, I used to base most of the time in Chicago at the Southwood Hotel. Right on the corner was a drugstore that served breakfast that had the most gorgeous girl for a cashier. Going in there every day for breakfast, for weeks on end. Keeping on trying to hit on her, every morning I'd say, 'How you doing, sweetie?' She'd take my check. And so on.

"'Hey, baby! How're ya,' doll?' Always, she was a little bit frosty, but after about two or three weeks of this, I finally asked, 'How would you like to go out with me?' Pleased and even a little bit surprised when she accepted, I took her out, and afterward we ended up in my hotel room. We hadn't done anything yet, but were both naked, with me lying up against the wall, and her at the other end of the bed. I was smoking then—it was 1947—and at one point I said to her, 'Sweetie, hand me those cigarettes.'"

"She turned to me and in a very flat voice said, 'What's my name?'"

"Sitting there and looking and looking at her for the longest time, finally I said, 'Well, I honestly don't know.'"

"She got up, got dressed, and walked right out."

"The next day, I said to her in the drugstore, 'What's your name, honey?'"

"She said to me, very angrily, 'Don't call me honey. My name is Avis!'"

"The moral there, I suppose, is always learn somebody's name before you start trying to get fresh.

Peg Leg Bates, the one-legged performer who went onto major tap dancing stardom, and who later in his career set a record for his number appearances on *The Ed Sullivan Show* on American television, played the Princess Theater while Reed was still working there. The colorful dancer was part of a T.O.B.A. revue fronted by popular comedian Eddie Lemons. However, it wasn't Lemons or Bates who really caught Reed's eye; instead, it was Lemons' wife, Anita. Wary of Zell's wrath, Reed meekly tended his tormentors and lines, and a few days later Lemons and company moved on to their next date in Oklahoma City. That would have been that as far as Reed's infatuation with Anita Lemons was concerned, except for a big decision Zell Roan had just made: She handed Leonard a wad of bills—traveling money back to Kansas City. The official version was that it was now time for him to be going back to school, but in fact, Roan was growing tired of her young lover. It was all the encouragement Reed needed to take off for—not Kansas— but Oklahoma City in hot pursuit of Anita Lemons: beautiful, older, and, most importantly of all . . .. married!

Eddie Lemons
Owner and Producer

Showman-comic Eddie Lemons—Reed's employer in the mid-1920s.

CHAPTER SEVEN

Next Stop, Seminole

"Lemons and his troupe had cut short their engagement in Oklahoma City and moved on by the time I got there. So, joining up with a carnival, the *S.B. Williams Show*—again as a barker— once more I was passing for White. Passing is a word I really don't like; as far as I'm concerned, I was working not "passing." The word implies deceit, and I really wasn't practicing that much trickery. Most carnival people were street-sophisticated; some were 'on to me,' and those that weren't probably sensed me to be somehow, well . . . different. All that finally mattered to them, though, was that I got my job done. That's what I mean by 'sophisticated.' By and large, carny and show people were live-and-let-live sorts.

"Ola Jones, a dancer out of Chicago, was light-skinned enough to be a part of Williams' all-White chorus line. Maybe this helped draw us together, because shortly after my joining the Williams show, we took a liking to one another. The next thing you knew, things were serious enough for us to get tattooed with each other's initials. When you tattoo someone's name on your arm at sixteen it's because you're in love, or you think you're in love. 'You love me?' 'Yeah, I love you.' 'Well, then, put my name on there.' And I did, and she did, both with little hearts around the initials. Seventy years and several wives later. the initials "O. J." (for Ola Jones) are still faintly visible on my right arm.

"When the *S. B. Williams Show* went on hiatus, the next job that Ola and I took was with a traveling T.O.B.A. revue. That turned out to be a big letdown after the Williams carnival. The show, *Trip to Cannibal Isle*, was led by the husband and wife team, [Henry] Drake and [Ethel] Walker. The highlight was a sketch called 'Twenty Minutes in Hell' featuring a comic by the name of Rastus Brown, not to be confused with the legendary dancer, King Rastus Brown. 'Twenty Minutes in Hell' was a pretty funny bit, and I enjoyed getting my feet wet doing comedy, but a week after joining up, just as we were getting ready to pull out of Jacksboro, Texas, Henry Drake, pleading poverty, wouldn't give Ola and me our salary—'If we could only wait until'—I'd heard *that one* before. Ola and I decided to cut our losses and leave, right then and there, and head for Ft. Worth, which was a good town for hitching up with a carnival.

"We took a bus to Ft. Worth, but after our fare we didn't even have the money to pay for a hotel. We had baggage, though, and were able to get a room. All I had to my name was a dollar, enough for an all-important shoe shine (a dime and a nickel tip) and two 15¢ sandwiches for Ola and me. That left 55¢.

"Across from the hotel, there was an upstairs pool room. After eating, I decided to wander over and check out the action. Just as I suspected, they also had a crap game going. First, I played pool, and with my 55¢, won $4 or $5 dollars, Then, I moved over to the crap game and proceeded to break everybody. That proved to be too much for the guy who ran the place; now *he* wanted to play. He should have resisted the temptation. When I beat him out of $5, he went back to the safe and got another $5 and another $5 and another. He must not have had too much in there, because he never got more than $5 at a time. After beating him five or six times, he said, "You wait, I'll be back." He went downstairs. This didn't look good because I've now got $60 or $70 on me. Scared to death, I handed the girl at the counter a $1 bill.

"'Give me some coffee and change this for me in nickels and dimes, no quarters.'"

"Then, taking the small change she gave me, I walked over to the pool table and said, 'Okay, fellers,' and threw it on the pool table all at once. And while the four or five guys there practically threw themselves on the table scrambling for not even a dollar's worth of change, I skipped down the outside stairs, five steps at a time, getting out of the place.

"Our next stop was Seminole, Oklahoma. There were rumors of great opportunity there, even for show people, because of an oil boom. Another reason for going there: *Eddie Lemons Revue* was set to play Seminole, which meant Anita Lemons would he there. Dropping Ola off in Oklahoma City, and going to have a look at the town for myself, what I found was that Seminole was unlike anything I'd ever seen before.

"There's no excitement in the world like an oil boom. You've got to picture the muddiest scene imaginable, horses and mules going down the street carrying telephone poles, oil gushing all around, and everybody is dirty and filthy. Planks are thrown across the dirt streets, the ground is oily, and the horses and mules come back from the oil fields tracking all that black gold back into town. Everywhere there's the smell of oil. There were no pavements, not even any boardwalks, and you're walking in all this oil and mud right up to your ass.

"Checking into a hotel, and getting some cardboard, I went door-to-door offering to draw up menus for restaurants and signs for barbershop and hotels—and that's how I paid for my room. My mechanical drawing teacher at Lincoln High back in Kansas City had been the painter,

Aaron Douglas, before he became famous, and so I was pretty good at sign painting.

"By the time Eddie Lemons and his revue arrived in town for a week's booking, a hooker had fallen so madly in love with me that I hardly even noticed they were there. Meeting her in one of the restaurants where I was drawing up menus, the next thing I knew she was living with me in my hotel room. She was making $200-$300 a day. Without even half trying, I was being kept, but it didn't last long. One night, we were sitting in a restaurant, and another girl walks in with a razor, and starts cutting up my girl. And all I could do was sit there, frozen to the spot. Something had happened between the two of them because of a trick. By the time it was all over, I was as bloody as they were. Looking down, my girl was cut ear-to-ear, and I was sure she was dead. Scared to death and thinking I was going to be killed, I ran out of there just like everybody else. Still haven't gotten over it. I found out later, the girl had died and they never even bothered to try and catch the killer. In those days, nobody cared about a nigger being killed.

"I went back to the hotel, threw my things in a bag, and caught the next train out."

For Reed, his brush with prostitution in Seminole was the beginning of a sideline enterprise that would continue off and on for nearly the next fifteen years. "It wasn't just a Black thing," he insists. "Practically everyone and his brother on the Vaudeville circuits were doing it." If that apologia happens to fall short, he clarifies further, explaining that he was impelled toward "the life" because, of all things . . . air conditioning, or, rather, the lack thereof. In the U.S., before the advent of sophisticated methods of indoor cooling, many, if not most, theaters were "closed during hot months," he tells you. Thus, making it necessary for many mid-range and bottom-rung entertainers to find alternate sources of income.

Reed has no inclination to pull punches on the subject. "Can I make it any plainer?" he barked in 1990. "I always looked for a whore in July or August to take care of me." Even in the early 1930s, when he and his partner, Willie Bryant, were a steadily employed act on some of the nation's top Vaudeville chains, the layoffs due to summer theater closure were considerable. Thus, the sky was the limit for Reed when it came to "turning tricks and running whores."

"When I was pimping in Minneapolis," he said, "I'd warm up bricks and put them under their feet to keep them warm in the cold outdoors. I had two whores and took them up there. We went from Chicago to Minneapolis because we heard it was a good place for whores. This was 1931. My show business partner, Willie, and I survived off of them. Ginger and Claudette."

Winter in Minneapolis? There goes the air conditioning rationale out an open window. However, what does parse is that it was The Depression, which meant that even popular Vaudeville acts had their fallow periods.

"I know it's hard looking at me now to believe that a woman would want to do that for me," Reed laughed, "but I had an awful lot of them wanting and begging to do just that. That was no hill to climb. The bottom line is, I wouldn't even go into a show unless there was somebody that I could screw. I've always had a woman to take care of me. When I got into a town with a show, I made it my business to find a restaurant with a waitress who looked good and who'd give me a free meal. Because half the time I didn't get paid. There were layoffs at least half the year. It was The Depression."

Inasmuch as he sought out such care-givers with a vengeance, Reed, having lost his mother at the age of two, suggested less pragmatic reasons why he always looked for women to "take care of" him. Such observations glanced right off of him. He couldn't or wouldn't deal with the concept of a surrogate mother. "If I had my way, I probably wouldn't have worked at all."

"With a woman taking care of you," he remarked, "it was beautiful when she said, 'Don't go to Philadelphia. Stay here. How much you making down there? I'll give you twice that much,' and to not have to go the next week to Philadelphia or Washington or . . . ."

59

... Oklahoma City, which was where Reed was headed back in 1924 after fleeing Seminole and the grisly razor-slashing of a hooker that took place right before his eyes.

Reed publicity photo circa 1930

CHAPTER EIGHT
I Learn While I Earn

"WHILE I WAS IN SEMINOLE, OLA HAD REMAINED IN OKLAHOMA CITY where she'd starting turning tricks. I was totally open-minded about it, though, and we got back together. There was a show we thought we might be able to hook up with called *Hits and Bits of 1925,* a T.O.B.A. revue that was just what the doctor ordered after several months that had seen us moving further and further away from show business. Tucker's show featured a Charleston contest, which I won hands down, as usual. [If Reed ever lost a Charleston contest, I was never able to get him to admit it.] Then we found out he needed a chorus girl, and Ola fit the bill, but in order to get her, he had to take me. It was the kind of show I was looking for, with comics, dancers, a band, and a line of pretty chorus girls.

"Everything I ever did at the Grand Terrace, the several Plantation Clubs, and Cotton Club in the 1930s, the Lincoln Theater in the 1940s, the Apollo in the 1950s, and at all the stops in between, drew upon what I'd learned in the year-and-a-half barnstorming around the country with Travis Tucker. All I'd ever really done up until joining up with *Hits and Bits* was some sideshow barking and the Charleston, and for the first few weeks with Tucker, all I ever did was my dance.

"Then, one night coming off-stage heading for the dressing room, Travis grabbed me by the elbow and insisted that I stand there and watch the show all the way through. He told me, 'I want you to learn everything that they're doing, and that even means the soubrette.'" [Few words in the language have disappeared from common usage so thoroughly and rapidly as has the once common "soubrette," which referred to the frivolous young female lead in a production, with its meaning having been more or less subsumed by "ingénue."]

"I already respected Tucker a lot, and was honored that he was trying to pass along some of his knowledge to me, even though the deal about learning the soubrette's part struck me as kind of pointless. I took him up on his 'offer,' though, and watched all of *Hits and Bits* every performance. The whole thing went over like gangbusters. And no sooner had I pretty much familiarized myself with everything when—you probably guessed it—the soubrette got sick, and I went on in her place. Didn't do it in 'drag,' but sang her number, 'I'm Looking at the World through Rose-Colored Glasses,' then did her dance routine, and after that was over, went right into my Charleston. All of this was right at the very beginning of the show. I experienced first-hand Tucker's philosophy of pacing a show, or *lack* of it: just hit the audience with your best shot right out of the starting gate and everything else will just fall into place. That seems to go against all common wisdom about pacing, but it works. Using this approach successfully all through the 1930s and 1940s, if it weren't for this bit of wisdom and a whole lot more that I learned from Travis Tucker, I doubt very seriously if show business would have become my life. He ended up teaching me every bit as much about that end of things as Dad Cook had taught me about life, and Zell Roan about sex.

Travis Tucker

"Travis Tucker's big thing was song parodies. In the 1920s, these were very big in comedy. People would have major arguments about which comic did the best parody of one popular song or another. Travis had his printed up. I'd sell them in the audience—they cost 10¢ apiece— and we'd split the money. In all likelihood, there's not a single copy of these little pamphlets left on the face of the earth. However, I can still recall many of Tucker's versions of the popular songs of the day:

63

"Irving Berlin's 'Always' became, 'I'll he drinkin' corn, Always. In the alleys and hallways, Always.' Tucker turned 'River Stay 'way From My Door' into ''Policeman Stay 'way From My Door.' And 'Bye Bye Blackbird' became the story of craps players and their attempts to evade the law: 'We were pickin' 'em up and layin' 'em down, shootin' 'em in, curvin' 'round, bye bye policeman.'

"Travis was a boozer, but not to the point where he was an alcoholic. When he muffed his lines, then you knew he was drunk. Another way you could tell was, instead of putting cork all over his face, sometimes he'd just put a ring around his mouth. Anyway, one day found me standing in the wings stage right watching the entrance of the other comic who entered from stage left, when Travis, who normally joined this guy from where I was standing, just gave me a big old shove and said, 'You're on. Do me.' Turning around and looking at him, I was petrified. He repeated, 'Do me.' So . . . knowing the bit, I did it! Before long, every time he didn't feel like it, I'd cork up and go on in his place.

"Usually we'd hit a town for a week, but there were also some split weeks. For example, Bessemer and Insley, Alabama were splits weeks before you played a full week in Birmingham. You played Bessemer for three days, Insley for three or four days, had a day off, and then go into in Birmingham. Most towns were a week. No more, no less."

Travis Tucker and wife Anna Gresham's comedy and dance act was the centerpiece of the traveling show, *Hits and Bits of 1925*. The couple had appeared in numerous other T. O. B.A. revues, such as the *Darktown Frolics of 1921*. Then in 1924, they took over the annual *Hits and Bits* series from performer Billy King. The revue, with its nineteen-member troupe of six chorus girls, a soubrette, a specialty dancer, a dancing act, two comedians, a straight man, a vocal quartet, and male and female vocalists, was typical for shows of the period. (Productions smaller than *Hits and Bits* usually made do without the quartet.)

Unlike many of the other shows that were touring the T.O.B.A., *Around the World* (Toby Time's east coast variant) or lesser Black circuits,

Hits and Bits didn't have a catchy, pointedly racial title, such as *Ebony Vampires, Brown Babies,* and *Chocolate Box Revue.* Why, one wonders, weren't such titles reserved instead for Black shows intended for all-White audiences?

Also in 1925, there was *Charleston Dandies,* which featured in its cast at one time or another that season John Snow, the Violin Wonder; Bob Davis, The Witty Gentleman from Chicago; Joe Bright, 1000 Pounds of Versatility (who plays a part in Reed's story a little later on); Patch-Head Smith, Exponent of Sparkling Humor; Julius Caesar Adams, Cyclist Extraordinary; Sun Burnt Jim: the Knight of Joke and Chatter; Sugar Foot Brown, the Mouth Harp Blowing Boy With the Fantastic Feet; and Pauline Montella, the Soubrette With a Thousand Qualities.

The star and producer of this popular T O.B.A. Show, *Charleston Dandies,* was none other Clarence Muse, who went on to great success in films, appearing in over 300 titles. Reed and Muse's paths crossed constantly on the road that season, and a year later Reed was even employed by Muse who, Reed claimed, still owed him unpaid salary. He laughed, "Boisey De Legg, S.H. Dudley, Clarence Muse, Joe Bright . . . all these dead guys owe me money from when I worked for them." (Muse died in 1979.)

Working the T.O.B.A circuit consisted of all the well-known physical rigors that have come to be associated with life on the road during the 1930s Big Band Era, plus the indignity of Black performers having only occasional access to convenient and decent overnight accommodations and to restaurants that would offer them table or counter service. The latter included: in New Orleans, Mom Phine's; and in Atlanta, an actors' hangout, with photos of famous Black performers on its walls, run by one Lonnie Hicks. Such ad hoc locales, however, tended to be in private homes. However, the lobby of the T.O.B.A. Palace Theater in Memphis featured a restaurant that served good food, and larger cities like Memphis also contained hostelries catering to Blacks, such as the Washington Hotel in Nashville. However, inasmuch as it was the former

A.N. Johnson mortuary and still had the look of one, performers tended to stay away: The barber shop was the former morgue, the rooms were all stark and white and, over all, a creepy feeling prevailed.

Barnstorming from city to city on trains that were racially segregated or on buses, performers had to put on two and three shows a day and often had to help in technically setting them up. At least one African-American entertainer, Duke Ellington, got around the problem of accommodations and food entirely by chartering entire train cars on which his band traveled: When they pulled into a town, the setup was shunted onto railroad sidings where the band resided hassle free for the run of the engagement. This was a fairly common White practice; however, very few (if any) other Black operations could afford a solution of this magnitude.

For the first half of this century, Black performers and actor-managers like Clarence Muse and Travis Tucker played almost exclusively to African-American audiences in the Midwest and the South. Aside from circuses, carnivals, and fairs, there were few others venues that would showcase their talents.

Though the T O. B.A. theaters themselves catered to an almost exclusive Black clientele, there were exceptions. Atlanta's 81 Theater on Decatur Street had a Thursday midnight "Matinee" for Whites only, at which time ultra-fashionable Atlantans turned up in droves clothed in glittering evening wear to witness the likes of Reed or Tucker or String Beans Price. The crowd paid a price for the privilege of "slumming," for this was indeed the atmosphere that prevailed; the price increased from the standard 40¢ and 60¢ to the (then) steep tariff of $2. Also, the Gay Theater in Birmingham, contained seven rows of seats around the projection booth reserved for the White friends of owner H. J. Fury.

Most of the (primarily) White theater owners treated the itinerant Black Toby Timers with dignity and kept well-maintained locations. In fact, some of the theaters were quite majestic, like the Lincoln in Kansas City and the Ella B. Moore Theater in Dallas, with its main floor of 600 seats, a balcony for 500, loge seats for 100, four boxes, a reception area, a roof garden, and seven dressing areas. Despite the fact that the Ella B. Moore Theater (named after the owner) was one of the nicest and most elegant on the circuit, even here there was a catch, said Reed. "It was located next to the railroad tracks. Trains would pass, and you had to stop until it had gone by so the audience could hear you."

In general, Reed recalled the T. O. B. A. and other Black theaters as being on a par with those catering to Whites, which is to say they were adequate: They had curtains; they had spotlights; they had a pit band. Many of the theaters were large. The Princess Theater in Kansas City was a thousand seats; the Koppin in Detroit, the same.

Not that there weren't some less-than-adequate Black theaters. St. Louis' Booker T. Washington Theater, located on Market Street, was an 800-seat theater that had once been an airdrome and was converted into an indoor theater by the simple means of putting on a roof. The floor was cement, and the walls were crawling with exposed steam pipes whose main purpose seems to have been to convince the audience of heat even when there wasn't any.

Reed remembers the Star in East Baltimore (not a T.O.B.A. Theater) as being an especially grueling experience. The stage held six or seven people and didn't even have a crossover, i.e., space to move across the backstage area from left to right wings. However, in such instances you knew beforehand what the theater was like and, generally, the show would be pared down to, perhaps, two comedians, a straight man, a singer and a dancer, to compensate for the reduced playing space. Reed says it was simply a case of "if you were good, the audiences would listen; if you were bad, they wouldn't."

The great Ethel Waters was far less charitable than Reed in her assessment of the T.O.B.A., and Black theaters in general. Wrote the singer-actress in her autobiography, *His Eye is on the Sparrow*:

"They [the audiences] did what they pleased while you were killing yourself on stage. They ran up and down the aisles yelling greetings to friends and sometimes having fights. And they brought everything to eat from bananas to yesterday's pork chops." Nevertheless, Waters agreed with Reed on one point: "If they liked you, they were the most appreciative audiences in the world. They'd scream, stomp, and applaud until the whole building shook."

CHAPTER NINE
Tales of the T. O. B.A.

"SOME OF WHAT ETHEL WATERS WROTE ABOUT ROUGH AUDIENCES might have been true, but she had more trouble with her men *and* women than with theaters, and, besides, she didn't really play the T.O.B.A. theaters all that much. I was on that circuit for almost two years and don't ever remember crossing paths with her. She worked Philadelphia and Baltimore. The Standard, the Royal, and the Howard. However, she didn't go down and play the Lyric or the 812 in New Orleans, or the Lincoln in Kansas City. Ethel was a bigger timer than that.

"*Hits and Bits* was almost exclusively T.O.B.A., and on the road nearly year-round in big cities, small towns, and in every kind of theater imaginable. The pace was every bit as tough as on the Charleston circuit. Bad food, accommodations, traveling conditions, money, health care, all of it, was just the worst. However, the fervor of the audiences, and the support and friendship you got from the other performers, made it all worthwhile. No matter how wild it got, we all stuck together. Like the time in the winter of '25 when we were booked into Chattanooga, Tennessee for an entire week and it was so cold, dogs were sticking to the sidewalk. The landlady in the rooming house gave us no heat or firewood, and the cold was blowing down the chimney and into the fireplace, and finally I couldn't stand it any longer. Taking her chairs and put them in the fireplace and setting them on fire, when I'd finished with them, I threw in everything else in the room that was flammable. We were gone by the time she found out, but apparently she was not amused. By the time we got to Knoxville, Tennessee, the next stop on the tour, the sheriff there was looking for me. Travis whispered, 'You better take the bus to the next town, and wait for us. I'll tell the law you're no longer with the show, and I don't know where you are.' I had to miss a week's worth of shows waiting around in Gadsden, Alabama for *Hits and Bits* to catch up with me just because of exercising my god-given right to stay warm when it was ten below outside.

"Just about everybody in the show was sleeping with somebody else. Regardless, you had to say you were married to your partner in order to stay in the same room with him or her; an arrangement that was desirable from an amorous *and* economic point of view. Sam Price, our piano player, told the rooming house lady that he was married to his girlfriend; Happy D'Nover, one of our dancers. She was supposedly married to the person he was shacking up with. I was 'married' to Ola, etc. There were even fake wedding rings. We'd gotten by with sharing rooms with our various lovers on the road for so long that we'd almost forgotten we were breaking the law. Maybe somebody let something slip, or forgot to put on a ring? Could never did find out why, but in Danville, Virginia, the police came in, raided the place where we were all staying, and dragged every last one of us from the show off to jail-and not just the ones who were sleeping together. We were violating cohabiting laws, they said, and anyone who couldn't produce proof of marriage would have to serve time.

70

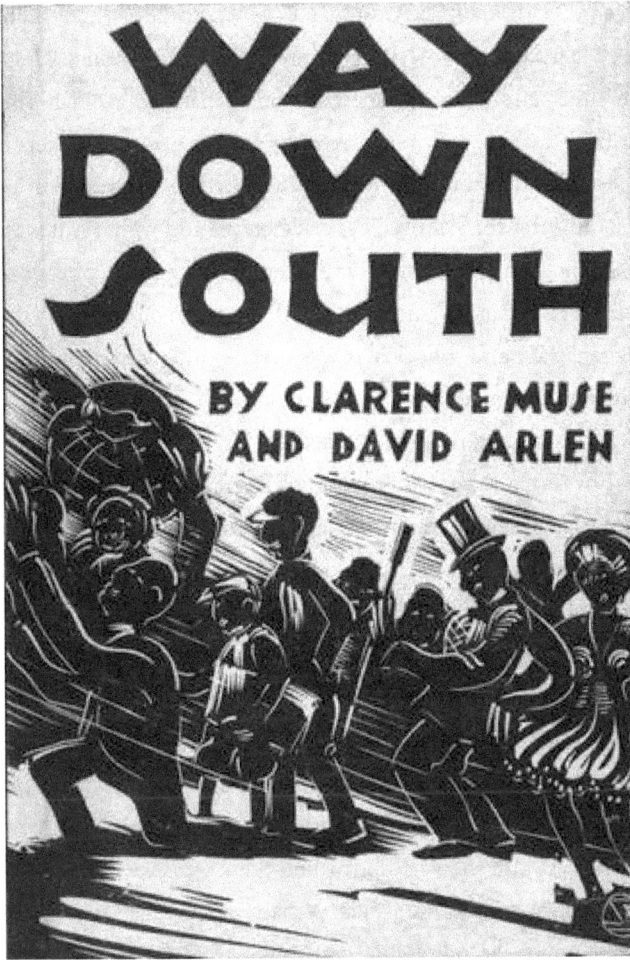

1932 roman à clef, real persons depicted as fictional characters traveling the T.O.B.A. circuit.

It had nothing to do with race, that's just the way the social climate was back then. There wasn't a single one of us who was legally married, and it looked like the bitter end for *Hits and Bits*, but the manager from the theater ending up bailing us out. Then, some strings were pulled and all we got was a fine.

"Not that there wasn't a lot of racism, especially if you happened to be traveling with a T.O.B.A. show all over the South where they didn't allow a Negro out of doors after nine o'clock. If the police caught you on the street after that, which was kind of hard to avoid if you were appearing in a show, you were arrested. However, the performers had an Open Sesame. It you were nabbed, all you had to say was, 'I'm working at the 81 Theater for Tom Bailey,' or wherever and whoever it was. Then they'd call him up and say right within earshot, 'I got one of your niggers down here. His name is (such and such). Is he one of yours?' 'Yeah, that's my nigger,' Bailey, or whoever it was on the other end, would say. 'Let him go.' And that was that.

"My being so light-complected, there were some towns and theaters where I wasn't allowed to perform. Either the manager didn't want it, or I'd play a day or two and the cops would complain. Most of my trouble came about because I looked *too White* not because I was Black. In Birmingham, Alabama, the police came and got me out in the middle of the night and made me move into the White hotel. Another time in Birmingham they let me stay in the Black hotel even though they thought I was White because of telling them that my father owned the show and it was important that I remain close to the rest of the outfit. It was fairly common for the law to make this kind of exception.

"Unlike White shows, I don't think there was ever a T.O.B.A. show that had its own buses or train cars. Perhaps the popular Whitman Sisters did at one point; I'm not really sure. However, *Hits and Bits of 1925* was public transport all the way; buses, but mostly trains. And when it came to travel, unlike the hotels, I was segregated from the rest of the cast all the way down the line. Had to ride the front of the train as a White man, while all the rest had to ride in the back; the same thing went for buses. Some members of the cast held bad feelings toward me because of that. They thought I actually enjoyed the privilege; in fact, it made me sick to my stomach.

"Restaurant people usually assumed I was White, and I was the one elected to go in and get food for the cast. Even though it wasn't true, sometimes I'd even get to thinking that the only reason I was with *Hits and Bits* was because of being so White and could get things like this done easier than a Black man. This was even resented by some of the cast, even though I was getting their food quicker. One time, the resentment reached a point of real craziness. Somewhere down South with *Hits and Bits* I went into a place, ordered the sandwiches and while I was waiting, I asked for a piece of pie and a cup of coffee and sat down (something that no Black man could do) and this *thing* from the show walked in, saw me sitting there, and said 'How come I can't if he's eatin'? He's a nigger, too.' We both got thrown out on our cans, and everyone had to go someplace else for food.

"What a world! Travis Tucker had a regular tour that lasted for four or five months. He always started in Chicago, played most of the T.O.B.A. cities, then did some east coast cities, on what was called the Around the World circuit. In 1980, I went through some of these towns on a trip across country. I kept an open eye for theaters I'd played with *Hits and Bits* and was able to take a picture of the theater in Richmond where I played in 1925. It's called something else now, they've changed the name—added to it—but it's still there. Every other theater I searched for along the way was apparently gone, though; demolished, burned down, or changed into something unrecognizable. *Hits and Bits* always finished up a tour playing a week in Baltimore, Travis' hometown. Then, the cast would go their own ways for a month or so while Tucker remained in Baltimore reworking the show (*Hits and Bits* of '25, '26, '27, etc.) for its next swing on the circuit. Usually, I took it easy during these layoffs, but in late 1926, I became a little more ambitious. The Charleston was dying out and I wanted to learn other steps and routines. While *Hits and Bits* was on hiatus, I took on a dancing partner by the name of Cut-Out (his real name was Maceo Ellis), who had joined up with *Hit and Bits* somewhere along the way. We called our act 'Leonard and the Cut-Out Kid.'

"Maceo did a dance called the Cut-Out; it was a peculiar little dance, so he was labeled with his name, just like another dancer, Buzzin' Burton, who got his name from a dance he did called the Buzz. There were a lot of new dances coming along around that time: Scratching and Grabbing, the Black Bottom, Truckin', and the Cutout. It was easy to find work. We played Washington, Baltimore, and Philadelphia, and other cities in the east on the Around the World circuit. Cutout and I performed as two sailor boys. We had purple sailor suits. Cut-Out was cork-faced and I was the light face. We did jokes and danced, with me as the straight man.

"Me: 'I don't like your running around with my sister!':

"Cut-Out: 'I'm not running around with your sister, I'm gonna marry her.'"

"Me: 'You can't marry my sister. You don't make enough money to support her.'"

"Cut-Out: 'I make enough money for the two of us.'"

"Me: 'Yeah, but suppose there's more?'"

"Cut-Out: 'What are you talking about?'"

"Me: 'Babies . . . children.'"

"Cut-Out: 'Were not going to have any children.'"
"Me: 'You can't say that. How can you stop having children? If you have an affair, you're gonna have children. Science will tell you, you GOT to have children.'"

"Cut-Out: 'Wellll . . . [Cutout knocks on wood] we been lucky so far.'"

"The audience fell out.

"Cut-Out also sang parodies, the kind that Travis Tucker did, and I'd do a solo dance. We not only wrote our material, we stole from other comics, which was common back then, because there was no such thing as getting someone to write your material for you. You just did the best you could.

"After we'd been working together a few weeks, somebody caught our act—I don't remember who—in Philadelphia at the Standard Theater where we were doing stock. As a result, we were hired to appear in New

York. It was the first time I'd ever been there. We were going to be on a bill headlined by Mamie Smith at the Lincoln Theater on 135th Street between Lennox and Seventh Avenue.

"I was excited about playing the Lincoln, but it was just as thrilling to finally get to New York. When we came through the tunnel, and they announced, 'Ladies and Gentlemen, get your coats and hats, in five minutes we'll be in Grand Central Station,' it was the greatest thrill I'd ever had. And when we saw Harlem, it was just the greatest thing ever. We had never played or even seen a theater as large as the Lincoln. This was the Big Time!"

The Lincoln Theater in New York, along with the larger Lafayette, was one of the two big-time Black theaters in Harlem. Built in 1908, by the time Cutout and Leonard arrived in Harlem in early 1927, the Lincoln was the longest-operating theater in the community specializing in staging shows for Black audiences.

After playing the Lincoln, and a date at the Pearl Theater in Philadelphia, Reed and Cutout completed another brief tour with *Hits and Bits*, then journeyed out on their own as performers once more. It was then that they appeared on a bill with Bessie Smith discoverer, Blues legend in her own right, Ma Rainey. Georgia-born Rainey was buck-toothed, squat, and wall-eyed, and was sometimes openly referred to as "the ugliest woman in show business." However, she worked at offsetting her ungainliness by decking herself out in elaborate, expensive jewelry made from gold coins, which resulted in her also being called, a bit more kindly as "The Golden Necklace Lady of the Blues."

By the time the T.O.B.A. shut down in the early 1930s, Reed had managed the extraordinary feat of working on shows with unarguably the five finest Blues innovators of their day: Ma Rainey and the three "Smith girls," as they were often called by the public: Clara, Mamie, and Bessie, and his personal favorite of all the early Blues singers, Ida Cox, who Leonard describes as:

"...a much smoother and more appealing style than any other Blues singer, although Bessie always gets most of the credit today. I remember once when Cutout and I were on a bill with Bessie at the Royal Theater in Baltimore, when she was also supported by a popular comic-female impersonator by the name of Dinah (that was the name he went by) Scott. Actually it was called a 'wrench act' and didn't employ full drag. Dinah Scott wore a bustle when he worked and tights pants. When he went to do the split one night at the Royal, his pants accidentally split, and everything just fell out; no underwear, no jock strap, no nothing. Alas, Dinah didn't know it and just kept on working. The audience was laughing so hard they were peeing, but the stage manager, and the emcee, Al Bratley, and everyone were gesturing and begging for him to come off. 'Not now, I got 'em!' Dinah shouted back. Then finally he looked down, saw what had happened, and fainted dead away right there on the stage. When we followed Scott's act that night, the audience just didn't have much left over for us (and not even for Bessie Smith)."

CHAPTER TEN
Uncle Will

"THE FIRST PERSON I LOOKED UP IN NEW YORK WAS MY UNCLE, WILL Marion Cook. I'd never met him before, because he'd mostly been in Europe giving command performances before kings and queens. He was a very important man: he had written the first Black musical to ever appear on Broadway, *Clorindy*, in 1898. A few years later in 1903, he began writing the music for the first of several hits for the team of Bert Williams and George Walker, *In Dahomey*. He was one of the major figures in Jazz and popular music, but just about the only other things I knew about him when I first met him in 1927 was that he'd done some work and arrangements for Ziegfeld, and was known as an s.o.b. because he'd rip up the scores if the musicians—especially fiddle players—weren't playing what they were supposed to play. He would walk right up and tear their music in half. I even saw him do it once. He knew what he wanted and went after it.

"The most famous story about him is that he was so angered by a review in the *New York Times* that called him merely the world's best *Black* classical violinist, that he walked into the office, smashed his violin on the critic's desk, and vowed never to concertize again, a vow he held to until he died in 1944, heartbroken and more or less forgotten. But when I was first in New York and said his name, almost everyone in show business, Black or White, knew him as an outstanding arranger and musician. Much of his training came from composer Antonin Dvorak, and from conservatories abroad, where he studied as a youth.

"In New York, I saw him almost every day and he was really nice to be with. He really loved Hartwell, my older brother. Harty had written a couple of good songs, and Will Marion had helped get them published. [Hartwell was also a dancer, who appeared in a number of New York shows. His wife was the well-known dancer, Louise Cook.] Duke Ellington once called Will Marion Cook, 'The master or all masters of my people.'

Will Marion Cook

"Unfortunately, Ziegfeld didn't make him known, unlike Paul Whiteman, who made it known to everybody that Gershwin wrote *Rhapsody in Blue*. The reason Cook was passed over, of course, is because he was Black. It doesn't matter how this sounds; he should have tried to pass for White, just like I did for a while a few years later.

"Johnny Nit, my tap guru from K.C., was another person I looked up after hitting New York. For a while, he'd even been with *Hits and Bits* at the same time I was, and he continued trying to show me how to tap dance cramps, rolls, wings, and so on. Just didn't get it, though. Starting again, in '27 whenever I was in New York, he spent time with me again, only this time I got it. How to tap!

"Later on, there was a wonderful dancer by the name of Teddy Watson, who nobody's ever heard of, who taught me how to do Trenches and Over the Tops [tap dance steps].

"During the next year, after teaming up with Cutout, we did little tours of our own every time Travis Tucker shut down *Hits and Bits* and took a breather in Baltimore. Arriving back there in the fall of '28, fresh from supporting Ida Cox at the Koppin Theater in Detroit, we were ready again to go back out on the road with Travis when I caught wind of a New York-bound all-Black revue playing in Baltimore that week that was still taking on talent. It wasn't just any ordinary revue; it was *Deep Harlem*, and the brains behind it were the team of J. Homer Tutt and Salem Tutt Whitney. And unlike most Black shows, which barely managed to limp into Manhattan while no one was looking, this one wasn't headed for the outskirts of Times Square, but Broadway proper. Set to open not during the summer doldrums when Black producers usually took owners up on offers to lease their theaters for a cheaper rate, but right after the first of the year at the top of theatrical season. It was too good an opportunity for Cutout and me to pass up.

"We auditioned for Tutt and Whitney at the Royal (in Baltimore). The brothers weren't interested in our comedy, though; they only wanted to see us dance. Instead, we both Charlestoned. Cutout did 'the Cutout, and we really gave it our best shot, and they hired us on the spot.

"Elected to tell Travis Tucker, I'd never given him a second thought when we auditioned. Now I knew I needed my mentor's blessings and acknowledgment that Cutout and I were 'ready' for Broadway and that there were no hard feelings.

"The day after the audition, I stopped by his house to see Travis and to tell him the news about Cutout's and my big break with Tutt and Whitney, heroes to almost every Black performer in the country, Travis included. Just like in all those backstage movie musicals, the ones where one-half of a team gets their big chance while the other partner has to stay behind, Tucker reassured me: 'This is your big chance. Take it!' And we did, and Tucker and I remained good friends up until the time he died in a car wreck in 1933. I'm still close with his daughter, and consider her my sister. As for my girlfriend Ola Jones and me, we'd come apart several months before, with no hard feelings. So there was no problem there, and we even managed to work again briefly as act during the early 1930s.

"December of 1928 found Cutout and me joining the cast of *Deep Harlem* at Washington, DC's Howard Theater, the show's last stop prior to New York and a final two week rehearsal period before opening on Broadway at the Biltmore Theater.

"We didn't have the proper costumes, and the show's wardrobe mistress had to make us some out of old theater curtains. That's how low the shows budget was, and I can still recall today what the mixture of fire retardant and sweat tasted like."

Brothers Salem Tutt Whitney and J. Homer Tutt were a prolific African-American producing-writing-acting team who, between 1910 and 1925, had produced and/or appeared in sixteen musical comedies and twenty-five revues, but until *Deep Harlem* they had never had a show on Broadway. *Deep Harlem,* with its all African-American creative team, had a score by (along with Homer Tutt) Joe Jordan and Henry Creamer ('After You've Gone,' 'Way Down Yonder in New Orleans'); a libretto by

Tutt and Whitney; and orchestrations by Will Vodery a *Ziegfeld Follies* regular and *aide-de-camp* to George Gershwin. In addition to Tutt and Whitney, the cast of *Deep Harlem* also included the popular dance team of Chapelle and Stinette, comedians Dusty Fletcher and John Mason, as well as the team of Grant and Sterling, Doe Doe Green, and the Four Northern Brothers. <u>And</u> Cutout and Leonard.

Also playing on Broadway the year of *Deep Harlem* were productions such as Elmer Rice's *Street Scene*, Preston Sturges' comedy *Strictly Dishonorable*; the war drama, *Journey's End*; and the trifle *Broken Dishes*, featuring an aspiring actress named Bette Davis. Laurence Olivier, whom Reed would eventually meet more than two decades later when he gave the actor-turned-icon a tour of Harlem's Apollo Theater, was making his first American stage appearance that year in the ephemeral *Murder on the Second Floor*, and the musical hits that season included *The Little Show, Fifty Million Frenchmen*, and *Wake Up and Dream*. The all-singing, all-dancing Black revue, *Hot Chocolates*, had also been well-received that year, as had been, earlier in the decade, such shows as *Runnin' Wild, Dixie to Broadway*, and *Rang Tang*, all brought into being to capitalize on the monumental 1921 Broadway success of the all-Black *Shuffle Along*. Clearly though, Tutt and Whitney were aiming for *Deep Harlem* to be something a little more serious than the high-stepping, down-on-the-levee Black shows that had come before it. For while act two of *Deep Harlem*, featuring Cutout and Leonard, adhered to the Black musical formula, act one represented a 180 degree about face from similar shows that had preceded it on Broadway, telling as it did, the story of an African tribe that had been defeated in war and abducted into slavery. The action follows them on their shackled journey through the African desert and the jungle, and finally to the slave ship and a nightmare of an ocean voyage to the United States; with the remainder of the act depicting their diaspora into slave markets and plantations. Reed, essayed the role of a slave ship captain cracking the whip and flogging Black captives being brought over from Africa. The Caucasian part came easily; He'd already had experience portraying White men . . . in real life.

Act Two found descendents of the slaves in the much more familiar surroundings of a Harlem night club, at which point *Deep Harlem* does more or less take on the trappings of a typical Black revue. However, the hard right into more conventional territory wasn't enough to save the show; most newspaper critics roundly panned it, with the one exception being the reviewer for the *Herald-Tribune* , who found it "interesting . . . because of its attempts to make something out of what wide-awake Negro minds have been thinking of possibilities for genuine Black drama."

Deep Harlem barely lasted out the week, opening on a Monday and closing on the following Saturday night. Since then, the Tutt-Whitney undertaking has come to be viewed by many experts in the field as a trailblazing effort; at the time, though, Leonard Reed had no sense he was part of a production that, more than sixty years after its production, would be remembered for its pioneer stereotype-shattering efforts. He was too close to be objective about *Deep Harlem's* sociological merit. Even though it represented a shot at a Broadway run, ultimately *Deep Harlem* was just a job like any other. When it was over, the act of Cutout and Leonard packed their bags, folded their tent, grabbed a red pencil and a copy of theatrical trade paper, *Variety*, and went to work . . . looking for work.

CHAPTER ELEVEN
Hustling and Hoofing

"IN THOSE DAYS THERE WERE SO MANY THEATERS CRYING OUT FOR talent that you had to be pretty *un*talented not to land something, and Cutout and I were certainly a lot better than average. Even though *Deep Harlem* was a failure, we'd started to make a name for ourselves. Bookings were no problem. We played Vaudeville, went on the road with Clarence Muse, and stock in Philadelphia with a company run by a character by the name of Joe Bright. He was a former member of the Black theater company—the Lafayette Players—who'd turned producer. His billing of '1,000 Pounds of Versatility' was an exaggeration in both departments, but he must have weighed at least 400 pounds. He was also a genius at getting himself out of the most impossible jams. Once, I remember, he committed some sort of crime, and they gave him sixty days in jail, and he went up before the judge, and he cried and cried just like a baby. The judge said, 'I'll make it day and night time,' which would have meant thirty days. Bright just kept on sobbing and the judge out it down to fifteen, and Bright just kept on with the waterworks. The judge finally ended up giving him one day in jail. Down from sixty! Once, Joe Bright got in a cab in Philadelphia and rode all the way to Baltimore without a dime in his pocket. He had the driver pull up in front of a Baltimore hotel, told him to wait, and went right on out the back door. One of the shows we did for Bright, in Philadelphia, was called *Why Girls Go Wrong*, a half-hour melodrama that was pretty much like its title sounds. It went on first, then the curtain came down and the variety part started. Cutout and I were working in both acts. We did bits in the drama and then our act in part two.

"Cutout and I had been working for Bright in Philadelphia for three or four weeks and still he had not paid off, beyond $2 here, $3 there. The rest of the cast was pretty much in the same boat. Finally, the company was getting ready to fold up for good, when Bright called everybody together. 'Gather round, everybody,' he said. And then I'll be damned if he didn't actually start crying. We all moaned amongst ourselves, 'Uh-oh, here comes some crap, man.' He acted like he didn't hear us. 'My mother just died. I'm not going to be able to pay anybody tonight . . . .'

"And just then, Cutout, who happened to be leaning up against one of the canvas wings, turned around and accidentally pulled one of them down. It fell over on top of Bright, whose head went right through the canvas."

"'Don't kill me, I'll pay you!' Bright yelled. 'I'll pay everybody!' And, he did pay us off.

During this period, I didn't only pair off with Cutout, but also teamed with several other partners. I also toured as a single in a show that featured eccentric dancer Boise De Legg and his Bandana Girls. However, teams were the thing, and so I got new partners practically every time I turned around; I'm unable to remember because there were

Harlem's Lafayette Theatre – 1985

so many of them. Somebody'd say, 'Hey, let's do an act.' And if you weren't working, more than likely you'd say, 'Okay.'

"Mostly, working with Cutout, we were doing stock at the Standard in Philadelphia when Garland Howard, a very popular comic of the day, saw us and put us in his headed-for-New York *Sundown Revue*, a much bigger and better show than the one we were in at the time.

"Howard portrayed a lot of different characters in his act, the most popular of whom was 'Hot Stuff Jackson.' Very funny and inventive, Howard did something I've never seen anyone do before or since. He didn't just do the voices and movements of his characters; he had a wardrobe trunk, and would quick change behind a screen right on stage. He did at least twenty costume changes during every performance. Eventually, like so many other Black performers, Garland Howard went to Paris where he became a big hit.

"After *Sundown Revue*, when Cutout and I weren't on tour, I always seemed to be on call at the Lafayette, usually working opposite the soubrette and was what you called the 'juvenile.' Could sing and dance, wasn't big and fat and out of shape, and looked good.

"Around the corner from the Lafayette, on 132nd Street, was Big John's, a restaurant and bar with a piano in the back that featured good cheap food and was run by a man who was a soft touch for performers down on their luck. In a basement, also just around the corner from the Lafayette, was the Rhythm Club. There you could almost always find piano players like James P. Johnson, Fats Waller, or Willie 'the Lion' Smith engaged in 'cutting' contests, i.e., trying to outplay one another. But the most important place as far as I was concerned was the Hoofers Club, the tap dancer's hangout.

"Today, for some reason or other, nearly everybody is under the impression that the Hoofers Club was under the Lafayette Theatre, but that just wasn't so. There was a breezeway on the uptown side of the theater where the exits were, then a storefront, then a hot dog stand that also sold newspapers, and right next to that were the stairs leading down to the Club; upstairs was a pool room.

"Another mistake people make today is in thinking that the Hoofers Club was just for dancing. Not so. As you walked down the stairs, you made an immediate left and there were two tables, one for poker, and one for blackjack; both were played openly. There was also a lunch counter, and at the end of that was the entrance to the room where the dancing happened. Everybody who went there didn't go there to dance. They went to get a sandwich, coffee, play poker, blackjack, or shoot pool.

"You didn't have to be a member or anyone special to be part of the Hoofers Club, just somebody who liked to tap dance. The room was about thirty feet square and had a piano. All the ones who didn't dance would watch the ones who got up to try. No one hooted anybody else down. We didn't practice just at the Hoofers Club. Inky (Freddy James), another dance partner of mine, and others of us sometimes could be found at two o'clock in the morning right out in the middle of the street in front of the Lafayette having 'cutting' contests. Speaking of such things, Bill Robinson once tried to arrange a contest between Alice Whitman of the Whitman Sisters and Ruby Keeler, because he told everybody that Alice was a far better dancer than Ruby. Even Fred Astaire didn't meet the high Hoofers Club standards for great tap dancing.

"Very few Blacks had the opportunity to take dance classes. Of all the dancers who hung at the Hoofers Club, I don't know one of them that ever went to a class to learn tap. The Hoofers was one of the reasons that New York produced more great tap dancers than anywhere else.

"When not hanging there, or touring with Cutout, or working at the Lafayette, you could usually find me hustling pool with the White boys at the Strand down at 47th and Broadway. Being around the Lafayette so much of the time, I even got the chance to appear with the Lafayette Players, who headquartered there. Granted, the parts were never big ones, a walk-on as a cop, etc., and I can't even recall the names of the plays. It still managed to be a thrill sharing the stage with Laura Bowman, one of the greatest actresses of her day, along with Jimmy Basquette [a.k.a. Baskett] . . . remember him as Uncle Remus from *Song of the South*? [The Players' alumni also included *Casablanca's* Dooley Wilson, Clarence Muse, and Charles Gilpin, who originated the title role in Eugene O'Neill's *Emperor Jones*.]

"At the Layette, I got my first exposure to a real producer, Leonard Harper. Travis Tucker and the others were performers who put shows together, but Harper was strictly a producer. Hanging out and watching him a lot, a few years later I got a chance to work for him when, appearing in his *Leonard Harper Revue* in 1932 at the Lafayette. I sang 'You're an Old Smoothie' and did a soft shoe with the wife of dancer Eddie Rector, Madeline Belt. [Also in the show were such popular acts as the Midnight Steppers; singers, The Palmer Brothers; dancers, The Two Black Dots; and comic Jazzlips Richardson.]

"In 1933, I worked for Leonard Harper, again at the Grand Terrace in Chicago, where I probably got one of the single greatest laughs of my career with an idea of his. At the very top of the show, I came out with this pageboy outfit on and a scroll in my hand. The trumpets played a fanfare and I said, reading from the scroll that I'd just unrolled, 'Hear Ye, Hear Ye, Hear Ye! Ladies and Gentlemen, I have been requested by the management of this theater to announce that at no time during this performance will you hear 'Stormy Weather.' Ever since Ethel Waters had popularized the song the year before, just about every other singer had sung it to death. So the audience laughed and applauded long and loud and gave me a standing ovation. That opening stopped the show . . . before it even started. That was Leonard Harper!"

In the 1920s, 1930s, and 1940s, nearly every Vaudeville or revue presentation featured at least one performer whose specialty was "laying down iron," i.e., tap dancing. This was especially true of Black shows. Most of the greats of the day, including John Bubbles, Bill Robinson, and Willie Covan, used the Hoofers Club as a kind of home away from home. One of the dancers there from whom Reed took his cue went by the name of "Piano." No one ever knew his real name, but Reed recalls he got his nickname because "he would hold on to the piano and do the most fabulous wings you've ever seen. Alas, if he turned the piano loose, he couldn't do nothin.' As long as he held on to that piano he could really wing."

New York's Lafayette Theatre, where Reed spent so much time in the late 1920s and early 1930s, was the nexus of African-American Harlem's theatrical and social life. This 2,000-seat venue, where all the biggest Black-oriented shows played, was built in 1911 and was also the home of the Lafayette Players. The Players opened a new show each Monday afternoon, which added up to some 250 plays from 1915 to 1928 during their residency. (The company, which disbanded in Los Angeles in 1932, also had troupes in Philadelphia and Washington, D.C.). Not only were original plays, musicals, and classics performed, but recently-closed successes from Broadway were also staged utilizing scenery from the original production, with the all-White casts being replaced by Blacks.

In front of the Lafayette Theatre grew the theatrical good luck charm, the Tree of Hope. Jobless African-American entertainers would touch its bark with hopes of landing work. Talent agents and producers who were casting shows also would regularly come by the talismanic tree to survey those congregated there. So just hanging out at the Tree of Hope might land you an engagement even if the superstition didn't hold water.

Tree of Hope and showgirls. Perhaps the only surviving photo of this legendary arboreal good luck charm

CHAPTER TWELVE
Two by Two

"CUTOUT AND I MUST HAVE WORKED IN A HUNDRED DIFFERENT theater and club shows all over the east and up around the Great Lakes. Two of the acts we appeared with were the husband-and-wife-team of comic George Williams and Bessie Brown (a great, forgotten singer) and comedian Gallie De Gaston, which illustrates my point perfectly about the need for having several performing partners that you could pair off with. When there was a call for a two-man comedy team but no singer, or else when Bessie was off somewhere appearing as a single, Gallie would often pair off with George in a comedy act they did together. Audiences were familiar with George Williams in both of these arrangements.

"It was during this time that Cutout and I managed to appear with all three of the Smith 'girls,' Clara, Mamie, and Bessie (with the latter in a show called *Steamboat Days*). We also worked with Butterbeans and Susie, who were as popular in their time as almost any act on the Black circuit. [Reed felt that no one was more popular during their time than Butterbeans and Susie with their put-upon wife/triflin' husband comedy presentation. The duo, whose real names were Jodey and Susie Edwards, and who were married in real life, also featured the latter's warm, expressive Blues singing, and played far and wide—and almost exclusively to Black audiences—for nearly fifty years up until the time of her death in 1963.] Butterbeans and Susie would end up playing together as a team into the 1960s, but that sort of thing just wasn't in the cards for Cutout and me. After a little more than two years together, we decided to throw in the towel. This was the usual sort of problem that plagued show business partnerships. I was the straight man and he didn't want me to turn a line around and get a laugh. If I got a laugh, we'd have a fight. In some cases, he was probably right. He was a few years older and knew much more about show business than I did, but I couldn't deal with the fact that he wanted to get all the laughs.

"Getting back together with good old reliable Inky in Detroit at the Koppin Theater, and meeting Sadie Montgomery, a chorus girl with the *Mamie Smith Revue,* I formed an act her. We were strictly a dance team—tap, soft shoe, exciting little turns, and it was a neat little act. She was nearly as light-skinned as I was, so we sometimes worked as a White act. We played independent theaters mostly around the Michigan area: Kankakee, Jackson, Michigan, Flint. She was a dominant figure over me, partially because she was older: Of course, we were shacking up together. It was while working with Sadie that my first experience with marijuana happened while moonlighting as an MC at a place in Detroit called the something-or-other Gardens. Just like nearly every town had a Plantation Club, they also usually had a this-or-that Gardens; let's just call it the Royal Gardens. At that time, a pool hustling buddy of mine by the name of Don Ramsey was working at the nearby Herbie's Black Cat with a woman who later went on to play a lot of maids in Hollywood movies. There were so many of *them* that I can't recall her name.

"Jap Branch and Wealthy Davis, two chorus girls in the show I was with, were friends of Don's, and I'd sometimes go in the dressing room to watch the three of them smoke pot. Afraid to try it myself, finally one night I gave in. Took one or two tokes. The next day, this is what I was told had happened: I more or less wove right out of the dressing and onto the stage—the floor show wasn't even on—and then said, 'Ladies and Gentlemen . . . I would like to introduce the girls.' However, glancing over my left shoulder, there were no chorus girls, and in the other direction there were no girls there either—only the manager shaking his head 'No!' and making gestures for me to get off. Just standing there looking dumb for a couple of seconds, then the band started playing, trying to cover for me. I said something about how they sounded like ten tin cans, which they did in my condition. Then, going blank again, I stared out into the audience and spotted a couple with their heads together whispering in one another's' ear, positive they were talking about me. Grabbing a waiter by the elbow, I demanded in a very loud voice that he stop them *at once*. Now the manager is *really* panicking. 'They're not saying anything about you. What the hell is wrong with you!? Are you alright? You're acting awfully strange.'"

"He tried to pull me off, but I yanked away and hauled myself back to center stage, again announcing, '. . . and *now* here are the girls.'" *Still* there were no girls. 'Awwww, the hell with it. I'll do it myself!' And with—sometimes—the band following me—sometimes not—I began to dance like a mad man.

"Don, hearing the ruckus going on, came out and whispered in my ear, 'Let me help you.' He tried to cover for me, pretending it was all just an act, but by now it was pretty obvious to the audience what was going on.

"Ramsey managed to half-dance, half-drag me off, right on down at to the corner White Tower, where I ordered a piece of lemon pie, a hot dog, and a bowl of chili, and washed it all down with several cups of coffee. Now, I was *really* wired.

"Heading back to the club, I began hallucinating all sorts of hideous masks laughing at me, which caused me to freak out completely, thinking I was going to die. It was at that point the club's manager told me to take the rest of the night off. A few years later, in Chicago, I sold the stuff, but never *ever* smoked it since then.

"The act with Sadie didn't last long. One night, I wanted to go out, but she didn't want me to, so she cut me with a razor. I still carry the scar on my leg. A razor cut won't leave; it stays with you. There's no way for it to heal. A knife will heal, but not a razor. Sadie sliced into me more than sixty years ago, but I still think of her every time I look down to put on my socks."

It is perhaps important to emphasize that there was nothing unusual about Reed's moving from engagement to engagement and partner to partner on a regularly irregular basis. He wasn't difficult to get along with, he wasn't unreliable, and he wasn't suffering from a bad case of Wanderlust. This was just standard operating procedure for thousands of entertainers of the era.

The team of Sadie Montgomery and Leonard broke up in Chicago, but there were much worse places for Reed to be without a partner, stranded, and out of work than the so-called Second City. Surpassed only by New York City in many areas of endeavor, and running a very close second when it came to theatrical activity, Chicago was a hub for both White and Black entertainers. Reed was not unacquainted with the town. Earlier that year, Chicago was where he and Cutout had headed right after the closing of *Deep Harlem*, and where, just after his arrival on the scene, he took singer Herb Jeffries up on an invitation to come along and witness the immediate bloody aftermath of the St. Valentine's Day Massacre. Now almost a year later, Reed was back there after his split with Sadie Montgomery. He was "between engagements," but his job search ended right at the top with the Whitman Sisters, in their time one

The Whitman Sisters

the highest-paid company of performers on the TO.B.A., and popular on White circuits, as well.

The Whitmans' show featured dancing, comedians, various girl singers, a chorus line of twelve or fourteen girls, a five-piece to six-piece Jazz band, and always a few first-rate dancers. The sisters owned their show and traveled over the United States, usually playing a full two weeks in the big cities. Over the years, from 1900 to 1943, May Alberta, Alice and Essie Whitman, and their twenty to thirty-member troupe provided jobs for hundreds of talented young Black performers. Tap dancer Bunny Briggs, influential scat singer Leo Watson, Count Basie, and Eddie "Rochester" Anderson are just a few of the African-American entertainers who got their start with the Whitmans and went on to fame and success. Youngsters learned the tricks of the trade with the Whitmans.

Dancer Briggs recalled, "You sang one week, danced the next, sold peanuts the next, and if you got caught breaking any of the rules, you got shipped home in a hurry."

In *Way Down South,* Clarence Muse's novelized look at life on the T.O.B.A., showman and performer, he wrote, "They always carried a bunch of clever kids with the show. These, they explained to their audiences, were friendless and homeless orphans. They'd picked them up in their travels and were trying to provide for them after God's commandment. Oft as not they were sending money back home to them parents of these kids. [It] was a tremendous sympathy getter and helped their business wonderfully."

Mabel , the eldest of the sisters, was the overseer of the troupe and generally conceded to be its creative spirit, as well as being rough-tempered and highly opinionated; a tough business woman whom it didn't pay to mess with. It was this ferocious survivor of the rough and tumble of the Black theater circuits who Reed would have to impress if he hoped to become a part of the Whitman Sisters company.

CHAPTER THIRTEEN
Tricks of the Trade

"THE STAGE DOOR WAS STANDING WIDE OPEN, AND I STROLLED RIGHT on into the Grand Theater in Chicago. Mom May was up on the stage rehearsing 'Tight Like That.'"

"'See that man standing over there; he's got no hat; he's got bald hair, oh, it's tight like that.'"

"I could tell she was having trouble staging the song. 'If you want me to,' I called out to her, 'I'll show you how to do it.'"

"'Who's out there? Who said that?' she shouted. My having broken her concentration, she was annoyed."

"'My name is Leonard Reed. I'm a dance director,' I told her, lying.

Reluctantly, she allowed me to join her on stage to show what I could do with 'Tight Like That.' Faking an improvised routine top-heavy on Charleston, when I was finished, she still didn't seem quite sold."

"'Show me what else you can do,' she snapped."

"I gave her a grab bag of dance tricks: the soft shoe, a couple of time steps."

"Somewhere in the middle of Shuffling off to Buffalo, Mom May shouted for me to 'Stop!' She liked how I 'sold" myself across the footlights; she offered me a job."

"By the time of my joining the Whitman Sisters, I knew how to 'wing' and do a lot of other tap business; I wasn't just a Charleston dancer anymore. Certainly no full-fledged dance director either, so I just faked it as I went along. It didn't take long, though, for me to exhaust all the routines that and I'd done with Cutout or Sadie. So, first with the Whitmans and, later on, on my own, I began to watch motion pictures and copy them. Busby Berkeley was just getting started and I took from him, and stole from MGM and from just about everywhere. Changed it all around, of course, and eventually, my own ideas began to come and I didn't have to stay one step of everyone else all the time.

"My best partner *ever*, and the most talented, was Willie Bryant. He first joined the Whitman Sisters in 1925; he left in 1928, but returned once again shortly after Mom May hired me. At some point before meeting him, Willie had originated a dance called the Goofus. Helping him expand upon it, we featured it in the Whitman show for not just one or two but a quintet of hoofers. In the middle, we put Alice Whitman, who was a tremendous tap dancer; Pops Whitman [Alice's son] was to one side of her; a dancer by the name of Joey Jones was on her other side; and Willie and myself were on either end. We did the Goofus, which I never thought much more about until a few years later when Joey was a member of a dance trio called the Three Little Words, and the Goofus was a popular part of their act, and they tried to take the credit for inventing it. By now they were calling it the Shim Sham Shimmy, and that's what it's been known as ever since then. Still . . . Willie and I originated it in 1929 when two of the Three Little Words were just babies, and Joey was with the Whitmans. The only credit he and/or they can take is for: a) adding the part where you shake your shoulders, and b) re-naming it the Shim Sham Shimmy, or just plain Shim Sham. I know it's a fact that some people say Willie and I didn't invent the Shim Sham, but I don't care who denies it. All that matters to me is that *I* know we did! I also know that I'm the inventor of Trickeration.

"Trickeration evolved in Chicago at a club called Dave's a few years after I worked with the Whitman Sisters. I said to my dancers, 'I'm gonna *trick* you girls today.' And from that came Trickeration.

"As opposed to doing a four-bar, two-bar break step, I did a sixteen bar step without a break. Using chorus dancing this way builds excitement, rather than just waiting for one step to happen, and then *another* step and *another*. With Trickeration, the audience keeps waiting for something to happen all the time.

"Something else I did at Dave's had not been done before in a night club, maybe in a theater, but not a club. There were two pillars holding up the building. I took a rope and ran it between the two posts that were on either side of the room, and put a swing in the middle of it and pulled it all the way back over the bandstand. Then, I wrote a song for the show called, 'Swingin' Way Up High' to go along with the effect.

"There was a girl named Mary Richards in that swing that went all the way out over the audience. She'd come flying at them right over the top of their heads and they'd be sitting there with their drinks, and the entire house would duck down. Some people even threw themselves on the floor. Just about the time they were back in their chairs, here came Mary at them from the other direction."

In borrowing from Busby Berkeley, Reed was unwittingly bringing a theatrical tradition full circle. The Berkeley films were blatant attempts at imitating and, in the process, outdoing the Broadway spectaculars of Florenz Ziegfeld. Camera movement, lighting, editing, and special effects techniques gave Berkeley the sort of tools a master snowman like Ziegfeld could only have dreamed about. Nevertheless, it was Ziegfeld upon whom Berkeley was dependent for the basic ideas behind his musical numbers. Naturally, working in a night club Reed couldn't possibly hope to duplicate Ziegfeld, much less Berkeley. However, by keeping Berkeley's effects in mind, he was able to give his shows an aura of spectacle seldom seen in cabaret.

When it comes to "Trickeration," there is usually far less controversy vis-à-vis Leonard Reed than there is when conversation rolls around to the subject of the Shim Sham. Nevertheless Reed's concern over his and Willie Bryant's failure to get proper credit for creating what has come to be known far and wide as the National Anthem of Tap Dancing is understandable. A degree of controversy still continues to swirl in the dance community as to exactly who devised the dance. Flash dancer Joe Jones, of the Three Little Words, claims the dance came about when, "I had been practicing something like a Time Step and we just changed it a little." Authors Marshall and Jean Stearns in their book, *Jazz Dance*, tried to settle the matter when they diplomatically opined that, "Actually there is every reason to believe that Bryant, Reed, The Three Little Words—and other dancers—all helped to create this routine, since it contains elements of various older steps." In her book, *Tap*, dancer Rusty Frank describes the Shim Sham as: "A four-step routine created in the 1920s by Leonard Reed and Willie Bryant, originally called the Goofus. Shimmying of the shoulders added. (The four steps are: 1) Shim Sham, 2) Push Beat and a cross over, 3) Tack Annie, 4) Half Break, and then the Walk-Off is tagged on.)"

Technical considerations aside, the great benefit of the dance is that within a short time of its innovation/evolution/invention, the Shim Sham became known by virtually all pro and non-pro tappers alike because it provided an instantaneous framework for ensemble dancing even amongst strangers, a lot of which was obviously going on in the Golden Age of nightclub club and theater, for as Reed told Frank: "They used to say there wasn't such a thing as not having a tap dancer in your show! 'Cause in my day, no matter where you went you would run into tap dancer. Everything had tap!"

Even if the Shim Sham question is never settled, Reed's reputation as a dancer and choreographer is secure; and, generally Reed and Bryant are accorded credit for inventing what is sometimes is even known as "the Shim."

"I didn't know that Leonard was the originator of the Shim Sham Shimmy for a long time," says tap elder statesman Fayard Nicholas, "because dancers have been doing it for as long as I can remember. I think my brother and I started doing it in 1934, but it wasn't until the 1980s that I finally found out that Leonard and Willie were the first to do it. I wasn't even aware of it, even though Leonard and I have been very good friends for more than fifty years. He doesn't go around making a big deal about it."

CHAPTER FOURTEEN

Scarface and the "It" Boy

"STILL SEVERAL YEARS AWAY FROM ESTABLISHING MYSELF AS, WHAT one member of the Black press would later call me, 'a swash-buckling, chestnut-haired young producing genius,' in 1929, I was still taking my cues from the Whitman Sisters, playing Chicago, Detroit, Columbus, Cleveland, Cincinnati, New York, Philadelphia, Baltimore, and Washington, D.C. With the company for about six months, Willie Bryant and I were just beginning to work up a nice little act of our own when I got into trouble. It seems that both of us were sleeping with Alice Whitman, and Mom May didn't like that kind of thing. One night, we were playing the Howard Theater in Washington, D.C., and I didn't think May was in the 'house.' Singing a song called 'Shake That Thing,' I walked right up behind one of the girls and began bumping and grinding against her, and generally stealing the show. May had seen it! She came backstage with a stick and started hitting and chasing me with it right on out into the snow where she fell down. I kept right on running, and never dared even to look back. Going to the hotel and packing my things, that was the end of the Whitman Sisters and me.

"Next, taking up with a dancer by the name of Willie Green who was also stranded in D.C., we went on the road together. The first job we had was in Georgetown, Maryland, at the Blue Mouse Theater. We worked a lot of nightclubs, but not many theaters. We'd hit a town, pick three or four local girls to be the chorus line, perform an opening with them, and then Willie and I would do solos and routines. Maybe we'd have one or two other locals in the show. He was a hell of a dancer, and I learned a lot from him: a lot of 'legomania' stuff with taps that I'd never seen before. [Just like it sounds, i.e., the use or extreme and jiggly leg movements.] Don't know why Willie Green never got bigger than he did, but few besides me ever recognized him as a great dancer. We went into all these little clubs and got a fair salary. We thought we were awful smart, and maybe we were. The places we worked were towns like Cleveland, Dayton, Toledo, and Canton, Ohio. And little stops like Willoughby, Ohio. Towns that nobody else would ever go to. We also worked Detroit at Herbie's

Black Cat, and broke up amicably after that upon my deciding to base in Indianapolis.

"The rest of 1929 and the early part of '30 consisted of training back and forth between Indianapolis and Chicago. There was little trouble getting work in both places. In Indianapolis, a hooker who was really fond of me set me up in a night club called the Nest, which I ran for a few months, along with producing shows at the Indianapolis Theater.

"In Chicago, I was a featured dancer and chorus boy at the famous— some would say "infamous"— Grand Terrace night club, where my billing was 'The It Boy.' [A reference to silent star Clara Bow's "It Girl" billing, and an acknowledgment of Reeds blue-eyed, wavy-haired good looks.] Supposedly, the *Terrace* was owned by a fellow named Ed Fox, but everyone in town knew that he was just a front for Al Capone.

"Unlike most places, they didn't sell whiskey under the table at the Grand Terrace. You came in with your own bottle [of Al Capone-bootleg hooch], and they'd serve you a cup of tea and you poured it in.

"Capone used to come in the *Terrace* and always would sit in the same seat down front dead center. He loved Earl Hines and [singer-dancer] May Alix. You didn't have any business relations with Capone if you worked at the *Terrace*. That was all taken care of by Ed Fox. You didn't approach Capone without being sent for. He had two men sitting there with guns, and anyone that approached his table knew what was going to happen if they got too close too fast. Just like he was later made out in the movies, Capone was a snappy dresser, right down to the tips of his immaculate white spats. He was a big deal in Chicago, and the cream of society and political bigwigs could usually be found at his table. He also liked to be surrounded by entertainers, but you stayed back in your dressing room and if he wanted to congratulate you or slip you an extra $5 or $10, he would send for you. I was invited to sit with him at the *Terrace* fairly regularly because he'd gotten to know me from when I worked for him before as a dancer at another club he owned in Stickney, Illinois. Still, no matter how nice he was to you, you didn't go somewhere else to work unless he said so.

"And you didn't cross Capone, like Billy Mitchell made the mistake of doing one time. A popular entertainer at the *Terrace*, by the name of Mitchell—not the Black Billy Mitchell famous for putting a whole lot of pool balls in his mouth but the 'yaller' Billy Mitchell who specialized in risqué material—was well-liked by the mob. Capone had great respect and appreciation for entertainers. The same held true with most of the Chicago mobsters. When they took you into their arms, you could do no wrong. "They loved you. But it went to Billy Mitchell's head. He began to get over-confident and started walking around with gin that he made at home in his bathtub. It was winter time, and he was going about the *Terrace* wearing this long old coat that had all these bottles of whiskey in the lining, and he'd hustle around the tables and whipping open his coat

105

ask, 'You like old King tonight, mmmmmm?' [Mitchell billed himself as the King of Comedy] 'The King was good tonight, Did you like Toby?' [The dog in his act] Then he'd slither up to you and whisper, 'Buy some gin? Buy some gin?"

"For several weeks, two of Capone's men, Ralph Bugelo and another we just knew by the name of Cowboy, kept warning him nicely, 'Billy, don't sell any more whiskey in here. You don't want to get us in trouble.'"

"'Yas, sir. Oh, I'm sorry, sir.'"

Still the next night it was the same thing, and the next, and the next. 'Buy some gin? Buy some gin?' Finally, one night Billy was selling this whiskey and they called him outside. It was raining like hell, and they grabbed him by the collar.

"'Didn't we tell you not to sell no more whiskey in this place?'"

"'Yah, yah, yah, Sir. Oh, don't hurt King.' He was shaking and trembling all over.

"And Bugelo took his gun and put it right across Billy's shoulder and shot. Boom!"

"And Billy fell right down on his knees. '"Don't kill King. I'll do anything.' And tears were coming down his face and he sticks his thumb in his mouth [miming fellatio] and says, '"I'll do anything. I'll do anything. Please don't kill King."'"

"The whole chorus line was standing at the door saying, 'They got Billy. They're going to kill him.' They're screaming, 'Please don't kill him!'

"Because when we heard the shot, we were all sure he was dead. Mitchell finally got the message. He stayed on at the *Terrace* but never dared cross Al in such a manner again.

In the Prohibition era, the Grand Terrace was to Chicago what the Cotton Club was to New York. Opening in 1928 at the corner of Oakwood Boulevard and South Side Parkway, the Terrace occupied the site of a former movie theater and was the grandest of the many popular entertainment spots in the city.

106

Grand Terrace Ballroom – Chicago

The Terrace ostensibly belonged to entrepreneur Ed Fox, but in reality the elaborate showplace had been taken over shortly after it opened by the Al Capone gang and handed over to the care of Capone's brother, Ralph (aka Mimi). Fox stayed on as a front and manager for the operations, but Capone began taking a large chunk of the profits from him in exchange for "protection." The Capone gang had a stranglehold on bootlegging activities in Chicago, but chose not to push the law too far by running the club as a speakeasy. Besides, nearly all the bring-your-own booze that was eventually quaffed in the club was of Capone manufacture.

Reed was doing some pot selling on the side, but it didn't encroach on Capone's whiskey-based activities. Unlike comic Billy Mitchell and his bathtub gin, Reed had the good sense to conduct his new pot-selling activities off the Grand Terrace's premises, thus remaining on the mob's good side. Reed insists: "I know it sounds funny to say this, but Al Capone was essentially a gentle man. He didn't kill off anybody except those that tried to take over his territory. He didn't, like most think today, just kill off people for the hell of it. He didn't go around kicking the little man in the ass. Capone probably gave the little man more money than he'd ever had in his life."

Pianist Earl Hines, another regular fixture at the Terrace, told his biographer Stanley Dance that Capone ran a restaurant that fed poor people and that he also bought real estate "where these same people could move in and live."

At the same time Reed was appearing at the Grand Terrace, he moonlighted during the day producing shows for Chicago's Indiana Theater. Early 1930 found him taking a smaller-scaled show from the theater on a projected tour that was such a success in its first stop, Indianapolis, that the company remained there for a period of several months (instead of its originally-planned run of five days). One of the musicians in the show was a pianist by the name of Willard Hamby, who had played with Louis Armstrong and Earl Hines.

According to Reed and other eyewitness, Hamby was equal in prowess to the great Art Tatum, but went entirely unrecorded during his lifetime. Another member of Reed's company was dancer Ralph Brown, who joined up with Reed's company when it landed in Indianapolis. Brown, who was one of the stars of the 1989 Broadway hit, *Black and Blue*, told author Rusty Frank in 1989, "Leonard Reed [who] was in my hometown, and he was a real professional dancer and producer. He had the knowledge of show business and helped me a whole lot with my beginning. Helped me when I needed help."

For the (then) seventeen-year-old, "help" consisted of giving him a job in the show in Indianapolis and then taking Brown on the road when Reed and his thirty-member troupe (including a shake dancer and twelve musicians) departed Indianapolis for Columbus, Ohio. Brown remained with the company until, as scheduled, the tour broke a few weeks later up in Cincinnati, where he and a half-dozen other members of the troupe then went their separate ways.

However, Reed and two others from the outfit, Orville "Hoppy" Jones and Mifflin Campbell, stayed on in the city hoping to take advantage of local radio station WLW's heavy reliance on Black talent for its daily broadcasts. Back in Chicago, the three of them had formed an on-again off-again singing group, The Peanut Boys. It was something Reed could fall back on when work wasn't necessarily plentiful elsewhere, and which proved popular enough that they had the honor of being tapped to be on the opening bill of the million-dollar Moorish showplace, the Regal Theater.

Reed with pre-Ink Spots group, the Peanut Boys

Now in Cincinnati, two years later, it seemed to the three of them that the trio—which found them accompanying themselves on the then popular eight-string instrument, the tipple, whilst singing in a somewhat jivey style best-seller songs of the day, such as "Sweet Sue" and "Exactly Like You"— would be perfect for the kind of programs the broadcasting giant, WLW, was pumping out all over the Midwest via its powerful clear channel signal. One popular singing group on the station, Four Boys and a Guitar, had just been launched into the big-time as the Mills Brothers, and, hoping for a similar break, The Peanut Boys gigged around Cincinnati, playing irregularly at such spots as the popular Castle Farms.

After a few months, Reed, tired of waiting for the call to come from WLW, departed The Peanut Boys but stayed on in Cincinnati, no exception to the many U. S. locales having a nightclub featuring Black talent and named after the famed Harlem spot, the Cotton Club. The Cotton Club Cincinnati was located just over the Ohio/Kentucky border in the notorious Midwestern "sin city" of Lexington, Kentucky, and, like most others throughout the U. S., this Cotton Club also catered to an all-White clientele.

Reed was employed at the Cincinnati Cotton Club for a short time, then once more hit the road as a specialty dancer with a Burlesque troupe headed by one Hinda Wassau, a short tour slated to land him back in New York in a few weeks.

Meanwhile in Cincinnati, The Peanut Boys and its two replacements for Reed, Deek Watson and Slim (Simp) Green, were doing well. Reconfigured, the group had changed its name to The Riff Brothers at just about the time the call from WLW finally came. [One name change later—two years down the line— found the ex-Peanuts-former Riffs known as The Ink Spots, an act that would soon come to rival even the Mills Brothers in popularity.] Reed, however, wasn't feeling left out because he'd not gotten in on the Riff Brothers' big WLW break. He was happy just to be back in New York where his appearances with exotic dancer Hinda Wassau ultimately did qualify as some kind of brush with greatness.

Like so many other great discoveries, the telephone, radium, etc., Wassau's happened quite by accident. One night in back in 1922, she was appearing at some historically unrecorded location as just another dancer when her bra strap broke. Instead of running for cover, though, she went with the flow and made artistic capital of the unseemly break, and thus was born the uniquely American art form of the striptease. Years later, when asked if he knew this to be ex-employer Wassau's claim to fame, Reed replied, "No! But it doesn't surprise me . . . I always only worked with the very best."

CHAPTER FIFTEEN
Brains As Well As Feet

"HINDA WASSAU FINISHED OUT HER WEEK AT HURTIG AND SEAMON'S Burlesque on 125th Street (two years hence, in 1934, it would become the Apollo Theater) and moved on; but I stayed in New York. Since there hadn't been a day in my life since leaving Cornell University six years earlier but what I hadn't been dancing, scuffling, hustling, pimping, or just plain running from the law, now seemed like as good a time as any for me to take my first-ever real vacation. Inasmuch as Atlantic City was as far away as you could get from the merry-go-round I'd been on and still be in this country, that's where I decided to go for a nice couple of weeks lying in the sun on the beach, with the salt air, doing the whole Atlantic City bit.

"While checking into the hotel, I learned that my old friend, musician Norman Thomas—not the perennial Socialist presidential candidate—

along with his Quintet, were in town that week. Since it couldn't hurt to just sit in a theater and enjoy a show—after all, wasn't that something you did on vacation?—after settling in at my hotel, I went to see them perform.

"The Norman Thomas Quintet was a rarity, a colored group that played almost exclusively to White audiences; they were a major RKO attraction when each White circuit only handled a few Black acts at a time. The Quintet was real crowd pleasers, and the night I saw them in Atlantic City was no different.

"First, dancer Freddy Brown came down into the audience beating a drum, pounding the floor with his feet, and keeping time on the arms of the theater seats to 'Runnin' Wild.' Then, Robert Shanks sang one of his specialties, the spiritual 'Oh, Lord Please Take Away the Darkness.' Next, Thomas' son, Sonny, came out and did a dance spot with a partner, and, finally, Norman finished up with a bang doing his trademark song 'Listen to the Mockingbird.' Afterward, I went backstage to say hello.

"Maybe I should have just stayed back on the beach gazing out at the ocean and eating saltwater taffy, for by the time of my leaving the theater that night I'd agreed to replace Sonny's departing dance partner when [The Norman Thomas] quintet opened in Columbus, Ohio the following weekend.

"The first few weeks with the Norman Thomas Quintet were uneventful: from Columbus, Ohio and the Ohio State Theater, we traveled to Pittsburgh, where we played the Pitt Theater, and from there to Washington and the Downtown Theater, then on to Asbury Park.

"The last stop on the first leg of the tour, though, was the Palace, the New York Vaudeville house that was such a big deal for show people back then that some spent their entire careers trying to get a booking there. And here I'd just stumbled into playing the Palace without even half trying. Looking back, it's something I'm proud of, even though appearing on a bill with Ethel Barrymore was anything but pleasant. [One of Barrymore's specialties in Vaudeville was *The Twelve-Pound*

Leonard Reed and Willie Bryant, i.e. Brains as Well as Feet

Look, an old James M. Barrie one-act warhorse that the legendary actress had been playing in Vaudeville since 1912. It's something she fell back on especially when she needed money—lots of it—and fast. In 1929, she was still trotting out the drama of female emancipation when she was headlining the Palace.] First we opened the show, but we were so good we went second, then we went third, moving closer and closer to her slot, but she didn't want us to steal her thunder by appearing just before her, so she had us relegated to being the closing act, the dog position in Vaudeville. Ethel Barrymore didn't allow anyone to stand in the wings when she was working and just had that kind of suspicion and dislike that a lot of legitimate actors had for Vaudevillians.

"When my tour with The Norman Thomas Quintet was over, I returned to Chicago and the Grand Terrace. One day, shortly after my return there in early '30, I walked into rehearsal and heard someone shout, 'Hey, pal, how you doin'?' Turning around, there was Willie Bryant, my old dancing partner and rival for the affections of Alice Whitman. Nothing in his voice suggested that there was any bad blood remaining between us. He walked up, slapped me on the back, and we resumed a friendship that would last for nearly the next forty years. In fact, he was even my best man at my marriage a few months later.

"People were surprised when showgirl Anna Jones and I tied the knot. I just didn't seem like what they called, back then, the marrying type. What they didn't know was I'd gotten married because of a robbery.

"Besides women, my only other vices were clothes and more clothes. I was a clothes freak. By then I had a wardrobe fit for a king: beautiful mohair, shantung and silk suits; a dozen tuxedos; at least a hundred shirts; and so many pairs of shoes that it was almost laughable. One afternoon after rehearsal at the *Terrace*, coming back to my apartment, which was right across the street. I opened the closet door to hang something up, looked in, and saw that every single stitch was gone. After pulling myself together a little, I went back across the street to the *Terrace* to tell people what had happened: I didn't even think about calling the police. Most of the chorus girls and orchestra were still there—thirty or forty people—but after learning of my rip-off, they couldn't have cared less. Everyone, that is, except Anna. When she put my head on her shoulder, and whispered in my ear, 'There, there now, Leonard. Everything will be alright,' I just broke down and cried like a baby. We got very close, very fast, and the next thing you knew we were man and wife.

"This time also marked the beginning of Brains as Well as Feet! That's what we called ourselves. 'Reed and Bryant, Brains as Well as Feet.' Willie and I got along so well working at the Grand Terrace that we decided to form an act. We also made the decision to put ourselves forward as strictly a White act. That's where the real money was; and we were both so light-skinned that we just might be able to bring it off: We spent about a month at the *Terrace* polishing up our act.

"We stole some jokes and rewrote them, and broke in our act in at the Halstead Theater in Chicago, a White Vaudeville house. That's where people from Balaban and Katz, a chain of White theaters, caught us, 63rd and Halstead in Chicago. After meeting with the approval of the bookers from the chain, Brains as Well as Feet were set for the B&K circuit which owned fourteen theaters in Chicago, eight of which (the Chicago Theater, the Oriental, the Tivoli, the Regal, the Palace, the Uptown, the Granada, the Marlborough) featured Vaudeville.

"After proving ourselves on Balaban and Katz, we also started to get booked by the Gus Sun Booking Exchange which provided entertainment packages for about forty independent theaters located in towns such as Altoona, Erie, Springfield, Ohio, Dayton, Columbus, and Cleveland. Gus Sun 'Time' could provide an act like ours with sixteen weeks of uninterrupted bookings throughout the East and Midwest. Sun 'Time' was considered by some to be inferior to most other Vaudeville circuits, but it wasn't so much so as not to feature some pretty big-name acts like my old friends from New York's Palace Theater, The Norman Thomas Quintet, and future 'Toastmaster General' George Jessel, along with the comedy team of Ma and Pa Crackenbush, who—and you'll just have to take my word for it—were very big in their day.

"Willie and I could have pretended to be White men masquerading as Black men; but we wanted no part of blackface, so we decided to put together a class act. We dressed sharp —tails, tuxedos, sports outfits. We opened our eight-minute routine with Willie planted in the theater pretending to be a member of the audience, and as I started playing the ukulele, singing, 'Rolling down the river, my wandering days are through, rolling down the river just rolling home with you.'

[Willie would] yell out, 'Hey, when is the show gonna start?'"

117

"L: What the hell you think I'm doing up here?'"

"'W: I don't know. That's what I've been trying to figure out..'"

"L: Oh, you're one of those smart guys, Why don't you find yourself a seat and sit down?'"

"'W: I've got a seat, but I've got no place to put it.'"

"L: Oh, I tell you what, if you're not quiet I'm going to have the manager take you to the box office and give your money back.'"

"'W: Oh, you're gonna get my money back?'"

"L: Yeah!'"

"'W: Well, let's go, 'cause I came in on a pass.'"

"L: Yeah. You're gonna get thrown out on your . . . .'"

"'W: Careful now.'"

"And so on . . . .

"In the East, we performed at places like the Massbaum Theater in Philadelphia, and the Fort Pitt Hotel and the Stanley Theater in Pittsburgh. And in New York City, we were booked into places like the Brooklyn Paramount, and in Manhattan at Loew's State and the gigantic 14th Street Academy of Music, which was the hardest theater I ever worked in my life. The Academy was open from early in the morning until past midnight, and even though it was a big-time house, bums used it for sleeping. If it was a joke they'd heard before, instead of laughing, they thought it was real funny to crack open their newspaper real loud.

"Finally, the Fanchon and Marco organization, which provided Vaudeville 'prologues' to motion pictures, hired Willie and me for one of their units and brought us west to cities like Denver and Omaha and, finally, to the coast: Los Angeles, San Francisco, and points north. Willie Bryant, like Reed, was of indeterminate racial complexion. Born in New Orleans in 1908, his family moved to Chicago in 1912. Then in 1926, after unsuccessful tries at learning the trumpet, Bryant became a soft shoe dancer with The Whitman Sisters company, where one of his specialties was acting as a foil for one of the most fondly remembered entertainers in all of Black show business history, Princess Wee Wee.

118

Willie Bryant with The Whitman Sisters' Princess Wee Wee.

A talented midget, whom the Sisters met up with sometime during the 1920s, the Princess was first taken into their family and eventually was put into the Sisters' show. It was with this yard-high entertainer that six-foot Bryant was paired when, as a sixteen-year-old, he joined up with the traveling unit. Bryant recalls that Princess Wee Wee "Sang in a cute, high-pitched voice, and then she danced around and between my legs" in a routine not unlike that performed in films a few years later by Shirley Temple and Buddy Ebsen. For a time, Bryant also partnered Blues singer Bessie Smith in the "Big Fat Ma and Skinny Pa" routine that was a part of her stage shows in the late 1920s.

Because Reed and Bryant stayed in White hotels, ate in White

119

restaurants, rode in the White sections of trains and buses and, even more forbidden, cohabited with White women, they were setting themselves up for arrest on an almost daily basis. Although the act of Reed and Bryant would end up lasting slightly less than three years, with the exception of a squabble of several years duration that began in 1936 over the copyright to a song, the two remained friends until Bryant's death in 1964 in Los Angeles, where he was a popular disc jockey on the 50,000-watt radio giant, KDAY. Among Bryant's many professional accomplishments was the Swing band he formed after Brains as Well as Feet. Among the personnel, in what turned out to be one of the most popular outfits of its kind during the 1930s, were such virtuosos as Teddy Wilson, Cozy Cole, Ben Webster, Taft Jordan, and Ram Ramirez.

CHAPTER SIXTEEN
A Fine Working Relationship

"Few Black performers back then really had a shot: There were a handful of acts like Bill Robinson, and Buck and Bubbles that made it, but mostly they just played the colored circuits. Occasionally, someone would get into Loew's State in New York. A few blackface Black acts like Howell and Bowzer or Harris and Radcliff also made it, because White people couldn't tell whether they were Black or White, like Al Jolson or Eddie Cantor, who corked up all the time. A team by the name of Glenn and Jenkins were probably the first two genuine Black comedians to play the RKO circuit. They dressed as porters, pushed brooms, and did eccentric dance steps.

"Moss and Frye were one of the really great Black teams. They made a recording for RCA of their famous 'How High is Up?' routine:

"How high is up?"

"'Up where?'"

"'Up, anywhere.'"

"'What do you care?'"

"Then came [Flournoy] Miller and [Aubrey] Lyles. Their trademark was a gimmick they called "indefinite talk." One of them would beat around the bush trying to finish a thought, and eventually the other would come in with the answer. And there was Swan and Lee, Bootsy Swan and Johnny Lee; Lee later teamed up with Miller to become Miller and Lee after Flournoy Miller died.

"Even if they were only doing the Black circuits, most successful acts could work for many months on the road without revisiting a town, and Willie and I, although 'working White,' were no exception, which meant that we seldom changed our act. During our two-and-a-half years together, we made only one major alteration: we stopped opening with Willie planted in the audience when we finally got permission from Bill Robinson to use a variation of his famous stair dance. [Reed knew of only one other act, the team of Worthy and Thompson, that Robinson allowed to do this.] Now, we opened up together with a moderate tap dance, a chorus or two, and then we would 'single out.' I played the uke stop-time while Willie danced. We did cute little jokes, nothing broad. Willie was very thin. We both were, but being 6' 1" or 6' 2", Willie just looked much thinner than I did at 5' 10½." He would dance and I'd say:

"'Boy, you're really something. If a shower came up, you wouldn't even need an umbrella.'"

"He'd say, 'No, I'm so skinny I can walk between the drops.' Then he'd do another step.

"And I'd say, 'Show me how you walk when you got plenty of money.'"

"Then he'd do a strut.'"

" I'd say, 'Show me how you walk when you're broke.'"

"He'd stumble along and drag.'"

"I'd say, 'Oh, I see you walking like that all the time.'"

"He'd say, 'I'm broke all the time.'"

"When he finished, I danced double fast with lots of wings. Then, in order to rest myself for the finale on the steps, I would sit down on the side of the stage.

"He'd say, 'What's the matter, are you out of wind?'"

"I'd say, 'No, the wind's out of me.'"

"We finished with 'the stair' routine. We'd go up them dancing, one of us on each side. At first, we'd meet each other at the top, face the audience, do a step, come down another step, go back up. We danced up and down the stairs, and then we'd run right over them and do this little flinch like we were going to run into each other: 'Look out! Watch out!' I'd almost fall off and he'd almost fall off. We'd then come down and do the finish bow and walk off.

"This was a format that worked. The only thing wrong with it was the steps we had some guy build for us; he made it with the heaviest lumber I've ever seen. It stood at least seven feet tall, and to try to get these things on the bus was something else!

"We worked with big-time White acts. Our first New York appearance was at the Grand Theater on the Bowery with the great Yiddish star, Molly Picon, in her show where she sang 'Heaven Help the Working Girl.' We appeared with Jean Harlow at the Oriental Theater in Chicago where she was doing a scene with Hattie McDaniel from a movie they were promoting.

"Molly Picon was so charming, and Sophie Tucker was a marvelous woman who we worked with many times. 'Go get 'em, kids!' she'd say as we were about to make our entrance. And she'd stand there during your act and applaud and laugh instead of waiting backstage in her dressing room until her turn to go on.

"We worked with Jack Benny at the Audubon Theater on 167th Street in New York. He did a bit lying in a bed dying, and saying in Jewish dialect, 'I am *dyink*. I *vant* to see all of my children here. Rosa!' And the girl says, 'Here, Father.' 'Rebecca!' 'Here, Father.' 'Samela!' And this big Black guy rose up from behind the bed and said, 'Here, Father.'

Blackout. People screamed. One time, the Black guy was slow getting out his line, but just rose up from behind the couch and they laughed even harder. [This doesn't seem so much like Jack Benny as, perhaps, the very popular Benny Rubin, i.e., a *mis*-remembrance? – B.R.]

"In those days, all the White performers, including Jack Benny, were prejudiced to one degree or another. What was Rochester to him but a pickaninny? They didn't want any Negroes on the bill with them to begin with, but if they used the Negro, he was a pickaninny.

"I first met Louis Armstrong in 1927 while doing stock with Cutout at the Walker Theater in Indianapolis. It was the first time I had ever seen reefers. Backstage he opened up his cigarette case and offered me one . . . but I refused. I never even drank. A year or so later, I made up for all of it, of course, the night I got so stoned at the club in Detroit [Chapter Twelve], so it's kind of funny that I ended up being Louis' pot dealer in Chicago in the early 30's.

"Willie and I were working at the Lafayette Theatre in 1932, and Louis was on the bill with us. I had just written the song, 'It's Over Because We're Through.' On one of the choruses, Willie imitated Louis. Opening night at the Lafayette, hearing it from the wings, Louis came out on stage and said, 'Let me finish it.' Willie did a good Louis Armstrong, and you could hardly have told the difference when Louis took over from him that night. Fats Waller was in the pit playing the organ for that engagement, and one evening his wife came in with a gun right during the middle of a performance, threatening to kill him.

"Fats' wife wasn't the only person I saw packing a gun. A little after that, one night backstage at the Pearl Theater in Philadelphia, Bill Robinson was on the phone, and a bunch of us, including Benny Carter, had just arrived at the theater, while some scenery was being picked up, and we *were* making a lot of noise. Putting his hand over the mouthpiece, Bill turned to us and said, 'Just cut out all that noise you sons of bitches.' And Benny said, 'Who are you calling a son of a bitch?' and he ran and he grabbed Bill and they started fighting. Finally, someone separated them, and all of us, except for Robinson, got back on the bus and we went on to Baltimore and Washington. The next week when we came back to New York, we were headlining at the Lafayette, me and Willie and Benny Carter, and when we got off the bus, Bill Robinson was waiting for Benny in front of Connie's Inn with a gun. There was a tussle; the gun went off missing Benny, and then Bill just pistol-whipped the stuffings out of Benny, who ended up being taken to the hospital for observation. He was released the same day, though, and he had hardly gotten home before Bill came around to apologize . . . with a cop in tow just in case.

"Willie and I had a very fine working relationship—not like Cutout and me—and we had been together from the end of 1930 until about the middle of 1932 when we made a serious mistake. Or I should say, when Willie made a mistake. We'd had a long layoff, were low on funds, and he said to me, 'Let's play the Lafayette,' which, of course, was a Black theater.

"'I don't know, Willie,' I said, thinking about what this might mean to our White booking.

"'Aw, shit,' he said, 'nobody'll know nothin'. These White folks don't know what the hell's going on.'"

"Famous last words. We played the Lafayette date, and our agent, Sam Bramson, found out. He figured out that we obviously had some Black in us—enough to hurt—and dropped us cold. Word got around fast. After that, there was no way we could get back into any White show where they had White girls, because we'd been having every redhead and blonde that we wanted up until then. That's what they didn't like, not so much the deception, but the fact that we'd been with *their* women. It confirmed what I'd known all along and been convinced of just as much ever since then; that sex is the only thing in this country that keeps Blacks and Whites from really getting together. I've been Black and I've been White and I know what I'm talking about.

"Career-wise, the break with Willie was probably for the best; tap dancing was going out, so we were probably only going to go so far anyway. Besides, we had both started to get work as 'singles.' Just before the Lafayette incident, for example, Willie had replaced Bubbles in the team of Buck and Bubbles for a couple of weeks when John Bubbles got sick.

"After that, we played the Black circuits for a few months with Butterbeans and Susie and others, and then we just kind of drifted apart. I became a producer. Willie became a band leader. Willie was clever; he had a good band and got recorded. Unfortunately, we eventually fell out for a long time over that song of mine that Louis Armstrong had sung back at the Lafayette, 'It's Over Because We're Through.' Now, Willie wasn't a songwriter. I wrote that song one night in 1931 while sitting by myself in a restaurant in Chicago thinking about how it was just about *over* between my wife Anna and me; we were having some marital problems. Sending the song to Washington and getting a copyright on it, when I appeared with Willie, we used to do the song and I'd say, 'Here's a song my partner and I wrote.' I guess he just got to believing it. Then shortly after we split up, in the latter part of 1933, Willie when formed his band, he used 'It's Over Because We're Through' as his theme song. And I was so happy and glad one day when somebody said to me, 'Hey, Leonard, I heard your song on the juke box!' Well, I went out and bought the RCA record, but looking at the label it said, 'Words and music by Willie Bryant.' We didn't speak for a long time. Eventually we patched things up by working out a co-author agreement, and Willie worked for me in the 1950s when I produced movie short subjects for Studio Films. When he moved to Los Angeles in the mid-1950s, he helped me to get an on-the-air job at radio station KDAY where he was a popular dee-jay.

Dancer Fayard Nicholas recalls: "Leonard and Willie were having all this success all over the country but Willie got homesick. He told Leonard that he wanted to 'be with my people.' And Leonard said, 'We're having all this success, making all this nice money'. Willie said, 'I know, but this isn't true. I don't like it. I want to go back home.' That sort of broke up the act. Willie started the band; and Leonard did his own thing."

Fayard and Harold, The Nicholas Brothers

So, perhaps it wasn't only scarcity of bookings in White theaters that saw Reed and Bryant playing the Black Lafayette Theatre and blowing their cover. Sixty years later, Reed admits that there may have been either a conscious or unconscious death wish for the act on the part of Bryant, who was by mid-1932 growing increasingly weary of the game of racial deception.

Reed was now twenty-seven years old, and had the experience of hundreds of medicine shows, carnivals, Vaudeville, Broadway, and night club appearances under his belt: His show business skills were sharpened to a fine point. The perpetual transience that went with show business had finally erased most of the fear Reed ever had about "passing" for White, and he could now move back and forth across the color line almost without premeditation. He had reached the stage, much like that of the character in Carl Van Vechten's *Nigger Heaven*, who tells the heroine, ". . . when I'm living with Whites, I have a White psychology, and when I live with Negroes, I have a Negro psychology." Clearly, this took a psychic toll on Reed, but he was so busy with his career that there was little time for sitting down to worry about who he "really" was. The only identity he consciously cared about was the one that could be strung up in lights.

"Following the dissolution of his partnership with Willie Bryant, Reed wasn't anxious to find another teammate and continue working as a hoofer. Now he wanted to apply all he'd learned over the years to creating shows all his own. The only arena realistically open to him, however, was Black show business; and the fastest way he could "make a name for himself" in that world was by striking the highest profile imaginable. Shrewdly then, building upon the celebrity he had already attained, Reed began to develop for himself an image as a dashing man about town. Before long, he had the Black press tracking his every move.

On April 29, 1933, the switch was thrown in Chicago opening the two-year World's Fair-like Century of Progress Exhibition, whose attractions—in addition to a partial reconstruction of a walled city in China, a Mayan nunnery, and a Japanese teahouse—included Sally Rand, whose then-daring fan dance made international headlines. It was against this backdrop of a Chicago, still going up to Roaring Twenties speed, that Reed finally got a chance to produce a nightclub revue.

The offer came from Dave's, the most popular of all the Chicago "Black and tan" clubs that featured Black performers but catered to a racially mixed clientele, which, in the pre-integration era, carried the alluring aura of the "forbidden."

"Leonard Reed is sparing no expense at giving the patrons at Dave's Cafe, 343 E. Garfield Boulevard, a real show," declared a Chicago Defender review of one of Reed's productions there. In addition to directing, Reed also composed and arranged most of the songs and incidental music, directed the dances, and wrote the sketches. In essence, he was almost single-handedly responsible for the monthly creation of a Broadway revue.

After a show was set and running at Dave's, Reed's days were freed up for two weeks until rehearsals for the next production were to begin. Since he wasn't actually appearing in the Dave's revues, he was seldom required to be at the club at night. So, he turned his attention to the Black show palace, the Regal Theater, where he lead his own band on Sunday nights, and also instituted a weekly Amateur Night that he emceed. Additionally, Reed and his stock company of Deluxe Players began popping up in shows in various theaters all over the South Side. One would also be likely to find him emceeing whenever there was a major Black community benefit in Chicago. August 11, 1934, for example, saw him hosting an N.A.A.C. P. affair highlighted by the somewhat incongruous apparition of White fan dancer, Sally Rand.

Reed was by now becoming one of the most famous Black impresarios in the country. Even though his domain was primarily the Midwest, he was known and respected nationwide. For all this success, though, Reed couldn't help but wonder "when the call would come" ushering him into the real big-time. The only question: was such a big-time available to someone like Reed? Today "crossover" artists in every form of show business are taken for granted, but in the 1930s the notion of a Black man rising to a position of power behind the scenes was a radical one. Operating in the world of Black show business was one thing, but to use it as a basis to evolve into someone along the lines of a White showman like John Murray Anderson was something else.

Still, like any reasonable person, the "bottom line" realities of racism notwithstanding, Reed continued to believe that talent would out. There was no question that he possessed directorial skills similar to someone like Vincente Minnelli, who during this same period had graduated from designing sets and costumes for Earl Carroll's *Vanities* and the *Ziegfeld Follies*, to directing *The Show is On* and *Hurray for What!* on Broadway. By the 1940s, Minnelli would be in Hollywood; Reed would continue to run in place.

It isn't difficult to understand why Reed felt he could eventually "beat the system." He thought he "knew" White people. When he had "passed" he had been privy to seeing and hearing close hand how they behaved interacting with one another, an experience few other Blacks could claim. In the last analysis, however, it wasn't enough. No matter how light his skin or sophisticated his manner, he was still Black, according to the "one drop of Black blood" law prevalent in most states. In 1934, however, Reed remained oblivious to such realities. He continued looking for a way to crash through the "invisible ceiling" of Black show business; doing everything he could to capture the attention of the powers-that-be.

CHAPTER SEVENTEEN
Rhythm Bound

"Even though I had the basic knowledge of how to stage a nightclub show from the ones I'd appeared in, there's a big difference between being in a show and producing one. Also, there were basic differences between the stage, where I'd gotten most of my experience, and night clubs, which generally didn't have prosceniums or raised stages. Audiences in most clubs were surrounded by the show in a U-pattern. This meant that performers couldn't just do their thing in one direction facing the people across the footlights; unusual staging was needed. For inspiration, cribbing from the movies, everything I did was just a little bit larger than life. Many of the numbers in my shows were done like brief one-act plays. Each song was part of a little story. With 'Singing in the Rain,' I had my two singers on the balcony that went over the stage. They were behind little cutout windows I'd built, and you saw just their silhouettes on panes of glass that had rain streaming down them. The lighting was very dramatic. My shows at Dave's weren't nearly as large as those at the Cotton Club or the Grand Terrace, but what they lacked in size were made up for with staging.

"In the fall of `34, I decided to try taking a production of mine on the road. Knowing I could come back to work at Dave's Cafe anytime, I offered to put another show in the club, while taking the current one touring. I groomed a guy named Joe 'Ziggy' Johnson—Ziggy was short for Ziegfeld—to take my place at Dave's. The show as called *Rhythm Bound*, and it must've had forty people in the cast. There had never been a Black touring show this big, and probably never a White one either. Our progress was charted in the Black press every step of the way as we headed east to our hoped for destination of New York City.

Page from Leonard Reed's Rhythm Bound (1934) scrapbook

"One item in the news around the time of *Rhythm Bound* revealed that 'Reed was recently wed to Beatrice Ellis, chorus girl deluxe.' I have no idea how anyone could get that into their head while I was still married to Anna Jones, but it's possible that Bea herself might have been responsible for spreading the rumor. Bea was a little girl that was as beautiful as she could be, who'd come to the Regal Theater in Chicago when I was working there. We started going together, and taking *Rhythm Bound* on the road, I brought Bea along as . . . my secretary. Anna, who was in the show, was aware of what was going on and was upset, but went along with it. Finally, Bea pushed the button that really made Anna see red. Anna had an infection in one of her fingers and they put her in the hospital. She was in a room on the third floor facing the street. At the time, I had a Cord convertible with a horn that went bee-bee-ooo-wee! So, one day between shows, Bea said she wanted to borrow the Cord. Didn't ask why, but just gave her the keys. A little while later, I found out from Anna that Bea had driven right up to that hospital, parked across from her room, and blew that horn: bee-bee-ooo-wee, knowing that Anna would recognize the sound and come to the window. When Anna looked out, Bea just waved at her, gunned the motor, and sped away. That was the beginning of the end for Anna and me. She quit the show and went to work at the uptown Cotton Club. Then, Bea and I separated, and she started going with Duke Ellington. She claimed to be Bea Ellington, just like she claimed that she was married to me. However, Duke's wife would never give him a divorce, and legal divorce or no, Bea remained with Duke Ellington for the rest of his life.

"Arriving in Pittsburgh with *Rhythm Bound* after a week each in Indianapolis and Columbus, it was doing so well that I called Frank Schiffman, who I had worked for at the Lafayette, who now owned the Harlem Opera House on 125th Street in New York and was soon to buy the Apollo just down the block from the Opera House. He came over to Pittsburgh, saw my show, liked it, and offered to bring it into the Opera

House providing that, first off, I get rid of my comedians, Spodie Odie and John Oscar. He said they weren't well enough known in New York and wanted to put in the team of Swan and Lee who were New York favorites. Anxious to get my show into New York, I went along with Schiffman. I took Spodie Odie and Oscar to New York and paid them just the same as if they were working. Schiffman paid Swan and Lee. Spodie Odie and Oscar got a free ride for the week. That was one thing, but then Schiffman insisted on adding Nora Holt Ray to the show. I said, 'Fine, but I won't fire any more of my people.' It wasn't just loyalty, because I had plans of continuing on after New York—Baltimore—Philadelphia—all these towns, and I knew Nora wasn't about to travel with us after New York. My singer, Callye Dill, was the real star of the show. She could out-sing Nora two-to-one, but no one in New York knew her. Schiffman wanted a 'name' and that was Nora Holt. I wouldn't let him fire Callye, but had to cut her part way down.

"*Rhythm Bound* was a good show. I conducted the overture, and originally it had opened with Callye Dill singing one of my songs, a ballad called 'Another Day,' right from the orchestra pit. [Dill continued to work in various Leonard Reed productions up through the mid-1940s, after which, marrying a minister and moving to Arkansas, she retired from show business.] She broke up the house. Nora, who wasn't really in the rest of the show but only had a featured spot, shouldn't have objected to Callye doing this, but she did. She put up a stink because she didn't want Callye singing before she had performed. Holt sang stuff like, 'A Good Man is Hard to Find' and 'My Daddy Rocks Me With a Steady Roll.' Slightly risqué, but nothing like, say, Sippie Wallace singing 'Some Black Snakes Been Sucking My Rider's Tongue.' Callye Dill was a singer more akin to Ethel Waters. In fact, I think she was better than Ethel Waters. My secret hope was that *Rhythm Bound* just might have a chance of making it to Broadway, and that I wouldn't have to go on the road again after we played the Opera House. I'd seen most of the famous Black Broadway shows like *Shuffle Along* and *Blackbirds* and honestly felt

134

mine was at least as good as any of them. It wasn't a big spectacular thing, but we had a realty good cast and Callye was just great; but when we got to New York, Schiffman had made so many changes in the show that he'd weakened it.

Nora Holt. was, according to one newspaper, "The toast of four continents. She was last in Shanghai, China and took some of the glamour to the East which has been thrilling London, New York, Chicago, and Sydney. in returning to Harlem [to appear in *Rhythm Bound*] she will be welcomed by a staunch and loyal following."

Much married, and frequently gossiped about in the press, Holt was the inspiration for Lasca Sartoris, the femme fatale anti-heroine of Carl Van Vechten's novel of the Harlem Renaissance, *Nigger Heaven*. Van Vechten biographer Bruce Kellner, describes her as, "a girl of surpassing beauty" who sang "a rowdy repertoire in a voice that ranged from deepest bass to shrillest piping." Holt, who also went by the names Nora Ray, Nora Holt, Nora Lena Holt, (and sometimes with the latter two names hyphenated reflecting her many marriages), had a more serious side, as well. She was a founder of the National Association of Negro Musicians, the first Black member of the New York Music Critics Circle and, in later years, the host of her own program of concert music on New York's WLIB for more than ten years. At the time of *Rhythm Bound*, Holt's notoriety sprang from a messy widely publicized divorce from her fifth husband, wealthy food concessionaire, Joseph L. Ray, a few years earlier. Because of this publicity, Schiffman thought the infamous entertainer would be an asset to the show. As far as Reed was concerned, Holt was a liability.

CHAPTER EIGHTEEN
Money in Their Stride!

"CALLYE DILL'S PART BEING SLASHED WAY DOWN TO MAKE ROOM FOR Nora Holt really killed *Rhythm Bound*. After a week at the Harlem Opera House, where it hadn't done too well, there was no place else to take the show. I had to let most of my cast go, but kept The Reedettes together. We played some theaters back out on the road: Newark, Washington, Philadelphia, and, finally, Baltimore, where Murray Waxman at the Royal Theater there offered me work week after week with my dancers. Jumping at the chance, each week I'd work up a different routine, and he'd bring in different stars and set them into the show.

"While in Baltimore, I started going with a hooker, a gorgeous girl ... let's call her Mary. One night, she and a friend were tricking with a business man, and while this other girl was in bed with him, Mary happened upon $10,000 the guy was carrying in a satchel. It was a complete surprise. Don't know why he was carrying around that kind of money, but he was. Mary grabbed the money, stuffed it into her clothes, and never even told her friend about it. That same night, she ran into the theater and out of nowhere gave me all this money to hold on to for her! I was scared to death, but gave each of my dancers some and told them to stash it away for me, and they did. With the bills stashed in their drawers and their bras, they were dancing with money in their stride! I took some more of it downstairs and hid it in an old broken down furnace. Then, getting scared the cops would look right there, an hour later I hid it somewhere else. The next day, just as I'd thought they would, the police came around to see me. They had busted Mary, her friend, and her friend's pimp for robbery.

"The pimp, who was furious, told the policeman that he knew that Mary had given the money to me. The station was in the next block from the Royal. So, they let me do the show, and after it was over, took me in. They kept asking me about the money. I lied and said I didn't know anything about it. 'Come on in the next room,' the cop ordered, and the pimp was there. He looked me dead in the eye and said, 'Yes, she gave it to him.'"

"'I never saw you before in my life,' I said. 'What's the matter? Are you jealous of me or something?'"

"But I was convincing enough to the police. After a couple of hours, they let the girls and the pimp go because they had no money and no evidence. I had the upper hand; I told the police, 'If this thing isn't over and done with immediately, I'm going to the newspapers. I'm a celebrity here.'"

"When the business guy got wind of what I'd said—being a married man—he dropped the case because he couldn't stand the publicity. The cops still kept trying to find the money, though, and after every show they began arresting me! They'd march me right out through the audience at the Royal. The audience laughed and applauded, and after a day or two, the theater began to get packed because of my getting arrested at every show! I ended up getting busted every day for nearly a month, because they thought they'd find the money that way. They didn't. I must be the only person in show business who nearly built a career on getting arrested.

"Since both Mary and I were now 'hot' with the authorities, it was probably a good idea for the two of us to split the money and go our separate ways for a while. In a few weeks, after things had cooled down a bit, we would rendezvous. She didn't show up, though, where we'd arranged, and I never saw her again until the mid-1940s. Running into her on the street one day in Los Angeles, the first words out of her mouth were, 'Don't say anything. I'm doing okay now.' She had just married a well-known person in show business and was playing it straight. It was a classic case of Hooker-Turned-Square.

"After Baltimore, traveling to Philadelphia to Parisian Tailors and with some of the money, I ordered suits you never saw the likes of. I tried to pay with $1,000 bills, but had some trouble. The cops came and asked me where I'd gotten that kind of money. They finally backed down, but I had to get out of town. Fast! Driving to the closest safe place I could think of, I went to New York for a breather before following through on plans to return to Chicago, but something happened to change all that.

"The Apollo Theater in Harlem had started to broadcast its Amateur Nights on WMCA, and Frank Schiffman, owner of the competing Harlem Opera House, where *Rhythm Bound* had played a few months earlier, decided to go up against the Apollo on WNEW with a virtually identical show of his own. [Schiffman had originated the Amateur Night tradition the previous year at another Harlem theater, the Lafayette, which he owned.] Like the Apollo program, Schiffman's radio show, too, was to be called 'Amateur Night in Harlem.' He offered and I accepted the job of emceeing, and his new radio show went on the air in March 1935. In an article referring to me as Chicago's 'Pet Son,' the *Defender* told its readers that 'Fan mail from all over the country [was pouring] in daily expressing the nation's enjoyment of an innovation which has taken the entire country by storm.' Maybe that's a bit of an exaggeration;

I swear I'd completely forgotten about the radio show until recently coming across a reference to it in some old clippings. As a matter of fact, even after seeing these write-ups about my broadcast career, I still can't recall ever having done the radio series. It's one of the few things I've ever done with absolutely no recollection of whatsoever, no matter how hard I try. However, there it is in black and white in the *Defender* and in several other papers, as well, so if they say I was a radio star, who am I to argue the point? This much I *do* know: shortly after the Harlem Opera House radio show went on the air, Schiffman bought the Apollo Theater. And instead of competing against himself, he probably decided to get rid of the copycat show on WMCA (the one I emceed) in favor of the established one from the Apollo on WMCA, featuring Ralph Cooper.

"I stayed on with Schiffman, producing shows at his new Apollo, where Andy Razaf was writing special material for some of our shows. Working with Fats Waller and Eubie Blake as writing partners, Andy had written the lyrics for such songs as 'Ain't Misbehavin,' 'Honeysuckle Rose,' and 'Memories of You.' Now at the Apollo, he was dashing off

*Apollo Theater marquee from the jacket of Reed's
1956 Vanguard Record's LP*

lyrics to my melodies right there on the spot. None of the songs were ever published, and they were really just lightweight throwaway things, sometimes not even complete songs. Still, Andy Razaf was the best lyric writer one could ever hope to have for a collaborator.

"Meanwhile back in Chicago, Ziggy Johnson had just quit Dave's Cafe to accept a better offer to produce shows in Detroit, just starting to boom as a night club town. And when Dave's offered me a very generous salary to come back to Chicago where, unlike New York, I was really a big fish in a really not so small a pond, I couldn't resist. Especially because I'd be returning to the Midwest in really high style, bankrolled by all that money from the Baltimore scam the previous year, with a wardrobe fit for a king, a limousine, and even a chauffeur."

Shortly after he returned to Chicago, one newspaper noted that "the young genius" had managed to throw together an entire show within the phenomenally short space of four days. "He is a hard taskmaster," the article went on to observe, "forcing his company to work night and day until they mastered steps, gesture." The end result, the paper suggested, "may not be eligible for a Pulitzer Prize, but it far surpasses the mill-run productions which have been fostered upon the public."

Despite all the Second City adulation, in January 1936 after a few months at Dave's, Reed accepted an offer produce floor shows at Detroit's Plantation Club, a spot notable for the way in which it carried racial segregation to undreamed of new heights. Although it catered exclusively to Whites, the Plantation was not only located in a Black district of Detroit known as Paradise Valley but in a Black hotel, as well—the Norwood. Reed's move, observed one news writer, "would do a lot to place this city on a big-time scale" (if not necessarily advancing the cause of integration). However, Reed said, "Clubs like that were a way of life then. Nobody ever questioned it. They had colored clubs in Chicago and Detroit that only Black people went to; Whites could go to these clubs if they wanted, but never did, but Blacks certainly couldn't go to a place like the Plantation, except during Sunday Blue Hour."

As for his decision to move on to Detroit, "Not only was the money better but I'd also started thinking seriously about radio in a way that I hadn't when I was doing that show in New York. I began to realize how big it had become, and I wanted to get in on it again. The best way was to become well-known in more than one city. Since by now I'd produced and appeared in shows in New York, Chicago, Pittsburgh, Baltimore, and several other cities, I felt I was on my way."

Even though the money was better in Detroit and the Plantation was a nationally known operation, the new job was still something of a sideways promotion. His arrival in the Motor City to produce at the Plantation Club was heavily touted not just in the *Defender* but also the *Detroit Eagle* and the *Pittsburgh Courier*. Reed's June show at the club, *Plantation Melody*, was heralded by the latter's theater critic as being, "one of his best . . . a cafe opera [. . .] more true to the life and folklore of the American Negro than was the Opera *Porgy and Bess*." Each ensemble number, true to the style Reed had forged, was described as an "episode, complete in plot and continuity. Each was a show within a show."

Another of Reed's Plantation Club revues had a Wild West theme, highlighted by a full tilt production number set in the Oklahoma territory, featuring such songs as "Wagon Wheels" and "The Last Roundup." In Reed's frontier, the cowboys were portrayed by the swinging vocal-instrumental group, The Rhythm Racketeers, and the romping, stomping The Reedettes essayed the role of Indians.

During breaks at the Plantation, Reed even ventured to the north end of Detroit to choreograph at the Bowery, a club that featured stars such as Sophie Tucker and Reed's old friend from the Chicago Century of Progress exhibition, Sally Rand. However, it was as a Black showman-of-all-trades that Reed continued to make his greatest impact. To nurture his increasing celebrity status, Reed began contributing a very Winchell/ Ed Sullivan-like weekly theatrical column, "Night Life in Detroit," to the *Chicago Defender*. Its ostensible subject was Black show business, but the column also featured a fair degree of self-serving plugs about Reed's own comings and goings. Behind this new publicity push was his growing belief that his true show business future lay in network radio, but he never got a chance to so much as try to crack the audio color barrier. His on-stage career as a snowman and his off-stage role as a figure of fashion completely absorbed his time. In fact his two-tiered lifestyle became so intense that it finally wore down his health:

"Leonard Reed 'Much Better' After Nervous Breakdown in Motor City" reported the entertainment page of the *Defender* early in October 1936. The truth, however, was actually a good deal more mundane than the newspapers let on. Reed had only come down with a serious cold verging on pneumonia. In the world of show business, he had finally reached that rarefied plateau of celebrity whereby a bad cold automatically translated into "nervous breakdown." His illness, though, had consequences far beyond generating tabloid-style headlines.

PART TWO

Bearcat and the Bomber

CHAPTER NINETEEN
The "Bomber" and the "Shack"

"I FIRST MET JOE LOUIS [A.K.A. THE BROWN BOMBER] IN '36 IN Detroit. It was Easter Sunday, right after he'd fought and won one of his first major bouts, the one where he ko'd Charlie Retzlaff in the first round. He'd come into the Plantation Club to see one of the Cotton Club-style shows I had been staging there for the past year or so.

"Detroit's Plantation, like New York's Cotton Club, was a Whites only club, with strictly colored entertainers, but on Sunday afternoons they had what was called a 'blue hour,' when Blacks were allowed to come to see the show. By then, Joe was such a big deal, especially in Detroit, that he could probably have come into the Plantation any time of the day or night he wanted to, but he happened to choose 'blue hour.'

"Often appearing in my shows, clothes horse that I was, I changed suits after every one of my numbers. Then, after the finale, I'd come out in a bathrobe, say, "That's all folks," go backstage, change one last time into something real sharp and come out to mingle with the crowd. I still remember my outfit after the show the day Joe came in: a linen suit with a purple shirt and tie, and tan-and-white shoes! The first words Joe Louis ever spoke to me weren't about the show, but my clothes. What was the material? Who made them? I told him I'd be happy to introduce him to my tailor in Cleveland sometime, but Joe couldn't wait. Come sun-up the next morning, a chauffeur-driven car with Joe and his girlfriend on board, picked me up and a dancer from my chorus line, Mary Stevens, and off we went on the 240-mile drive to Cleveland.

"The store, Lyon Clothing, was over on Euclid Avenue, and when my tailor saw me walk in with Joe Louis, he got so excited and made such a fuss that, within a few minutes, the entire neighborhood had begun to crowd around the place. Joe walked up and down the aisles saying to the tailor, 'Gimme two of those, some of these, and lotsa those.' By now, all of Euclid Avenue was blocked by crowds of people as the four of us walked out of the store into the mob wearing wraparound camel hair coats—the rage that season—that Joe had bought for us.

"The next time Joe and I crossed paths was few weeks later, under much different circumstances. Flat on my back with the flu—for some reason the newspapers had reported this as 'a nervous breakdown'—I heard a knock at the door of my hotel room, which was over top the Plantation Club, and in he walks.

"He looked down at me for a second, then asked, 'What you doing in bed?'"

"'I caught cold going up and down these damn stairs. One of these days I'm going to get out of this goddamn show business and do something else.' I was just babbling.

"'And if you got out, what would you do then?'"

"I thought a moment, then I said the first thing that came to my mind. 'Open up a restaurant. Maybe a Chicken Shack, I suppose. There's none in Detroit.'"

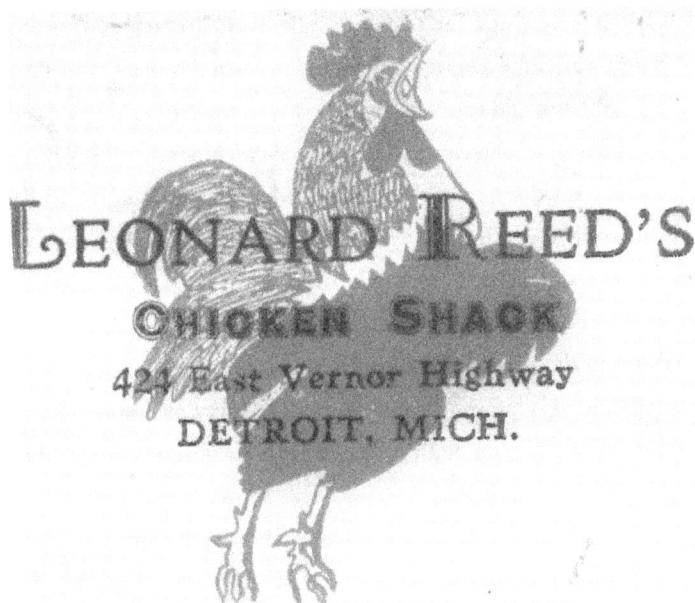

Letterhead for Joe and Leonard's Detroit restaurant

"'Well, if you opened up a chicken shack, you'd have to have a lot of money.'"

"'Yeah,' I said."

" 'How much?'"

"'I'd need about $5,000 to open up.' I really didn't know: I was only guessing.

"'Well, if it takes $5,000 to open it,' Joe said, 'it'd take another $5,000 to run it, wouldn't it?'"

"'Yeah.'"

"'That ought to be a good business. I'll be back,'" he said.

"Three hours later, he returned with $10,000 in large bills, put it on my bed, saying, 'Let's open the Chicken Shack. Use this for your expenses, and after I get my money back, we split everything 50/50.'"

"Who ever heard of a deal like that? No papers. No contract. No nothing."

"'I'll talk to you later,' he said and walked out."

"Here I was, not even knowing where to open this place, and already I had $10,000. I would soon discover, that was typical Joe behavior; and, some years later, he even came to playing fast and loose with my money.

"Locking my door, I hid the money under my mattress, and thought about the whole idea hard for the next twenty-four hours. Joe knew what he was doing, because even though he didn't have an education, he wasn't dumb like some people think. He had good sense.

"The next day, I began looking for a place to open up our business, and finally found one over on East Verna Highway, at number 424. An old house for sale costing $6,000. I put $2,000 down, moved in, and then started hiring help to fix it up.

"In early December 1936, the headline over my 'Nightlife in Detroit' column in the *Chicago Defender* announced: 'Len Reed Forsakes Show Biz For Chicken Shack Adventure in Detroit.' Further down, I revealed my New Year's resolution 'to never appear before the public as an actor throughout the entire year of 1937 for pay.'

"However, 1936 had not quite turned to '37 yet, and I was still not only producing and appearing in my shows at the Plantation, but also continuing to write my newspaper column and pulling together the Chicken Shack. I never worked harder in my life. By night, still barking out orders to a stage full of dancers and singers; now, by day, had turned into some kind of crazy interior decorator from outer space.

"'Upstairs,' I told my builders, 'I want it to look just like a barnyard. I want booths. Put some sawdust on the floor. That pipe that's running up there should be a tree. I want real tree bark on it.'

"In the front, I had them put an old dray carriage with a table right in the middle and throw in two more chairs so it would seat four people. My plans grew wilder and wilder.

"I got an old wagon wheel and had lanterns hanging down from it, then put a big circular bar against the back wall in one of the bedrooms. Between the living room and the house's original dining room, I knocked out a wall, but for safety's sake I had to leave the huge doorway. Between the kitchen and an adjoining bedroom another wall was knocked out, doubling the size of the original kitchen. I put a baby grand piano in. Real plush. The finishing touch was three little Ford coupes I bought. There were heaters in their trunk so that takeout orders stayed warm till they arrived—our motto was 'We Deliver It Hot'—and I put little electric signs on the back that said 'Leonard Reed's Chicken Shack.'

"Growing up in the wilds of Oklahoma where I grew, I knew all the names of chickens: Plymouth Rock, Rhode Island Red, the Dominecker, and over the next four weeks I learned how to buy and cook them. Found out how much flour it took to make biscuits, how much each pat of butter cost. My instructor, a guy by the name of Ernie, was a friend of Joe's from Chicago. Ernie was a restaurateur, another dumb-uneducated-but-smart guy who had made a mint like Joe. He was the sort who'd say he was taking the 'twah' instead of T.W.A. Ernie not only taught me cooking, he also showed me how cashiers could steal from you, and things like how the butcher and the seller could work together to con you.

"All the while, my private life remained as wild as ever. The *Pittsburgh Courier* had me 'slated to wed a Detroit girl. Guess who?' However, I wasn't even divorced from my first wife, and the so-called engagement was nothing more than a big romance that was going on between myself and this 'mystery girl,' who happened to be the daughter of a General Motors executive.

"Around this time, my still-legal wife, Anna Jones, swooped into town from Chicago. She'd been carrying on a big affair with the gospel singer, Mahalia Jackson, but a local column made it seem like things were all sweetness and light between us: 'Mrs. Leonard Reed (Anna Jones) is another charming and beautiful lady who seems to have met Santa Claus on the way here. She has upset Detroit with her stunning Parisian creations and that continental speech of hers with that broad A is too ducky for words.'

"She'd come to town because she smelled money coming from my association with Joe, but when she found out that none of it was coming her way, she left as fast as she'd come. Things were civil between us when she was there, but that was about all, and just as soon as possible, I planned to get back to Chicago to file for divorce. She'd messed up several important deals in my life already, and I wasn't about to let her screw things up between Joe and me.

"We were set to open the Chicken Shack a couple of days before Christmas, but I was doing double duty putting together my final show at the Plantation, *Santa Claus Comes To Town*, so the opening was pushed forward to Xmas Eve and finally to New Year's Eve, a deadline we were, at last, able to meet.

"During all this time, Joe's connection with the Chicken Shack wasn't made public, because it wouldn't have seemed right to have the Champ's name associated with something like a chicken restaurant. However, most people 'in the know' in Detroit were aware he was a silent partner, and a lot of the pre-opening publicity featured his name.

"Opening night of "The Shack" was just like the first night of a Broadway show or a movie premiere. Search lights lit up the sky, and there was even a real Broadway star on hand—Tallulah Bankhead. She brought along the cast from a show of hers playing in Detroit, and we played piano and sang all night. Being from the South, Tallulah loved chicken and biscuits, and for the next few nights, while her show was in town, she stopped by after every performance. Of course, Joe was at the opening, too, and so was just about everybody else—Black or White— who was anybody in Detroit. "The Shack" was a *smash,* as big as any I'd ever had in show business.

CHAPTER TWENTY
Flat on My Back

"It was January 23, 1937, but you couldn't prove it by me.

"I had just awakened to the two most beautiful smells in the world: flowers and fresh baked bread. The roses and daffodils were all around where I lay stretched out . . . wherever that was; and I could feel that I was coming out of a very deep sleep. Opening my eyes and looking around, everything was white on white, including the walls and the snow piled up to the windows.

"*Maybe*, I thought, *I've died and gone to heaven.* Then, I heard a noise, looked over, and there standing in a doorway was Joe Louis. That, at least, seemed real enough. Or could my friend Joe be dead, too?

"He stood there for a minute; then slowly began moving toward me. When he reached the side of my bed, though, he didn't look me in the eye; instead, he was staring at my mid-section. I tried to do the same, but all I could see was a body cast and a mess of tubes plugged into my body.

"Finally, I began to sense what was going on: I hadn't died and gone to heaven at all, but was lying flat on my back in a hospital somewhere . . . next door to a bakery."

"'What's happened to me, Champ?'"

Slowly he raised up the sheets, glanced down at my nether regions, and gasped, "'Oh, my God, NO! They had to cut off your, your . . . ,' then he turned and quickly walked right on out of the room."

"'Joe, Joe!,' I called out, panic-stricken. 'Oh, God, no!' He was gone. Laying on the buzzer non-stop, the nurse came running."

"'Mister Reed, are you alright, what's wrong?'"

"Telling her what Joe had said, when she'd finished laughing, she reassured me that my manhood was still intact, but that maybe the car wreck had done something to my sense of humor.

"Car wreck?

"Slowly, it all began coming back to me, and it couldn't have happened at a worse time: Everything that I had worked for the past six months was now on the line.

"Today, it might be a little difficult for people to understand that in 1937—even before he became the champ—Joe Louis was already world famous, even more than most movie stars or politicians. Here I was, thirty years old, having just gotten into a business association with this great athlete. Now, the whole setup might go down the drain. The events leading up to my lying flat on my back in a Michigan hospital slowly became crystal clear.

"Five days earlier, the restaurant that Joe and I had just set up in Detroit, the Chicken Shack, was running smooth as silk, so as a reward to myself I had gone to a performance of the show, *Shuffle Along*, in Detroit. In the chorus, there was this real beauty, and since I could never resist a gorgeous show girl, almost before the curtain went down I was backstage coming on to her. She couldn't go out with me that night, but I wasn't about to give up that easy.

"'If I drive to Flint will you go out with me?' I asked. Flint was about sixty miles from Detroit and was where *Shuffle Along* was headed next."

"'Sure,' she said."

"Maybe she thought I'd forget all about it, but a few nights later, borrowing Joe's car, and asking a guy I knew by the name of 'Big Hat' to come along as company, off I went to Flint hoping to get laid.

"Seeing *Shuffle Along* again, when it was over, I was backstage in a flash. The girl, though, was acting kind of funny. She hemmed and hawed, and then let me have it. 'I can't do nothin',' she said. 'My old man's here. I didn't know he was coming down . . . .' And so on and so forth . . . love's old sweet song.

"Talk about pissed. Here I'd driven all the way to Flint, sat again through a show I hadn't particularly liked in the first place . . . and now this routine. Without even trying to snag another date, but with 'Big Hat' at the wheel of the car this time, I just climbed in the back to get some sleep, and off we started back to Detroit.

Alert the media!

155

"I don't know how long I was out, but the next thing I was aware of, I was jolted awake by the screech of brakes and honking of horns. Looking over the back seat, blinded by lights heading straight at us, I reached around, hit 'Big Hat' under the chin, and at the last second managed to grab the wheel to steer us out of the path of an oncoming truck. Right into a telephone pole! Upside down we went, with 'Big Hat' thrown free, but with me remaining in the back seat to go down with the ship. Even though I could feel that I was broken nearly in two, all that was on my mind while losing consciousness was my promise to Joe never to let anyone ever drive his car but me.

"*God damn that Big Hat!* I swore to myself, and then went out like a light.

"The headline splashed across the front page of the January 23, 1937 *Chicago Defender* told it all:

'LEN REED HURT IN AUTO OF LOUIS' KIN; FIGHTS FOR LIFE

Actor-Emcee Tossed From Car At Flint.

Auto Is Demolished As It Hits Post Coming Out Sharp Curve

"It said that my pelvic bones had been crushed and that my bladder punctured. A suspected 'possible fracture of the skull,' though, turned out to be a false alarm.

"However, where the *Defender*, the Black Chicago daily, had been pretty much low key about what had happened, the headlines and story in the *Pittsburgh Courier* were right out of today's super market tabloids.

"'Leonard Reed, Nationally-Known Producer, Is Seriously Injured In Automobile Accident' its headline read, followed by a screwed-up account, which suggested that a woman had been in the car with me, thus causing 'a shroud of mystery' to hover over the crash. Just below the main headline was another nearly as large: 'Leonard Reed Known In Theatrical World As Great Lover.'

"This one was accompanied by yet a another story ticking off a number of women with whom I'd been linked romantically, along with a photo of me in a tuxedo next to a photo of 'Alma Smith, former Grand Terrace beauty.' The caption read, 'Great Lover And One Of His Friends.' The *Courier* also got it wrong about me being at the wheel when the accident happened, but that wasn't the paper's fault. Not wanting it to get back to Joe that about my letting someone else drive his car, I told one of the cops that.

"Just as fast as it had come, Joe, the Chicken Shack, it seemed as if it might be all over because of the car wreck. Spokesmen for the hospital told reporters that I had no little or no chance of surviving, and as a result, one newspaper jumped the gun and ran my obituary."

Even though Reed didn't "look" Black, if the Pontiac, Michigan hospital authorities been aware of certain factors regarding Leonard's lineage, all merciful considerations would surely have been swept aside and he would have been shipped off to the "colored" hospital area faster than you could say Hippocratic Oath, a disruption that would certainly have meant his death and another addition to the list of perhaps thousands of African-Americans killed—murdered—by such practices.

CHAPTER TWENTY-ONE

In Passing

"IN A COMA FOR NEARLY A WEEK SINCE THE WRECK, AFTER COMING TO, I began with the questions, trying to piece together what had happened after going out like a light. 'Big Hat,' I learned, had suffered only minor injuries, was taken to a nearby hospital for observation, then released after a few hours. However, the authorities, thinking I was Caucasian through and through, had rushed me to the best hospital in the area, Pontiac General. As it turned out, I might have been better off where they'd taken 'Big Hat.' Brought into the emergency room at Pontiac, I later learned nobody would touch me because no one wanted to be responsible for what is known in the trade as a 'dead case.' The doctors on duty were more or less content to just let me lie there, waiting for death to take me off their hands. No one thought I stood a chance.

159

"There was one person, however, who happened into the hospital that night who was willing to deal with me: Doctor Robert F. Baker. I'll never forget his name as long as I live. Baker told me later that, ordinarily, he wouldn't even been have come in that night, but was in the neighborhood and decided to drop in to check up on one of his patients. Seeing me lying there on the gurney as he passed through the emergency room, he said that, unlike the others on duty, his attitude was that he had nothing to lose by trying to save me; I guess he thought of it as a challenge. When he x-rayed me, he discovered that among the more serious internal injuries were a crushed pelvis and a ruptured bladder. The first operation lasted more than six hours.

"A few days after coming to, Baker visited my hospital room and let me have the good—and the bad—news. I was going to live, but would probably never walk again, much less dance.

'You'll be all right in a wheelchair,' he said. 'You'll even get used to it.'

Just like in the movies, though, I swore, 'I'll walk again, Doc. You'll see!'"

"One of the ways to pass time in the hospital was dealing with Joe Louis' practical jokes, like the one about my privates. A few days after coming out of the coma, the phone at my hospital bedside began ringing off the hook with calls from almost every available girl in Detroit calling up to check out the truth of what Joe had just told them . . . that I'd lost 'IT' in a car wreck.

"After about the tenth call and giving up, 'Yes,' I admitted, 'it was all true. They had to amputate my penis.' One example of just how far Joe would go to get a laugh requires a little background:

Since, until fairly recently, there were hardly any hotels below the Mason-Dixon line that catered to other than Whites, when performers toured the South, they were forced to make do with whatever lodgings they could muster up. This was the situation in 1953, when Joe and I were touring our standup comedy act as part of a package called *The*

160

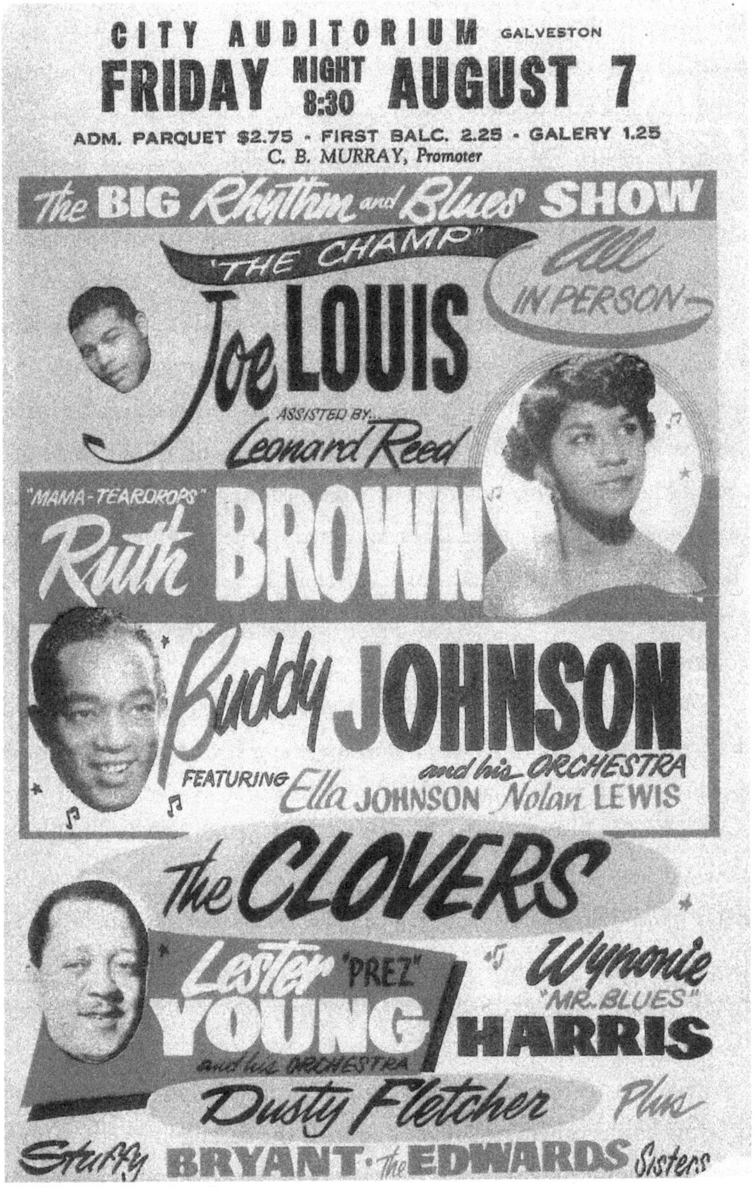

Bearcat and the Bomber on tour – 1953

Big Rhythm and Blues Show. Ninety cities in nearly as many nights! Joe was the headliner, but the others on the bill were fairly big stars in their own right: Ruth Brown, Buddy Johnson, Ella Johnson, a sixteen-piece band, comic Dusty Fletcher, singers Wynonie Harris, The Clovers, The Edwards Sisters; and for jazz spice, Lester Young.

"Naturally, the housing problem proved especially great for a traveling unit as large as *The Big Rhythm and Blues Show* with its two busloads of nearly fifty Blacks. Or, I should say it was a problem to everyone in our troupe but me! Looking too White to stay in most places that catered to Blacks anyhow, I usually stayed in White establishments. Most rooming houses in the South, though, were willing to allow a manager traveling with an all-Black show to stay with his cast, but still things could get messy. Many more times than I care to recall, during the first two decades of my show business career, I'd been routed by the local constabulary in the middle of the night and thrown out of my lodgings, bag and baggage. On one occasion, I was even arrested. The charge? Being a White man cohabiting with coloreds!

"With *The Big Rhythm and Blues Show,* the bus would pull into a town, I'd get off at a White hotel, and the rest of the cast and crew would head off to the Black side of town to scuffle. Not everyone in the company accepted my excuse that I was checking into the White hotels to avoid trouble with the law, and others were annoyed by the fact that many of the places I stayed just happened to be located conveniently near the nice Whites-only golf course in town. A few just thought I was being uppity. Mostly, though, there were no strong, hard feelings and things went smoothly. Except once, in Houston.

"Getting off the bus at the swank Shamrock Hotel and waving goodbye to the others, after checking in at the desk, going to my room and just getting comfortable, there was a knock at the door. Getting up and opening it, there stood the manager of the hotel."

"'I'm sorry, sir, but you can't stay here,' he said in this very starchy voice.

162

"'Why, what's the problem? I paid in advance and everything,' I said.

"'We'll refund your money. I think you'll be happier elsewhere.'"

"I began to catch his draft. Back then when Blacks sensed White prejudice, they called it feeling a 'draft,' and this was a positive hurricane. Knowing that there was no use in bothering to protest, I told him I'd go, and packed up to leave.

"Reaching the lobby, the reason for his attitude became obvious. Actually, three reasons. There stood one of our show's star attractions, Ruth Brown, and pulling up the rear were two of the most pathetic little wide-eyed waifs you ever laid eyes on playing the part of her children. She strode angrily across the lobby, and when she reached me, shook her finger in my face, grabbed me, and as she dragged me toward the hotel entrance, shouted back over her shoulder at the two little 'picks' 'Come along, children, we've found your daddy.'"

"Needless to say, Joe had put her up to it.

"I got into some horrible jams due to my light complexion, but some of them were pretty amusing, too. At least, thinking back on them now. One of the funniest involved my Vaudeville partner, Willie Bryant, who was as light as I am (you can still see Willie on TV all the time, hosting those old *Showtime at the Apollo* movie shorts that I produced in the 1950s).

"We had this little Black guy valeting for us. His name was Frankie, and he could out-dance both of us, but we never gave him the chance. Since Willie and I were working White, we'd bring him out on stage and introduce him us as our dancing discovery, and we'd let him do a few steps, but not enough so as to outshine us.

"Willie tended to curse a lot and had a great, gruff sense of humor. Backstage, he'd say to Frankie, "All right, yo' little Black sonofabitch, get my shoes.'"

"We were playing these New York theaters, and Frankie needed this job, so he put up with it. Besides, he knew Willie was kidding, didn't he?

"Frankie'd say, 'Yes, suh! Mister Bryant, I'se coming.' Seemed like he enjoyed going along with the routine."

"Then . . . we played Birmingham, Alabama, Frankie's home town, the fact of which Willie and I weren't aware. We got to the theater and Willie said, 'Hey, you little Black son of a bitch, bring my shoes.'"

"Frankie said, 'I want to tell you something, Mister Bryant, and that is that this is last time I'm calling you Mister Bryant. I'm at home, now, and I'm going to tell all the White folks that you're both colored.'"

"Willie panicked. 'Now, wait a minute, son, let's get together here.'"

"'No,' Frankie said, 'I want a better working situation. I don't want you to call me Black any more,' because back then it was an insult to call anybody Black. 'I don't want you to call me a nigger anymore, either. And I want a raise.'"

"I guess he hadn't enjoyed playing along with the routine after all. We had created a Frankenstein's monster."

"'Plus I don't want you to say that you found me.'"

"We used to say, 'Here's a little feller we found in the alley dancing.'"

"He said, 'I want you to tell them I'm a new find that you're presenting.'" Just about all he didn't ask for was top billing.

"So the next show , Willie went out and said, 'Ladies and Gentlemen, a new find . . . .'"

"And Frankie was standing in the wings shouting at Willie, 'Atta boy! Atta boy!'"

"You never saw such a turnabout in your life. From then on when Frankie said 'Jump,' Willie jumped . . . at least, until we got back up North."

"Another time, this was in the late 1940s, I almost blew the whistle on myself. I was at a football game in Dallas and became real friendly with an attractive woman seated next to me. At some point during the game I turned to her and said, 'Gee, I don't see one colored person here.'"

"'No, and there never will be as long as this stadium stands,' she said."

"I decided to teach her a lesson. I came on to her, took her back to my hotel room, and when we'd finished having sex, said to her, 'You don't like niggers, do you?'"

"'No!'"

"'Well, you just got through fuckin' one,' I revealed."

"She went completely off her nut, started screaming, and picked up the phone to call the police right there in the middle of redneck country. It was probably the most dangerous thing I'd ever done in my life. Fortunately, I managed to convince her I was joking.

"Five years later, I ran into her in—of all places—Times Square. She was with a Black guy. I took her aside and whispered, 'You sure you don't like niggers?'"

"'He's just a friend.'"

"'Well at least you got a friend that you didn't have back in Dallas. And,' I said, referring back to her earlier remark, 'by the way, is the stadium still standing?'"

CHAPTER TWENTY-TWO
Back on My Feet

"Despite what I'd said to the doctor about my walking again, I was still flat on my back after several weeks. Even starting to get into kind of a funk because of all the pain, when one afternoon this guy came into visit me from one of the other wards and he was in a wheel chair: all chrome, bright, and shiny, one of the most beautiful man-made objects I'd ever laid eyes on. Just had to have one."

"'Is that your own wheel chair?' I asked him."

"'No, they got 'em here.'"

"Getting one, before you knew it, every day at one o'clock this guy and I would have a wheel chair race. People would come from all over the hospital, bets were placed, other wheel chair-bound patients got in on it, and we had a ball. Still I didn't have any incentive to walk.

"The contests went on for a couple of weeks. Then one day, my pal showed up, but now he was on crutches and was heading home. I decided it was time for me to get some, too . . . and to think about leaving the hospital. Got a pair and was soon discharged. Like a homing pigeon, I headed straight for the Plantation Club, where Ziggy Johnson, who'd taken over for me when I went to work on the Chicken Shack, let me choreograph a special number for the girls. Instead of 'Truckin' on Down,' the dance step that was so popular around that time, I had all the girls up on crutches doing The Crutch: they were 'Crutchin' on Down' in my version of the dance. All my friends were worried about my health, though, and warned me not to get back into action full-time just yet. Joe Louis watched over me like a hawk. He had his brother, Don [DeLeon], follow me around wherever I went.

"A few weeks after getting out of the hospital, I was still on crutches and having a rough time making the transition to my own two legs, when Don took me downtown to a sporting goods store to buy some shirts. Hobbling my way to the clothing department of a sporting goods store, out of the corner of my eye I saw just the very thing I thought was needed to help get me back up on my feet. First, though, I had to get rid of Don by telling him to go to on to the nearby Hudson's Department Store and buy me a cravat."

"'Joe told me never to leave you,' he insisted."

"I talked him into it, though, and the minute he rounded the corner on the way to Hudson's I made the purchase of a real life saver—a cane that opened up into a seat. Throwing the crutches in a trash can behind the cash register, I headed back to my hotel on foot . . . alone! I'd hobbled along for as long as I could on the cane, then open it up into a seat, and rested. Walking and sitting, walking and sitting, all the way back to my hotel. A distance of a mile or so that took me several hours to navigate. Arriving back there, Don had already returned. Joe was there, too."

"'If you were any bigger,' Joe yelled at me, 'I'd put you in the ring and beat your brains out.'"

"Cards and letters poured into Pontiac General from all over the country from fans and friends while I was in the hospital. Also, my medical progress was a subject for constant items in the national Black press. This all bolstered the old ego. Alas, my wife Anna proved to be a big problem. We were estranged, but this didn't stop her from beating a path to my hospital bedside, visits which were reported in the press in a very corny manner.

"'Anna Jones At The Bedside of Injured Hubby: Pretty Stage Star Refuses to Talk About Divorce Until Dear Leonard Recovers' went one headline.

"A month later, the *Pittsburgh Courier* reported that 'Love And Kisses' were the order of the day between us. 'Cupid' was 'in Power' reported the silly headline over an interview between Anna and reporter Rollo S. Vest, which took place at the Chicken Shack, still rolling along despite my absence.

"The marital bliss was all just a figment of Anna's imagination. She was waiting around to see what she could gain from the situation, especially if I happened to croak before her high-tailing it back to Chicago and the arms of Mahalia Jackson. I wasn't the only one who was wary of Anna. Joe's advisers and handlers also had a cynical view of her bedside vigil. Around my third or fourth week in the hospital, I was paid a visit by Frank Roxborough, the brother of Joe's manager. Frank was an attorney, and instead of flowers, he was carrying a briefcase.

"He said, 'I waited until you were able to talk with me and answer some questions and.'"

"'I rose up out of bed to face him. 'What do you want?'

"'I brought some papers for you to sign,' he said. 'I want you to sign the Chicken Shack over to my brother, John.'"

"The gist of it was, the newspapers still had me near death, and since nothing was legally in Joe's name, his people, who were against the idea of the Chicken Shack in the first place, were afraid Anna would swoop down and grab the restaurant it I kicked the bucket."

"'Joe and I have a verbal agreement,' I told Roxborough. 'If he asked you to do this, you tell Joe to come to me. He doesn't need your signature or mine or anybody's. Just tell Joe to come to me.'"

"He walked in a huff.

"A couple of days later, Joe came in. He'd been out of town doing some exhibition matches. Telling him what happened, he denied sending Roxborough. 'Don't sign nothing! That's our Chicken Shack; that ain't theirs,' he said."

"'Joe, you know all you have to say is, 'I want the Chicken Shack and . . . .'"

"'The hell with them,' he said. 'Don't give 'em nothing. That place is mine . . . ours!'" Then he stomped out of the hospital room. And that was that!"

"I lost the 'Shack' anyway, but what finally did me in wasn't Joe's management—who never did like me very much—but my own people. I'd hired a very pushy type by the name of Sonny Wilson to take care of my personal affairs before the Chicken Shack was even a gleam in anyone's eye. After the 'Shack' opened, he went to work for me there. While I was in the hospital he *really* went to work.

"He had all kinds of locks around the place changed and, after a few months, when I came back to the 'Shack' in a wheelchair, I couldn't even get into the safe. The sign outside still had my name on it, but Sonny was soon telling anyone who asked, 'I'm just letting Leonard use his name up there, but I bought it from Joe Louis. It's mine now,' he lied to people."

"He was Real Takeover, trying to push me right out. Fighting back, I had the locks changed again, but being in a wheelchair, I wasn't up to playing those games. I'd give up; it just wasn't worth risking my health over."

"Joe more or less agreed with me. 'Look,' he said, 'you're in no position to operate the Chicken Shack. Then he handed me that $1,500. 'Kinda get yourself together until you're able to get around. I'll talk to you later.' Then, more like an afterthought than a command, he added, 'Give the Chicken Shack to my brother, Lonnie.'"

"This was fine with me, because Joe, and someone from his management, had told me to do it.

"So off I headed to California. The 'Shack' was doing quite well when I left and Lonnie took over. Not exactly sure when it closed, but I came back to Detroit the next year, and it was gone. I don't think it lasted too long after my departure to California to recuperate."

Reed is right; it wouldn't have seemed right to have the Joe Louis' name associated with something like a mere chicken shack. The fact is Louis remained a beloved public figure long after his glory years, even after he was reduced to acting as a kind of living logo for Caesars Palace in Las Vegas in the 1970s, only slightly was the luster of this modest, low-keyed, and soft-spoken sports hero tarnished. When, more than three decades earlier, Louis had rushed in to become the World Heavyweight Boxing champ, he was the first Black to cinch the title since the 1913 dethronement of the much-maligned and despised (by Whites) Jack Johnson. America's attitude toward Louis in 1937, however, was anything but hostile. So great was the respect accorded him almost from his beginning of his career that he was able to override all but the most vehement racism. At a testimonial dinner held shortly before Louis died, nearly a half-century after he'd first won the crown, L.A. Mayor Tom Bradley saluted him as the first 'Black symbol of achievement for Black youth.' Bradley was just the right age to know what he was talking about.

By then, however, Louis was broken in spirit and in pocketbook, and it is a source of annoyance to Reed that part of the Louis legend holds Reed himself partly responsible for the boxer's much publicized financial problems . . . millions gained and just as many millions lost. It saddens and angers him, for example, that one TV dramatization of Louis' life points to the Chicken Shack venture as playing a part in Louis' fiscal problems.

Says singer Herb Jeffries, who was friends with both men during the period of the "Shack":

"I don't think that Leonard was in any way responsible for Joe Louis' financial demise. There were two men who managed Joe. One was a great policy baron in Detroit; the other was a policy baron in Chicago. Both numbers men. I think that they pacified Joe. Gave him everything he wanted. A home, car, everything. His bank account never got as big as people thought, because his people divided it up. I believe it was his handlers and business managers who were responsible for Joe's finances going on the rocks. If Leonard had to do with money losses with Joe Louis, he'd be living in some super mansion in Spain or South America. Joe spent a lot of money, gave a lot of it away. When the game was over, I believe those were the guys who wound up with the money. The Chicken Shack that Joe opened for Leonard might have cost $50,000. However, what was that to a guy who could give a $1 million gift to the Navy Relief fun? $50,000 isn't even gas money for all of your automobiles."

For nearly fifty years, Louis just couldn't seem to get enough of Reed's companionship. For long stretches during that span of time, the two lived a high, wide, and handsome existence over much of the globe. Louis, however, set the pace for the spending and Reed gladly fell into step. Who, after all, wouldn't want to sport around the globe side-by-side, all expenses paid, with such a larger-than-life legend as Louis? Besides, Reed insists, he earned his keep.

Reed is described in one Louis biography merely as the boxer's "secretary," thus strongly diminishing the significance of the relationship between the two. Reed's duties, in fact, ran the gamut from procurer to Pygmalion of sorts, and creator of and partner in a comedy act with Louis that barnstormed U.S. and Europe off and on for nearly a decade.

The Louis-Reed friendship kicked into high gear shortly after the boxer cinched the heavyweight title on June 22, 1937 while Reed was in California recuperating. When Louis packed Reed off for the west coast, and told him he'd "Talk to you later," it wasn't the brush-off. A few weeks after Reed arrived in Los Angeles, Louis phoned asking him to come to the New Jersey camp where he was in training, to help him get ready for his upcoming bout with British heavyweight Tommy Farr. Reed caught the next train east, and by the time he arrived, the compound was jumping with newspaper reporters, and the Champ's daily training regimen was already in full swing.

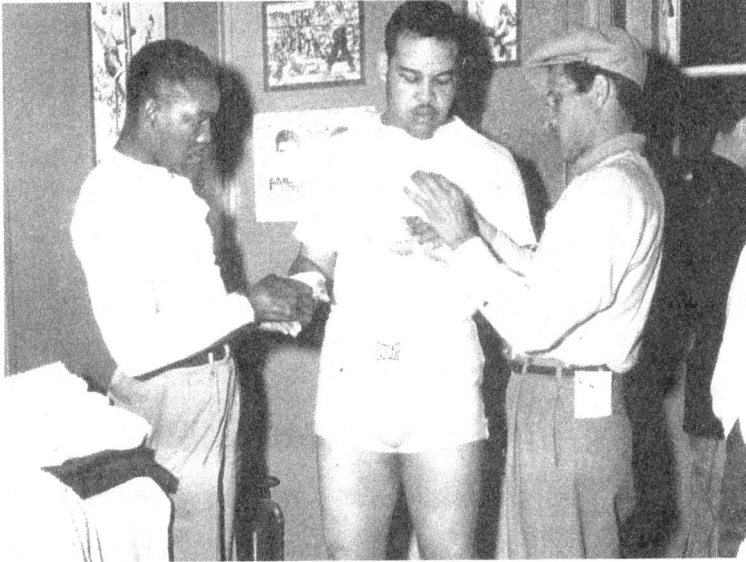

Reed and Louis at the latter's training camp

Leonard Reed at the Cotton Club – 1937

CHAPTER TWENTY-THREE
T. T. & T.

"Joe had his breakfast at 5 a.m., and then did his early morning run, with me at the wheel of a car pacing him. Three minutes running, then I'd honk the horn and he'd walk for one minute; the idea was to approximate the three-minute round and one-minute rest period of a boxing match.

"This routine went on for a few weeks, then one morning we came back into camp around nine o'clock, and in addition to the press, lots of big shots were also on hand. Joe Glaser, Louis Armstrong's manager, was one of those who had made the trip over from New York City to Pompton Lakes. Because of his association with Armstrong, Glaser also had a business relationship with the Cotton Club, where 'Pops' appeared regularly.

"When Joe got a break from sparring, he and Glaser sat down and began shooting the breeze, while I hung nearby trying to catch up on the latest show business gossip. At first, the talk was about boxing and Joe's upcoming match with Tommy Farr. I was just about ready to give up on getting any Broadway chatter, though, when the conversation finally turned from the fight racket to show biz.

"What Glaser told Joe was something I already knew: that the Cotton Club's regular producer, Clarence Robinson, was off to Europe with 'Blackbirds' and wouldn't be back in time for the '37 edition. What *did* manage to catch me by surprise, though, was Joe's next topic of conversation:

"'Well, here, here's a producer right here,' he told Glaser, turning around and pointing at me. 'Leonard's a great producer.'"

"Glaser asked me a little bit about myself, then said, 'Go on in and see Herman Starks. Tell him Joe Louis sent you.' A few days later, that's all it took to satisfy Starks, the Cotton Club's manager.

'Joe Louis sent me.'

"I got the job producing the 1937 Cotton Club revue, *Tall Tan and Terrific,* starring Cab Calloway and Bill 'Bojangles' Robinson.

"My credit read 'dances staged by,' but what it all boiled down to was *producing,* to which I was no stranger by then (at age 31), having overseen shows at most of the major clubs in the mid-west that featured Blacks. Chalk it all up to dumb luck or talent, by the time I went to work at the Cotton Club in 1937, the people I'd worked with and for constituted a Who's Who of Black *and* White entertainment.

"The first thing I did after being taken on by the Cotton Club was to sit in for the last few performances of the current revue, *Cotton Club Express,* starring two friends of mine, but definitely not of each other, Ethel Waters and Duke Ellington. "Contrary to what you might think, Duke Ellington was not always the easiest person to get along with. Having worked with him on a number of occasions, every show of mine he played he wanted to use his music for my chorus line.

"'Well, can't they do the soft shoe to 'Mood Indigo'?

"'No, Duke,' I'd say. "'We're going to do it to 'Swingin' Up High in the Sky' just like we've been doing it.'"

"He played my shows at the Apollo in the 1950s a lot, and every time he worked for me, I always had a problem of some sort, but we got along.

"However Duke was a pussycat compared to Ethel Waters, who had the reputation of being the meanest woman in show business. Like another great entertainer, Al Jolson, she was afraid of even the least important of her supporting cast possibly stealing her glory. This meant that no one else in the same show could do an act even remotely resembling hers. Ethel was always The Star.

"Like a lot of folks, I'm of the opinion that Ethel Waters is the greatest entertainer this country has ever produced. Alas, Ethel was a bitch. You can't get much more insistent than she was on opening night of *Cotton Club Express*, the 1937 revue that came before *Tall, Tan and Terrific*. She stopped right in the middle of a song, turned to the audience, and said, 'Ladies and gentlemen, I ask you to forgive me because these sons of a bitches [the Ellington band] are not playing my music correctly and tomorrow they won't be playing it or else I won't be singing it.'" And the next night she brought in an outfit of her own led by her husband-to-be, trumpet player Eddie Mallory. The way she got Eddie Mallory was . . . she going with a girl by the name of Florence Hill, who was married to Eddie Mallory. Ethel finally became so jealous of the two of them that she took Eddie Mallory away from Florence and dropped *her*. That was a big thing in show business at the time. Everybody was going around saying, 'How about Ethel . . . took her old lady's man away from her.'

"By the time of my association with the place in 1937, the Cotton Club was no longer located in Harlem, but had moved downtown to the Broadway-Times Square area. Otherwise it was pretty much business as usual; great stage shows and bands, like Jimmie Lunceford, Cab Calloway, Duke Ellington, and still . . . the Whites-only policy. People talk a lot about that today; almost as much as they do the shows themselves.

However, we really didn't give it much thought back then. You more or less accepted it. There was definitely a mob element involved in the operation of the Club. Still, I agree with my friend Fayard Nicholas, who said, 'However, they were *nice* gangsters.' I personally never saw anything, so I'll leave reminiscences about the mob to others.

"In our cast was a wonderful singer-comedienne by the name of Mae Johnson, who billed herself as 'The Copper Colored Mae West'; there was also a great singer by the name of Avis Andrews; dancer Freddy James; Tip, Tap and Toe; and Cab Calloway's band. Altogether we had a cast of 175.

"One number Bill Robinson and I choreographed together was called 'The Bill Robinson Walk' and featured sixteen chorus girls all wearing Robinson masks. [Perhaps Reed was unconsciously—or otherwise— still drawing upon film for some of his inspiration: The Astaire-Rogers vehicle, *Shall We Dance,* released in May 1937, featured a line of chorus girls all wearing Ginger Rogers masks.] During rehearsals, he was full of give and take. I didn't know exactly how he'd feel about a whole bunch of people on stage copying his style, but he said, 'Do you need any help with this, Leonard?'

"'I sure do, Uncle Bo.'"

"And he really pitched in. A lot of people thought he was difficult mainly because of expecting a lot from those he worked with. If you were a slacker, he could be get pretty mean, Or, if you crossed him, like when he pulled a gun on Benny Carter. Otherwise, I never saw much of the legendary Bill Robinson temper. Rehearsals went smoothly.

"Then, one week before our late September opening, Bill, who was under contract to 20th Century-Fox, got a call to return to Hollywood for the film, *Rebecca of Sunnybrook Farm;* which threw everything into chaos because much of the show was built around him. It was a real blow, but we were able to get the Nicholas Brothers, who were in town in the Rodgers and Hart musical, *Babes in Arms,* to fill in for him until he was scheduled to return east in a mid-November.

"The show opened a week or so later than was scheduled, but it was a hit, so much so that a 2:30 a.m. show had to be added to accommodate the crowds. I stayed on for a couple of months as production manager . . . long enough for Bill Robinson to get back from Hollywood and re-join the show. When Bill had to be dropped, the 'Robinson Walk' routine was taken over by Harold Nicholas. It was a smooth transition.

"I never got the chance to work the Cotton Club again; it closed up forever on June 10, 1940, a victim of changing tastes and rising rents."

In a movie short with the Nicholas Brothers from the mid-1930s, an emcee asks them "Are you boys professionals?"

The younger Harold answers, "Mister, we're already wayyy beyond that!"

They then proceed to burn up the screen with their mixture of tap, acrobatics, and youthful energy. Six decades later in December 1991, this longest-running two-man act in show business received the prestigious Kennedy Center honors.

Long active in every area of performance, today the brothers are best-known and remembered today for their high-energy specialty appearances in a number of classic MGM and 20th Century Fox musicals of the 1930s and 1940s. Stars almost from the moment they turned pro in 1930, by 1931, they were ages eighteen and fourteen respectively. Fayard and Harold were already capable of stepping in to fill the Bill Robinson slot in "Tall, Tan and Terrific." By then, they were regulars at the Cotton Club, having first appeared there in 1932 when it was still located in Harlem. However, in 1937, eighteen-year-old Fayard Nicholas still had stars in his eyes; he continued to be thrilled when coming into contact with the performers who had inspired him as an adolescent.

He recalled, "I first saw the team of Leonard Reed and Willie Bryant at the Standard Theater in Philadelphia, where my mother and father had an orchestra called The Collegians. And I used to go there to see all these all these wonderful entertainers. These were the people that I copied from when I was first learning to dance. Leonard and Willie were among my main inspirations. I especially was impressed by the elegant way they dressed and carried themselves. It showed me that just because you were Black, you didn't have to indulge in the kind of stereotyped behavior that a lot of entertainers did. That was very important for me to know as a ten-year-old with dreams of going into White show business."

Reed's activities following the successful opening of *Tall Tan and Terrific* were detailed by Detroit newspaper columnist Rollo Vest in a story datelined December 10, 1937. Under the headline "LEN REED QUITS WEST END SPOT," Vest writes that Reed was definitely set to oversee the next Cotton Club revue—which never came to pass; the Cotton Club closed forever—but that unfortunately his attempts to set up his own Vaudeville house just down the street from the Apollo at the West End Theater had failed. 'The problem,' says Reed, 'was Frank Schiffman. In 1937, the Apollo was the only game left in Harlem. At first, I was able to get talent the caliber of Pigmeat Markham and Dusty Fletcher. However when Schiffman realized that we were competition, he began threatening to blackball from the Apollo anyone who worked at the West End. We did well for the first couple of months, but when Schiffman sprang into action we went out of business . . . fast.'"

Library and book store shelves are lined with volumes that deal with the professional world of Broadway and spectacle producer John Murray Anderson, perhaps the most opposite number than Reed that there is in show business. Alas, while books abound that are of use to an Anderson chronicler, there is virtually nothing for someone wishing to write about Reed.

One turns then to the African-American press of the period: New York's *Amsterdam News*, the *Pittsburgh Courier*, the *Chicago Defender*, etc., where items like the above by Rollo Vest proved invaluable in jogging Reed's memory. For example, it wasn't until Reed was presented with the news item about *The Sun Tan Follies* that he began to recall appearing in the live stage unit that toured as part of a package with director Oscar

Micheaux's film, *The Exile* (1931). And, although he remembered it vividly when presented with hard copy documentation of having done so, Reed failed to ever mention having briefly paired off with comic Ole Olsen of the team of Olsen and Johnson during a time when the latter was ill and indisposed, thus forming what must surely have been the world's first bi-racial comedy team.

The Black press of the period chronicled Reed's professional activities in the late 1930s and early 1940s, as he raced about the area of the Great Lakes, the Midwest, and the East Coast performing his producing wonders at such sites as the Congo, Zombie, and Bowery clubs in Detroit (the latter being a strictly White establishment); Pittsburgh's Harlem Casino; the Cedar Gardens in Cleveland; and the Little Harlem in Albany. However, the most memorable and eventful of these engagements was, perhaps, the one immediately following the failure of the West End Theater. In the early part of 1938, the management of Chicago's Grand Terrace was unexpectedly set scrambling to find a replacement for departing dance director-producer Sammy Dyer. Because of Reed's long association with the club and recent Cotton Club success, he was the natural choice for the job. A generous offer was made, and the wayfarer began making plans for a return to Chicago, the city that, for him, still came closest to qualifying as "home."

CHAPTER TWENTY-FOUR
Scandal in St. Louis

"Prohibition had come and gone, the Depression was over, and Al Capone was in jail, but the Grand Terrace just rolled on. Anna was working there as a show girl and we were cordial. Apparently, though, Earl Hines, who was in residence there with his band, didn't feel the least bit comfortable with the setup. A couple of days after I was back on the job at the Terrace, an attorney by the name of Euclid Taylor came to me and said, 'Earl Hines says that he would marry Anna, but you won't let her go.'"

"I still have no idea where Earl might have gotten that idea, but I said, 'Hell, I'll let her go. I haven't got her now.'"

"He said, 'However she doesn't have a divorce.'"

"My mind on the subject of alimony, I said, 'Shit, if I had the money.'"

"'I'll get it for you for. $40,' Euclid offered. 'You got $40?'"

"So Anna and I went down to his office. We were very agreeable, and that was the end of that. $40 and I got my divorce. Nobody wanted anything.

"Ultimately, Earl and Anna ended up not getting married anyway, but something that Earl Hines took from me at the Grand Terrace *did* give me grief. We were featuring Earl's band at the club, with Fletcher Henderson in a guest spot. I'd written a routine about Fletcher's being the King of Swing: a trumpet player blew a flourish, and he came on wearing a crown. He did some business with the band, then Earl made his entrance for which my rehearsal pianist Tiny Parham and I had written a song for the band to sing:

"See than man sittin' on the stool?

He's a ghoul, a pickin' fool.

Piano Man, Piano Man,

There's no one that spanks those ivories like he can.

All about biology he knows not a thing,

But all pianology, he's really king."

"A light hit the piano, and Earl would play a figure, and then they sang, 'Swing it Fatha Hines,' and he'd play his solo. Then back to the band, and so on. Not too long after that, one of the girls in the show had heard it, told me it was on the juke box. I went straight out and bought the Bluebird recording, but my name wasn't on the label. It was just like Willie Bryant and 'It's Over Because We're Through' all over again.

"Acting fast, I walked down the street, sold 'Piano Man' to Gene Krupa, whose band was playing nearby, for $50. As far as I was concerned, it was my song. I could do anything I wanted to with it. Let Gene sort it out, and a lot there was soon to sort out! Krupa recorded the song, calling it 'Drummin' Man,' which lists Krupa as its composer, and that temporarily stopped Earl Hines' recording from being distributed. When the dust cleared a few weeks later, it all turned out to be an honest mistake on Earl's part. He had truly thought his arranger, Budd Johnson, had written the tune. For whenever a band member wrote a song, it didn't matter who it was—Duke, Cab, whoever wrote it—the leader more often than not claimed the song. Earl didn't know he was stealing from me.[To this day, both songs exist in their two slightly different versions as "Piano Man," which credits Hines as the writer, and "Drummin' Man," which credits Krupa and my rehearsal pianist, Tiny Parham, as the writers.] That is the true story of how 'Piano Man' and 'Drummin' Man' came to be written. There's a book out right now about Earl that still claims he wrote the song.

Snapshot taken by Reed of Ella Fitzgerald "on the road" – 1940.

"In the summer of '39, the club's star (we brought in a new headline act about every month) was Ella Fitzgerald fronting the band of Chick Webb. He had died that June. Ella had decided to keep the band together in Chick's memory and was taking it on the road. She asked me to come along to be the band's road manager, and even though it was a step down—with my being sweet on Ella—I accepted. The arrangement didn't last too long, though; a couple of months, maybe. We had pulled into Indianapolis, and were piling out of the car when she turned to me and said like she was a queen, 'Pick up those bags.'"

"And I said, 'Not me.' It was in front of a lot of people."

"It was the way she said, 'Pick up those bags and bring 'em in.'"

"So I said, 'Okay,' got the bags, set 'em beside my car, got back in, and drove off for Chicago and didn't see Ella again for a number of years. By which time she was a really big star, so I guess she was just trying out her new prima donna act on me there in Indianapolis.

"Back in Chicago, I got a job at the Regal Theater as the Master of Ceremonies for every show that came in. I also ran the amateur hour at the Regal for the South Center Department Store. One of those shows featured two people who both turned into big stars: a young blues singer named Ruth Jones, fresh out of her church choir, went on to become the great Dinah Washington. The other was Dorothy Donegan, who, even at age fifteen, had all the skill that she demonstrated later in Jazz concerts and clubs practically all over the world. Guess you could say both of them won that night, even though, technically, Dorothy was the prize winner and Dinah came in second.

"Dinah supposedly once said from the stage of the London Palladium, 'There is but one heaven, one hell, one queen and your Elizabeth is an imposter.' She was probably every bit as temperamental as she's made out to be in books and articles about her. Several years of one-nighters on the road in the segregated South with the Lionel Hampton band in the 1940s were really the cause of it; and while someone else might have had their run-ins with her, I never did. You cannot be a weakling in show business; you've got to be tough. Unlike Ethel Waters, Dinah was not nasty. I guess I saw a different Dinah than the one portrayed by the press. They called her the 'Queen of the Blues.' And she was! But she really had the common touch. No matter how great a star she became, Dinah never forgot me because, after that Regal Theater amateur near win, I started

186

teaching her how to walk on stage, walk off, all the little tricks. Whenever she came into the Apollo when I was there in the '50s, or we were in each others' vicinity, we were always doing things for one another . . . still helped each other out.

"Getting back to Chicago in '39: word about my work had begun to circulate, and a fellow by the name of Jim Scaparelli came to town to find out if I had any interest in coming to work for him in St. Louis. He had a club called The Plantation. Scaparelli had seen my Cotton Club show."

"I asked him, 'You want me to do that kind of show?'"

"'Whatever you think it takes. Come down and see the club.'"

"So, taking Scaparelli up on his offer, I got to St. Louis, checked into the Coronado Hotel, which, of course, was Whites only. They didn't even allow Blacks to work there much less check in. So prejudiced, I don't even think they had a Black porter. However, I hadn't even given such things a second thought when I phoned Scaparelli."

"He said, 'Oh, you're in town. Good. Where're you staying?'"

"'I'm at the Coronado.' I said. Let me give you the number.'"

"'Dead silence.'"

"Then he said, 'You're at the *what*? What are you doing in the Coronado?'"

"'I'm living here.'"

"'I'll be right over,' he barked. 'I want to talk to you. They don't allow niggers there.'"

"'WHAT did you say?' I snapped."

"'Well, they don't allow *Colored People* in there.'"

"'That's better,' I answered. 'I'll be right over,' he said, and hung up."

"Now, when he had been in New York and asked me to get him a girl out of the chorus line—a Black girl—that sort of thing was alright for him, but not for me. Well, we'd see about that! There was a show in St. Louis just then—I think it was the *Scandals*—playing at the Fox Theater, and I knew a couple of the girls who were in it and staying at the Coronado. So, asking them to get a couple of other girls and put their pajamas on and come to my room, they all came down and took off their robes and were lying all over the floor and all over the bed when a knock came at the door. Opening it, there he stood with his mouth wide open. You could have put a watermelon in it.

"I said, 'I don't care what you think, but I'm as much White as I am Black.' Then, I pointed in to all the girls in the room. 'And that proves it. So I'll stay where I want to stay.'"

"We went out in the hall to talk. I said, 'Checked in, didn't I?'"

"'Yeah, I guess it's all right,' he said grudgingly, and turned and walked off."

"Opening night of the show at the Plantation, they were having a party for the cast at the Bellman and Waiters club. Everything in St. Louis closed at 2 a.m., but they reopened for this special party just for the show people and their guests. Getting there a little after two and walking into the vestibule, one of the members of The Bellmen [a Black fraternal organization] came running up to me nervously. 'What can I do for you?'"

"'They got a party here?' I said."

"'Yes sir,' he answered in that humble tone of voice Blacks of that era reserved for Whites. 'However, no White people can come in. Tonight is strictly for The Plantation show.'"

"Telling him that I was the producer made no difference. Calling out to Charlie Pillars the band leader who was just finishing up a number, he turned around and saw me."

"He yelled, 'Hey, Leonard, come on in!'"

"The man at the door called back to him, 'Pillars, we can't let this man in. He's a nigger, man.'"

"Pillars said, 'Let him in.'"

"'You're not going to make me lose my license,' the guy at the door shouted back."

"And he wouldn't let me in. Being turned away from what was really a party in my honor wasn't the end of my problems in St. Louis.

One night after The Plantation show opened, I drove Tony Scaparelli's daughter home. She was about sixteen. Jim, his brother, had asked me to chauffeur her.

"When Tony learned about it the next day, he had a fit. He said, 'What did you say to her?'"

"I told him, 'Good night. I hope you enjoyed the show. What else did you *want* me to say to her?'"

I didn't last much longer in St. Louis."

After the debacle of "Piano Man" and "It's Over Because We're Through," Reed became increasingly careful regarding the copyrights of his songs. By 1990, he would not even demonstrate a new tune of his until it has been properly copyrighted. Thus, numbers he wrote in the late 1930s and early 1940s, such as "Another Day" and "Smile Up at the Sun," and recorded by the likes of Lionel Hampton, Fletcher Henderson, The Cats and the Fiddle, and Sonny Til and the Orioles, continued to bring him regular royalties due to the increasing frequency of compact disc releases of anthologies by these artists.

Because of the democratic protection accorded by the songwriters union, the American Society of Composers and Publishers (ASCAP), Black lyricists and composers had a much better chance of transcending the stigma of race than their counterparts in almost every other field of show business. Unlike almost any sector of the entertainment profession, songwriting abounded with African-American composers and lyricists who made a major mark in this field in the first quarter of the century. [The team of Henry Creamer and Turner Layton ("After You've Gone," "Way Down Yonder in New Orleans"); James P. Johnson ("Old Fashioned Love," "Charleston," "Runnin' "Wild," "If I Could Be With You One Hour Tonight"); Fats Waller and Andy Razaf ("Ain't Misbehavin'," "Honeysuckle Rose"; Noble Sissle and Eubie ("I'm Just Wild About Harry," "Love Will Find A Way"). There was, of course, a state of affairs against which ASCAP was virtually helpless at protecting its members (regardless of race). That was the practice of songwriters selling their wares outright for not much more than spending money, followed by little or no legal recourse to recoup further money if a song in question became a hit. In 1929, for example, Fats Waller sold the copyrights of twenty songs—including "Ain't Misbehavin'"—for the bargain-basement sum of $500. This tendency to take the fast money seems to have been especially rampant in the case of Black songwriters. Reed himself was no stranger to the process, having, during the 1930s sold a number of song copyrights to others.

Alongside songwriting, Reed continued to harbor notions of making it big in radio. A radio career was synonymous with big-time money and fame. To Reed, it also seemed to offer the possibility of something more: a way out of the racial double bind that had haunted his entire career. Theoretically, as a disembodied voice, his race on the radio needn't be of any consequence. He reasoned that if two men, Freeman Gosden and Charles Correll, could make a fortune playing Black as "Amos and Andy," why couldn't he do something like that in reverse? It wouldn't be a question of "passing" exactly; it was simply that the urbane, sophisticated character he'd created for the Vaudeville stage wasn't Black in any identifiable way. He had, after all, been able to break into radio as an emcee in New York. Why couldn't he go even further and carve out a niche for himself along the lines of Bob Hope?

However, there were any number of reasons why not. Being the powerful medium that radio was in the 1930s and as image-conscious as television later became, a network executive aware of Reed's Black show business past might have been willing to look the other way, but no sponsor would ever do so. Reed may have sounded as White as he looked, but the knowledge that he was legally Black would color—in every sense of the word—everything he might do on radio. Even working in a neutral emcee's capacity would have been frowned upon. A Black man doing nothing more than complimenting a singer on her appearance, would have been more than enough to incite racist wrath. A more acceptable and plausible scenario would have found Reed working in radio as an openly Black performer; doing the same kind of comedy he'd always done, but with a heavy dialect . . . "Tomming" it to the max. However, there was even a catch-22 involved with that approach: radio might very well have been willing to feature such a Black player, but only in a supporting role, never a starring role. Black performers, however talented, were always positioned as subservient to Whites, such as the situation comedy *Beulah* or Jack Benny and his manservant Eddie "Rochester" Anderson. At this point in his career, though, Reed wasn't about to forgo his hard-won headliner status to play second or third banana to any man. While trying to figure a way out of this double bind, he continued to hop sideways from Plantation Club to Plantation Club. After departing the so-named one in St. Louis over the dispute involving the car ride that he had given the owner's daughter, he moved back to Detroit to head up the new Spring 1940 show at that city's Plantation Club. After which, he hired on at a popular Motor City spot known as Broad's Club Zombie.

Pearl Bailey. Erie, PA – 1936

191

CHAPTER TWENTY-FIVE
A Wide Awake, 24-Hours-a-Day Town

"I HAD A VERY GOOD DEAL AT THE ZOMBIE. GETTING 20% OF THE door, plus $60 a week, which amounted to a couple of bills a week or more, and in those days that was pretty good money. I played attractions like Peg Leg Bates, Billie Holiday, T-Bone Walker, and the Cats and the Fiddle. [The vocal-instrumental quartet recorded one of Reed's songs, "Another Day," for Bluebird in 1941.] Pearl Bailey also worked for me at the Zombie. I'd known her brother Bill, a fine dancer, for years, and I met Pearl around 1936 at the Standard Theater in Philadelphia. Then a couple of years later, I was doing a show in Buffalo, New York, and some fellow said to me, "You ought to go down to Erie, Pennsylvania. There's a girl working there in a joint. Get her out of there." Meaning he didn't know her name, but that she was good, and I should hire her and get her away from some pretty dicey surroundings. So I went down to Erie, and it was Pearl performing in the goddamnest dump you ever saw; basically it was a whore house. I took her back to Buffalo with me and gave her a job doing stock for me; then she worked for me in Chicago, and in Detroit, everywhere I had a show. That was all starting in 1938, and by the time I hired her to come into the Zombie in Detroit in 1940, she had become pretty big and was my headliner.

"The first day of rehearsal at the Zombie, after she had done her music I said, 'Okay, Pearl, in a minute we're going to run down the finale with all the other performers.'"

"'I ain't going to do no finale.'"

"'Pearl,' I said, 'I hired you to do my show.'"

"'I don't give a damn, I ain't gonna do no finale.'"

Back and forth it went.

"'Well, I hired you to do my show.'"

"'I don't give a damn. I'm not gonna do it.'"

"'Come on, Pearl, let's not get into this. We've known each other for a long time.'"

"'I don't give a damn,' she said. 'I don't let friendship interfere with what I'm going to do,' meaning that she thought she was too good to be seen on the stage with everybody else in the show."

"'Fine,' I said. "'I'll call Joe Glaser and tell him I'm canceling your contract.'"

"'I don't give a fuck. You ain't canceling my contract.'"

So I called Joe and told him Pearl refused to do the finale and if she didn't do it, I didn't want her in the show.

"'Let me talk to her,' Glaser said."

"I put Pearl on the phone, and she came back a few minutes later and said, "'I'm gonna do it, but it's against my principles.'"

"'Fine,' I said. And that was that.

"We fell out and didn't see each other for years. Then in 1960, she was doing a TV show from the Palace Theater in L.A. and my friend, Marie Bryant, was doing the choreography. I had just moved there, and so I said, 'Let me go back and holler at Pearl.' Going backstage, I said, 'Tell her Leonard Reed's calling.'

"And I heard her from her dressing room say, 'Tell him I'm busy.' She was *still* holding a grudge for more than twenty years over that finale. So, I never bothered to speak to her again. Then one night around 1980, my wife, Barbara, and I went to see somebody, who was being accompanied by her husband, drummer Louis Belson, and we went to see whoever it was. Anyway, we were there, and Pearl came up and threw her arms around me just like an old long lost friend. She gave me an autobiography of hers, cookbooks, a nicely autographed photo . . . just like nothing had ever happened between us. Her problem with me, finally, really had nothing to do with the incident at the Zombie but instead with something I've observed in a few other talented people before they hit it big. After they 'make it,' they begin to feel uncomfortable around people who knew them 'when.'

"Pearl was just a very difficult woman to work with. She did a pretty good hiding from the public the fact that, behind the scenes, she could be a real bitch to work with; talented, but a bitch.

"All the while after the Chicken Shack dust-up, Joe Louis and I had remained in pretty close contact. He loved the way I dressed. I picked out his suits and things, took messages to his women, and dropped whatever I was doing to join him. One day, the summer before the Chicken Shack, he said to me, 'Come on out and watch me play golf.' At the time, he was taking lessons from a pro by the name of Clyde Martin. But I knew next to nothing about the game, so thought I'd go take a look.

"I followed Joe around the course for a while before he asked, 'You want to play?'"

"'I said no.'"

"But he insisted to the guy in the clubhouse, 'Give him some clubs.' He bought me a set of golf clubs, the shoes, the gloves, the works, before I'd ever even swung at a golf ball. I went along with it because I figured if I could hit a baseball, why not a golf ball? Watching everybody, what they did, I tried to swing at it like a baseball. And I hit it. Everywhere . . . in the creek, in the woods. Joe loved it; thought it was the funniest thing he'd ever seen. Shortly after that, however, he went away boxing, and I didn't pay any more attention to goddamned golf . . . at least for a while.

"In high school, I played semi-pro ball. Then in the 1930s whenever there was a break-in engagement, we played softball. Everybody in Black show business had teams, and some even toured with the teams in semi-pro leagues. Joe Louis had a team called the Brown Bombers; I had one, but it wasn't in a league, so we just played wherever we could get games. We did this in the summertime when most clubs and theaters were closed due to the heat. Even during the rest of the year, if I was in a city for five or six weeks, I'd have myself a basketball team or a softball team. All the bands had them: Basie, Lunceford, and I would play everybody who came to town. Nobody made any money. This was all for fun. Maybe you bet $1 a man. If you hadn't made enough of a living the rest of the year to take you through the summer, then shame on you. Until coming to California in the 1960s, I almost never worked July and August. Besides, managing to have somebody to take care of me, I didn't have to work those months. Sometimes I even had a woman looking after me when I *was* working. The man who owned the Club Zombie didn't believe in banks and would just stuff his money under a carpet; and nearly every day for the almost two years I worked there, his daughter, in between shows, would take me to the family's house . . . usually to screw. Afterward, she'd roll back the carpet and tell me to take a C note, her old man would never miss it. This is an additional $100 a day I'm getting, besides my $75 a week salary and 2 percent of the door.

"Staying at the Zombie until the war broke out was the longest I'd ever been in any one spot up until then, Besides, how could I resist? Then everybody started getting drafted, but before I'd even gotten my notice, I went down to the Draft Board and got rejected because of the car accident I'd had back in '37. Throughout the war, I formed little companies and did local Army shows all over California, where I

196

ended up in 1941 because of a letter I received shortly after Pearl Harbor Day. Postmarked Hollywood, California, it was from a guy named Nate Krevitz. He invited me to come to work for him at a place called the Hollywood Casino. Didn't know Krevitz, but he knew me.

"'Oh boy, Hollywood! This is for me!'" I'd go to Hollywood, work for Krevitz at first, and then find a way of getting into pictures. And that's where I headed in January 1941 with a suitcase containing the $40,000 saved from Broad's Zombie."

Los Angeles was never much of a place for nightlife until the 1930s. Part of the reason was that Los Angeles was basically a city without a geographic center. With the coming of World War II, the town began the slow process of coming alive after the sun went down. People of all nationalities, races, and backgrounds began streaming into the area seeking work in defense plants and other war-related industries. African-American entertainers—many of whom were leftovers from the glory days of Vaudeville—were also being lured there by the promise of steady work not only in the many night clubs and other entertainment venues that were springing up but also in the film industry.

When Reed arrived in Los Angeles in winter 1941, no part of the city was more alive than fabled Black-populated Central Avenue. It stretched from downtown area streets numbered in the teens all the way past Watts. Ground zero on the Avenue was the block of Central between 42nd and 43rd Streets, where nighttime and daytime fun and games approached critical mass that evoked the atmosphere of Times Square on New Years Eve.

In close proximity to the popular intersection of 42nd and Central there stood the mother ship, the spacious Club Alabam, which, even long before the War from the late 1920s on, had been a focal point of Black Los Angeles' nightclub and jazz scene. As luck would have it, Club Alabam was located directly next to the jumping and equally popular Dunbar Hotel.

Veteran musician Buddy Collette was fond of reciting a partial honor roll of the clubs that lined this Afro-American Via Venetto. "There was the Lincoln Theater at 23rd. Across the street was the Jungle Room, Jack's Basket Room was at 34th and Central. Then there was the Last Word, Down Beat, Memo, Crystal Tea Room, and Clark Hotel Bar. Ivy's Chicken Shack [owned by Duke Ellington vocalist Ivy Anderson] was across from the Club Alabam. The Turban Room was in the Dunbar Hotel at 41st and Central, Lovejoy's was upstairs at Vernon and Central, Honey Murphy's and the Plantation Club were way out at 108th. And there were after-hour spots and eating places everywhere in between, and music was the theme that ran through it all."

Dancer Frances Nealy, who worked for Reed in Los Angeles during this epochal period of entertainment recalls that the action wasn't just centralized on Central; clubs and theaters fanned out all over the Los Angeles Basin, and on into North Hollywood and the San Fernando Valley. "I drive past so many places today in Los Angeles and say to the person I'm with that I used to work there. Now of course, they're all laundromats and vacant lots. There's a place on Third and Main that was Victor's, the Burbank Theater on Main Street, the Linda Lee Theater on Main, the Follies on Main, the Orpheum Theater on Broadway, the Million Dollar Theater at Third and Broadway. Slapsy Maxie's on Wilshire near LaBrea. On Cahuenga near Yucca, there was a club I worked at; something called the K-9 down on 9th and Figueroa. There were all kinds of little clubs nestled around everywhere and they all had shows and bands and kept you working all the time."

Reed spent most of the 1940s in Los Angeles. He crossed the threshold of most of these establishments, which have now gone the way of swap meet, bodega, paint store, and mini-mall, all designed to serve the needs of a much more convenience-minded time.

The clientele of the clubs and ballrooms ran the gamut from solid Black to racially-mixed Black-and-tan. Since Los Angeles was no more progressive than most of the rest of the country at that time, the city also abounded with standard-issue night clubs with entertainment bills of fare that might alternately consist of Black or White performers, but whose admission policy was strictly Whites Only. There were even a few remaining places in Los Angeles that harkened back to the Cotton Club that featured strictly Black performers but barred Blacks as clientele. The Hollywood Casino, where Reed came to work on the west coast in early 1942, was one of them. The club was located at the comer of Sunset Boulevard and Gower Street (and later became a recording studio.) Nearby were a number of film studios. So hectic was the professional pace that Reed got immediately swept up in—in the strictly live branch of entertainment—that producing and choreographing for the adjacent Hollywood Casino was as close as he ever came to his dream of "getting into pictures" while he remained in Los Angeles.

CHAPTER TWENTY-SIX
Hollywood Days / Harlem Nights

"I WENT OUT TO L.A. TO TAKE A LOOK AT THE HOLLYWOOD CASINO. Not having actually made an agreement to work for the owner Nate Krevitz, nevertheless, he'd sent me first-class train fare and put me up at the Roosevelt. I went in to the Casino and checked it out. I didn't say, 'Yes, I'll do it,' didn't say 'no.' I said, 'I don't know. How many people you gonna have?'"

"'How many do you need?'" Krevitz asked.

"'Twelve, fourteen, sixteen chorus girls.'"

"'You got it,' he said. 'Who's the band?'"

"'Noble Sissle's band [which was a big hand], and we've got Benny Carter coming in later.'"

"'Oh, you've got big bands. Fine.'"

"A little more negotiating, and I went in, but right off there was a problem. A girl by the name of Patsye Hunter, who was a fine choreographer, wanted the job ... except she was local, and Nate Krevitz didn't want any local ideas. He wanted Cotton Club ideas. So she didn't get the job, but the girls didn't like that, because they had a clique and loved Patsye, which made it difficult for me to even show them a simple dance routine. So, I sent for one of my girls from Chicago, Mary Stevens, to come out. I'd put her in show business at age thirteen; she worked for me in *Rhythm Bound* and ended up with me in most of my clubs. I could say to her, 'You know the routine we did in so and so? Show the girls the steps,' and I wouldn't have to do the steps. If Mary came out from Chicago and taught them, things might cool down. I was wrong. They didn't like that either. So I said to myself, *All you got to do is get in with one of these girls.'*

"One of the dancers, Artye Brandon, looked awfully good to me. She was not only the most popular but the prettiest. I began courting her, dating her night after night. Soon, the girls began to warm toward me. Before, they'd straggled up, taken their time. Now, I'd say, 'Okay, girls!,' and they'd come running. We also just happened to fall in love. A month after we met, we got married.

"In California, I met a whole mess of my blood relatives for the very first time. My half-brother, Howard, had tracked me down in the early 1930s after seeing my name in the entertainment columns. This branch of my family had moved west during World War I with Major Reed, who had long since passed, but my aunt was still alive then and living with my half-sister, Hermie. My kin also included my three half-brothers, consisting of the twins, Ronald and Donald, and Harvey, who was never able to deal with the fact that we were also cousins (sharing the same father and having mothers who were also sisters). To the day he died in 1980, he denied that I was his kin. The twins and I became good friends, though, especially Donald; we played golf a good deal when I eventually moved to California in 1960. However, I was closest of all, and continue to be so, with my sister, Hermie, the only one of them still alive. She still lives in Watts [in 1985] in a house I helped her buy in the early 1940s.

"Shortly after arriving in California, Joe phoned me and said he was coming out in a few weeks and that, when he got there, he wanted me join him on the golf course. I still had the set of clubs he had bought me back in Detroit, but had never hit a golf ball since that one embarrassing time in Detroit a few years back."

"He added, 'You better take some lessons.'"

"At first, not taking his advice, I just started putting around, but without really knowing what I was doing. Then one day out at Sunset Fields playing about, there wasn't anyone else on the course except this one guy over on the first hole getting ready to tee off. I said, 'You by yourself?'"

"He said, 'Yeah.'

"'Wait a minute. I'll join you.'"

"So I ran up, bought my ticket, and went with him. Again, hitting the ball everywhere but where it supposed to go. We finished the ninth hole, and he said, 'Well, it was nice playing with you. I'm not going to play the back side.'"

Going into the restaurant to get something to eat, I'm sitting there half way through my sandwich and look up and there he is, going out on the tenth hole after all. I left my food and ran out after him like some kind of dumb kid,"

"'Oh, God? Oh, well,' he said when he saw me. "'C'mon.'"

"On the 18th hole, after he hit a ball that just *soared* through the air, I said to him, 'If I could just hit a ball like that'd be all I'd ever want out of life.'"

"'Do you *really* to learn to hit a ball like that?'"

"'I sure do,' I said. 'Then, I'll show you!'"

"Well, that thrilled me. We walked off the 18th tee, and he accompanied me up to the clubhouse. When we got there, he pointed to a door with a name on it that read 'Golf Pro: Paul Mangrum.'"

203

Unidentified pre–PGA players.

More pre–PGA players.

African-American women golfers.

Ted Rhodes.

Tup Holmes

Unidentified player

"'See that name over there? Go over there and talk to him and tell him I sent you and said you should take a lesson'.

"Well, that infuriated me. I thought he was going to show me, himself. Going up to the door anyway and sticking my head in, I said, 'I want to take some lessons.'"

"'How many lessons do you want to take?'"

"'Enough to beat *him*,' I told him, and pointed to the guy I'd just played with who was now on the putting green."

"'Well,' he said, 'you're going to have to take an awful lot of lessons. That's my brother, Ray. He's the club champion here." [There was yet a third brother, Lloyd Mangrum, who ended up being the most well-known of the trio.]

"When Joe arrived in California, I went out with him and Ted Rhodes and we each took a hundred lessons with Paul Mangrum. Ted was already an excellent golfer and would go on to great fame on the Black pro circuit. Then, he was like a singer who'd been singing for a long time, but then just suddenly decided one day that he needed some more lessons.

"I never played a game until Paul Mangrum told me I was ready. Today, that's what I tell my singers: 'Don't go anywhere and sing until I tell you you're ready. Because, once people hear you, if you're bad, they're never going to want to buy you again no matter how long you wait after the first time you strike out.' Mangrum showed me all the technical aspects of the game. How to hit it high, how to hit it low, how to fade it, how to hook it, how to come out of the sand trap. He showed me everything but putting.

"'See those fellows up there?' he said one day. 'They're putting for 10¢ a round. Go up there and learn from them, because putting is individual.'"

"So, I watched everybody else, and that's how I learned to putt *and* how to play golf.

"Late in December 1943, I got an offer to appear in a Los Angeles show called *Sweet and Hot* that was scheduled to open in January at the

Reed's 1944 stage appearance (and more!) in Hollywood.

Mayan Theater. Two years before, Duke Ellington had made west coast theatrical history there with his production, *Jump for Joy*. Coincidentally, one of *"Sweet and Hot"*'s star, Dorothy Dandridge, had also been in Duke's show. [Also in the cast, among others, were the comedy team of (Flournoy) Miller and (Jonny) Lee. Jonny was Flournoy's latest replacement for his old partner Aubrey Lyles, who died in 1932. Also in the cast was Flournoy's daughter, Olivette Miller, the dance team of Sneaks and Emil, and a big line of chorus girls.] I was hired to be the

208

The Sweet and Hot basketball team, including Charlie Mingus in the back row second from left.

emcee and the juvenile. Before this, I never had never done stand-up comedy; was always a Master of Ceremonies doing little bits between the acts. So, when they came to me and said they wanted me to do six minutes in front of the curtain before the show opened, I told them I didn't have six minutes that I was good enough. They got a fellow by the name of Joe Greene (he was also a popular songwriter) to write an act for me. This was the first time I had ever done material in a show that someone else had written especially for me.

"The first bit Greene concocted had me coming out and opening absolutely cold, no music, no nothing. We had a split curtain, and while people were still walking in and the lights were up, I walked through this curtain and stood shock still in the center and looked at them with a blank stare for at least thirty seconds while the lights were going down. Then, all of a sudden, I just said, 'Hello.' Opening night, I don't know why, but the audience died laughing. In rehearsals, I hadn't trusted the material. It's a fairly understandable response that when you've been doing your own thing for such a long time, and somebody gives you something new, it's difficult. Green had said, 'Just do it like I tell you, and I promise you it will work.' And he was right. After I looked the audience over, I said, 'If you came to see a show . . . forget it.' Then I said, 'Look on page 25. That's me. Nothing in the program is in the show except me. Go and ask them to give your money back. They ain't gonna do it, but you've got your legal rights to ask 'em anyway.'

"Then I told jokes, especially ones about California weather that were big that season. One that Joe Greene wrote for me went this way: 'This is the only place in the world where you can get pneumonia and sun stroke at the same time.' That's the joke Bob Hope stole from me. He came to see *Sweet and Hot* and used the joke on his show the next week.

"And more Southern California climate material—all good laughs. I closed my six minutes with, 'I know you expect when I walk off that the band will start playing, the girls will start dancing . . . .' Then I said, 'That's just what's going to happen.' And I walked off and the band started playing and the girls started dancing and right in the middle of it there was a break—silence—and walking back on

I said, 'See? What did I tell you?' and I walked off again. That was my first attempt at doing standup comedy.

"After my opening, though, it was pretty much downhill all the way for *Sweet and Hot*. Not because I was so good and couldn't be topped, but because the producers had this crazy idea for a band: just four pianos, no drums, no rhythm, just four pianos to do a Black musical. They thought it would be different, classy. However, it just didn't jibe, because the girls couldn't dance to four pianos.

"Then, somebody suggested that they let me re-do the show, because

Sweet and Hot just was not going to make it like that. So, we shut down for two weeks, and I reworked it from top to bottom. In came Benny Carter to lead the band in the pit. It was a pretty impressive lineup including Lee Young on drums, Calvin Jackson on piano, and a very young Charlie Mingus playing bass. From then on, everything was fine with the show. It ended up running eighteen weeks, but I never got any credit for saving *Sweet and Hot* because of contract stipulations.

"By now I had begun to establish some fairly solid relations with most of my half-brothers and sisters—except for Harvey—all of whom were now in California. Harvey still refused to accept me as blood kin, claiming I was just trying to scam the family out of money; just trying to 'get warm,' he claimed. Inasmuch as I had a suitcase with nearly $40,000 in it, nothing could have been further from the truth. One afternoon when we were playing baseball, I got so angry with him that I began peeling $5 bills off a roll and giving them to team members on both sides just to spite him.

"After *Sweet and Hot* closed, I began hopping all over L.A., doing shows from the Club Alabam at Central and 42nd, to the Lincoln Theater at 23rd, and yet *another* Plantation Club way out on Central

Reed on stage with two of the original Lafayette Players, Laura Bowman, Jimmy Baskette (Basquette), Margaret Hatch (far left), and Sybil Lewis (far right).

211

at 105th. I also emceed shows at the downtown Million Dollar Theater, which had stars such as Billy Eckstine and Lena Horne.

"Starting in 1944 and for about a year, I put together the shows at the Lincoln Theater, which was the closest thing there was to a west coast Apollo Theater. From back east, I brought such stars as Dusty Fletcher, John Mason, Ashes and Bilo, and Pigmeat Markham. We alternated between Johnny Otis' band and Bardu Ali's. That outfit had Charles Brown on piano. Charles was a star in the 1950s, but after that couldn't 'get arrested' for the next twenty years. Now [1985], he's hot again! I also used two of the biggest names from the now-disbanded Lafayette Players from time to time, Laura Bowman and Jimmy ("Uncle Remus") Basquette. Since the Lincoln had been the group's west coast home back in the 1930s, when these two were in my shows, it almost felt like a revival of the Players.

"One of the things I did at the Lincoln was a book musical I wrote called *Lulubelle*. We had three popular dance acts in the show: Sneaks and Emil, who played a paperboy and a milkman; my old friend Peg Leg Bates; and The Step Brothers. I finally got to make up for being forced to short-shrift singer Callye Dill when we'd done *Rhythm Bound* together; she was the female lead. Marie Bryant was my soubrette; my two comics were Dusty Fletcher and Johnny Taylor of Rutledge and Taylor; Bill Day was my lead male singer. We also had Eunice Wilson, who'd worked for me a lot at clubs in the Midwest. *Lulubelle* ran for eight weeks at the Lincoln, which was very good for a theater whose audience mostly expected to see revue-type setups. The performers like Dusty; Pigmeat; Ashes and Bilo; and John Mason, who worked for me at the Lincoln, were no big deal on the west coast, but back east they were big stars, especially at the Apollo.

"The money I was getting at the Lincoln was just okay, and besides I wanted to get back to club work, so I talked a guy by the name of Sheppard into opening up a club for me at First and San Pedro in L.A. At Shepp's, I got a salary, $75 a week and 20% of the dollar at the door.

Plus! They gave me the cloakroom concession, which I put my sister Hermie in. You could make a lot of money there, because in those days everyone wore a coat and a hat.

"Shepp's had a mixed racial clientele, but I still continued to stick to a strictly Blacks-only policy of performers in my shows. Whites simply didn't know how to play to a colored audience; they didn't feel comfortable. I remember once in Detroit, Joe Louis and I went to see this White magician at this Black club and he was just super, and people were applauding and going crazy, and he came back out after the applause died down and he said, 'This is wonderful. You don't know how you make me feel, because I've never worked for niggers in my . . . oh!' And he put his hand over his mouth and said, 'Excuse me.' And people just fell on the floor laughing, but he was never invited back there.

"Most people probably still recall that in the '40s and '50s, Sammy Davis Jr. was part of the Will Mastin Trio. The act was Sammy, his father, and Will Mastin, who everybody thinks was Sammy's uncle, but they really weren't related; no kin. Having known Will Mastin for some time, I kept them working at Shepp's while Sammy was in the service. I almost got fired for that because Sam Sr. and Will really weren't that good by themselves. They were getting old and couldn't really kick it anymore. However, I kept them there in production numbers.

"Then when Sammy got out of the service, I brought the three of them into Shepp's. Writing their opening number, I had one of my old tuxedos cut down to fit Sammy, who didn't have one since he had just gotten out of the army. They were good at Shepp's, so good, in fact, that their manager yanked them out of there and put them on tour right away. I know it's not unusual for people to put Sammy Davis Jr. in the category of performers like Jolson, Danny Kaye, and Bert Williams, but, really, Sammy was better than any of them, the best all-round entertainer of them all. Not only was he a great singer, but unlike these others, he could also dance, play musical instruments, do imitations, and he also had a way with patter that really grabbed an audience. The latter he

213

probably cultivated out of sheer necessity. After all, not even Sammy was superhuman enough not to have to stop and catch his breath occasionally. I was working at the Apollo Theater in Harlem when he appeared there several times in the 1950s. He was always at his best then, for he was superstitious about giving less than a hundred per cent in front of his 'own people' (Sammy's words). He once said, 'If you fail at the Copa, they'll break your knees. At the Apollo, they'll break your heart.'

"Sammy was often a guest of a radio show we broadcast nightly direct from Shepp's Playhouse, I had a great opening format. The show with train sounds, bells, and whistles:

"'All aboard. All aboarrrrrrrd. Rhythm train leaving now on track five. Heading for points south, Watts . . . .' And then do an opening pitch for our sponsor in Watts. I'd say stuff like, 'You can leave your pants off to have 'em pressed, and by the time the train gets back they can have them ready for you. You think that's a lie? Well, why don't you try? And say, you can get a really tasty sandwich right next door at . . . .' And we'd name the sponsor and read off part of their menu. And the conductor would come along taking up tickets. And I'd say, 'Conductor, I forgot to ask you a question. Who's riding this train tonight? We have Nat King Cole! Really!? Eddie 'Rochester' Anderson!? Wonderful! Joe Liggins . . . Gerald Wilson and his band!? You can't beat that! And Eddie Heywood!' Then, I'd call out the next stop, which would be some place like Inglewood, or Downey, California, and we'd name another sponsor, a beer company, and so forth. We also had interviews with celebrities in the audience just like the guy who owned the Stork Club started doing on TV a few years later."

Frances Nealy, self-described "chorus girl, hoofer, and [in films] queen of the one-liners" was a fixture of Reed's chorus line, The Reedettes, in Los Angeles in the 1940s. First, at the Lincoln Theater and then at Shepp's Playhouse, which was, she recalls:

" . . . THE place. Leonard brought in Eddie Heywood when Eddie was at his peak with 'Begin the Beguine,' and the house band was Gerald Wilson. You came upstairs and on the first floor, which was actually the second floor, was the bar and the cocktail lounge. Then you went up another flight of stairs and this is where the dancing shows were. It was on First and San Pedro. They had run all the Japanese out and into concentration camps, and Black people took over down there. They had the Civic Hotel and the Morris Hotel on Fifth Street. Sammy Davis [Jr.] stayed there; just everybody stayed there. It was jumpin' down there. When Leonard claims that he had affairs with just about all the chorus

Advertisement for Shepp's Playhouse from which Reed also broadcast in 1944

girls, he's probably telling the truth. He was a charming, good-looking man. I worked with Eric Dolphy, Buddy Collette, Gerald Wilson, Count Basie, and that's one thing that disillusioned me in later years, to work with musicians that couldn't read your music. That's the trouble with Rock."

Nealy continues: "Leonard had sent for all these people he had worked with back east, like Lawrence Criner, Monte Hawley, Sibyl Lewis, Jimmy Basquette, Pigmeat Markham—he brought them or some were already here—because he was trying to do at the Lincoln what was going on in New York at the Apollo. However, the Lincoln never became as famous. There's only one Apollo. Today they call people like Leonard, the 'choreographer.' At that time, we called them the 'producer.' Now, the producer and the choreographer are two different people, but then they were one and the same. Leonard put the shows on, hired and fired, and picked his people. Shepp's is also where I met a comic by the name of Willie Lewis—Della Reese swears by him—who I ended up marrying."

"The shows at Shepp's were not exactly like the ones at the Lincoln," Nealy adds, "because at the Lincoln, Leonard, Pigmeat, and the others were doing blackout bits, like the sort of thing Benny Hill used to do, but at Shepp's we didn't do blackouts. Otherwise, things were pretty much the same except the chorus line was maybe six girls at Shepp's instead of twelve. At both places, the number featuring the chorus girls, was always ... hot! The middle number they called the 'production number.' That was our pretty number; maybe featured the exotic dancer, or maybe one of the vocalists. Sometimes it would be built around one of the principals. And the finale was our big number. Maybe it would be the jungle number, something exotic with lavish costumes. Shepp's had a big floor large enough to get six girls and five principals on stage at one time for the finales with plenty of room left over. Mostly all the clubs followed this format."

Perhaps much too much of a good thing, Shepp's Playhouse was fated for a very short run. Recalls Hermie Crowder (Reed's sister), "Mr.

Sheppard, the club's owner, had a thing for the ladies, and even though business was booming, he got messed up and went bankrupt after a couple of years."

That still left a number of clubs in the area that still could have used Reed's services, but his Los Angeles days were numbered. He remained there for almost four years, the longest he ever stayed in one place. There was still no doubt in his mind about how good he was. He remembered, "I was as good as Bob Hope any day. There was a point at which I could have chosen the White path and never looked back, but by the mid-1940s, I was past that point. Anyway, I'd long since stopped regretting that I didn't because being on both sides of the racial fence was really starting to pay off as an education in life. I began to feel—and still do—that I saw the world in a way that no Black man could ever hope to view it, nor any White man, for that matter."

CHAPTER TWENTY-SEVEN
The Champ Branches Out

"Artye and I didn't last very long as man and wife, and by the end of 1945, I was shacked up with another woman, who every night when I'd come home would hassle me with, 'Where you been? What've you been doing? What's that lipstick on your ears?' While taking a shower, she'd be out in my car going through the ashtray to see if there were cigarettes or Kleenex with lipstick on them.

"I'd ask her, 'What the hell are you doing?'"

"She'd say, 'I know you're out there with one of them bitches. You get off at 2 a.m., and you're not home till 5.'"

"'Well, goddamn, when I get off at 2:00, I'm not out of there until 2:30 or 3:00, then I go to a restaurant, it's 4:00, and then it's a half-hour driving home.'"

"Never could explain that missing half hour to her satisfaction. One

Sunday morning, going to play golf at Sunset Fields, I got up at 5:30, and tried not to wake her up, but she did and said, 'Where're you going?'"

"'To the golf course.'"

"She said, '"On Sunday?'"

"'Yeah. Why? What's the difference?'"

"She said, '"We have someone coming.'"

"'I don't give a damn. Have them wait until I get back.'"

"She said, '"If you're really going to the golf course, keep going.'"

"I shot back, 'Really? You mean that?'"

"'Yes I'm serious. I'm tired of this shit. First, it's one woman; then it's another. Now it's the golf course.'"

"She had a lot of money. Her father either worked for or owned the Fox Theater chain. They were pretty well off.

"I said, '"How much money have you got?'"

"She said, 'Whatever's in the purse. I don't know, but you can take it.'"

"Looking in the purse, there was only a hundred dollars or so, but she had some rings and a watch, so I took them and the money. We had two cars, a Packard and a Chrysler Windsor, one of the little convertible jobs. I said, 'Which one of the cars can I have?'"

"'I don't give a goddamn. Whichever one you want. If you're leaving, take it and go.'"

"Forgetting all about the golf course, I just packed up my clothes. A Chrysler trunk is huge. Putting all of my things in, I hit the highway. I wanted to go east anyway, so didn't even think about the golf course. I just hit [Route] 66, and the next day was in Albuquerque, New Mexico. Staying there and golfing, I hustled and made some more money gambling. Then went on from there to Oklahoma City, and Tulsa, and Kansas City, right into Chicago, where I started back at the Regal Theater putting together shows. Before long, I got a phone call from Joe Louis fresh out of the service."

"'We're gonna do an act,' he announced."

Louis and Reed perform "The Act" on TV.

"That was news to me, but what else can you do when the most famous man in the world tells you he wants you as a straight man? If you're me, you drop everything and catch the first train headed east. Joe was always interested in show business, and after he got out of the army, he returned to New York to find at least one other boxer had beaten him to the punch: the fighter Barney Ross was doing an act with Joey Adams.

"So not to be outdone, Joe got Goodman Ace—absolutely the top comedy writer in show business at the time—to write us material for which he charged a lot of money. Looking at what he'd written, though, I had to tell Joe the truth that it was no good. Ace might've been great for Milton Berle, but he had Joe doing all these god-awful Uncle Tom jokes. Telling Joe I knew a guy who could write good material, I left out that the guy was me. Finishing the act I'd whipped up, I took it to Joe."

"'Goddamned, this is good. Who did this?'"

"'Me,' I said. 'You paid Goodman Ace $5,000 for six minutes. So I want a third of whatever you get for the use of this material and me.'"

"He agreed, and we put the act together. We rehearsed it and broke it in at in a couple of places. We did our comedy routine; Joe sang, 'Baby, Baby, Baby' and did the Shim Sham with me.

"Before it was all over, we ended up doing that same act over and over again for more than fifteen years all over the world, and never changed a thing. [For a further description of *The Act*, see Appendix I.]

"Joe had a dry sense of humor and when he delivered a line he always had a smile on his face. The reason we never changed the act was because it just seemed absolutely perfect the way it was; like they say, if it's not broke . . . We never failed with it once during the hundreds of times we performed it. How could we? Here's Joe, one of the most famous and beloved men in the world, and here I come, this annoying little punk buzzing and nattering at him like some kind of pesky mosquito. Then when I'm finished, he just kind of smiles, says a couple of words, and destroys me, first verbally, and then when that doesn't work, he goes at me physically. The audience ate it up. Joe always ad-libbed though, trying to mess me up. One night I said, "'Let me make my comeback.'"

"And he said, "'Where you been?'"

"However, that wasn't supposed to be the line. It was supposed to be, 'Come back from what?' The audience died laughing."

"In almost every book about Joe, they try to make me look like I swindled him. My first dealing with Joe was the Chicken Shack and I did not ask him for a dime. He offered to give me that $10,000 on my word and we shook hands. When I got hurt, he gave the Chicken Shack to his brother Lonnie, and I never set foot in the place again.

"My next thing with Joe was when we returned from doing the act in Europe in '48. I had earned $18,000 and saved every penny of it, with a cashier's check for that amount. We were on our way to the coast, and for once in my life I promised myself to put the money to good use. This was what I'd made from writing and performing with him. When we came into Chicago, there was a fellow by the name of Charlie Glenn, who owned a club called the Rhumboogie at 343 E. Garfield Boulevard.

[Located on the site of the old Dave's, where Reed got his first producing job in 1933.] He had borrowed money from Joe many times without my knowledge and Joe didn't tell me he was going there to collect. We got there, and there was a little bar outside the main club, and it's daytime, and we're sitting there talking, and the girls are rehearsing."

"Joe says, 'I'll be back in a minute. I want to go talk to Charlie.'" He was trying to get his money back."

"Charlie evidently said, 'I don't have any money to pay you, Joe.'"

"Joe comes back and tells me, 'Give me that check. I want to show Charlie something.'"

"Those were his exact words. Giving him my check, he went back in to Charlie, came back a few seconds later without the check and said, 'You and I now own the Rhumboogie. Sign this check over to Charlie.'"

"I did. So, whatever Charlie owned Joe plus this check of mine gave us the Rhumboogie, which I never had any desire in owning in the first place.

"We closed the place down temporarily and started rehearsals. We were going to do a whole new thing there. I brought in the likes of something which the south side of Chicago had never seen before: a band of Mexican mariachi musicians playing Rumba music and dinner music. Dinner was from six to nine. Then the mariachis go off at nine. There'd be a half-hour for the staff to clean up and get everything ready, and at 9:30, the big band would come on, and at ten o'clock, the show started, for which I'd brought in Valaida Snow, The Four Brown Buddies, Marie Bryant, and Erskine Hawkins' band. [In this one renegade package were two of the most legendary entertainment professionals of the era, Snow, a multi-talented performer star of the 1930s—singer, dancer, trumpet player—was interned for eighteen months during World War II by Hitler because she was a non-Aryan. Upon her return to the U.S., she was never quite able to regain her pre-war momentum. Bryant was a similarly talented entertainer, fondly remembered by her contemporaries, who somehow never managed to achieve the headliner status she so obviously deserved.]

"Right off the bat, there were problems. Charlie Glenn had failed to tell Joe that there was an outstanding debt with the musicians union for a local band that he had already hired for ten weeks. The union came in and said 'you've got to pay this band for the ten weeks they were hired for.' Telling them we couldn't pay Erskine Hawkins *and* the hired band, we got into a hell of a fight. They had to pull us off of each other. I said, 'This is my money and I'm not letting you close up my place.' However, they did, and Joe went down and talked to them. That's when they had separate unions: a Black union and a White one. We finally got the show opened, but it was operating at a loss because we had to pay two bands. On top of this, after she closed, Valaida Snow raided my chorus line and took three or four of my girls, including Marie Bryant, and went to the west coast.

"Finally, we had to let Hawkins go and bring the original band back in. Several weeks after we opened, Sarah Vaughan was brought in at $3,400 a week, and she packed the place every night. They had to send out for extra chairs to accommodate the patrons, but still we were barely making it. Shortly thereafter, Joe came to me and said to forget about my $18,000. He said, 'Give the Rhumboogie to Pat.' Pat was his half-brother."

"I screamed, 'Do what?'"

"Pat had been there every night trying to learn the business sitting there at an upstairs cash register. Not being able to squawk too much because of Joe helping me out after my car wreck injuries, I said, 'Okay, but why?'"

"'Because we're going South.'"

"That's the way Joe did things. He said, 'Teach Pat everything you know about the operation of the place.'"

"He could hardly read or write his name, but I spent two days just showing him how to clear the register when the night was over. Leaving

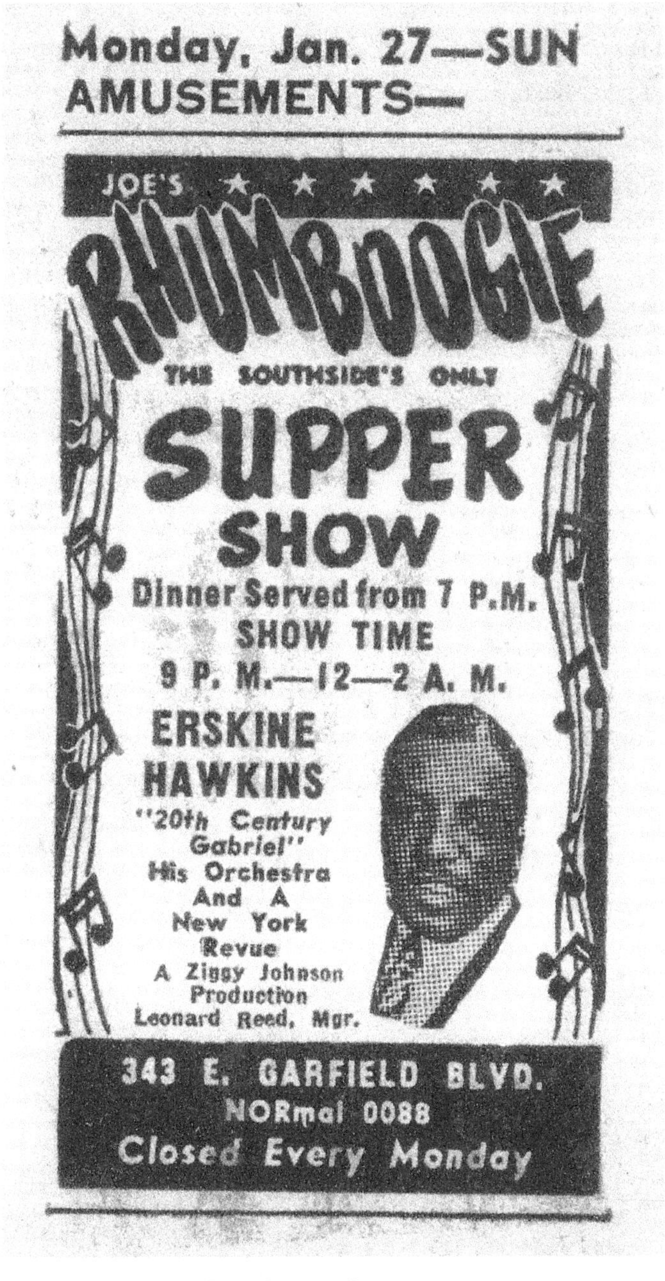

Rhumboogie advertisement

it with Pat, the Rhumboogie ran two, three weeks after we left. We were in Mexico when Joe told me, 'We closed the Rhumboogie. What should I tell Pat to do?'"

"I said, 'Tell him to go home, goddamnit.'"

Joe Louis' attempt to get the Rhumboogie up on its feet and running was indicative of the fact that he was anxious to retire from the ring. Still heavyweight champ at age 33, he wanted to quit the ring while he was still ahead. On March 1, 1949, shortly after an exhibition match in Jamaica, the champ announced his retirement from the ring, a decision made public just before the next leg of the exhibition match tour scheduled for March 1st in Havana, Cuba. The reason for these out-of-the-U.S. locales was to insure that profits accruing from this farewell tour (of sorts) could not garnisheed by his estranged wife, Marva, who had tied up his June 25, 1948 earnings from the Walcott fight. By this point, Louis also had serious back tax problems and needed immediate infusions of cash to stay afloat in the high, wide, and handsome manner to which he was accustomed.

No stranger to exhibition matches during the earlier part of his career, (wags then had dubbed it the "Chump of the Month" tour), Louis once again partook of such events on a regular basis for the next two years. Between March 18, 1949 and December 16, 1951, he engaged in sixty of them, often in such diverse locales as Taipei, Formosa; Rio De Janeiro, Brazil; Waco, Texas; and Tokyo, Japan. Always, Reed was by his side in the capacity of what was usually described as Louis' "personal secretary." However, the relationship between the two was a good deal more complicated than that.

CHAPTER TWENTY-EIGHT
Fear of Flying

"AFTER THE FAILURE OF THE RHUMBOOGIE, JOE AND I BEGAN HOPPING all over the place. Sometimes we did the act; sometimes it was exhibition matches; occasionally both. And wherever we were, there were two constants, golf and women. Once in Manilla, we took a couple of girls out, going out for a round of nightclubbing. Afterward, Joe and I returned to our hotel rooms with our dates. Helping my girl undress, I then took a quick shower, dried myself off, and walking back into the bedroom, not only was Joe standing there fully dressed but so was my date, who had her clothes back on."

"'What the hell's going on here?'"

"'I go home now, I no sleep with you,' the girl told me in halting English."

"Joe said nothing, while I stared at the girl. She was now mute, but her lower lip trembled with what appeared to be a slight touch of anger."

"'Why not you no sleep with me? What's wrong?' I asked her. 'What'd I do wrong?'"

"'I no sleep with you,' she repeated. 'Joe say you have gonorrhea!'"

"With that, the Champ hustled her out of the room, took her downstairs, put her in a cab and sent her home. What I found out later was that Joe had discovered too late that his date was having her period. The gonorrhea story was a phony; if Joe couldn't have a girl, neither could I!

"One night, we were in Birdland just before going to Europe and had this big party, and Joe came in with a girl on his arm, who had the worst goddamn outfit and was as ugly as anybody you ever saw. Everybody's face fell, and I said, 'Joe, what . . . ?'

"'Well, I gotta kinda brighten up the party don't I?'"

"Max Schmeling said Joe had a bad habit of jabbing and dropping his left. Maybe he did.

Still . . . he could jab and hook you at the same time. He didn't get battered and beaten. He was the only fighter I know who knocked out a whole lot of opponents with a left hook, not with a straight right. He didn't go 'headhunting.'

"Arturo Godoy, a fighter from South America who Joe first boxed in an exhibition match in February 1947, fought in a crouch. Godoy must have been six feet, but when he fought he was 5' 1" down in a crouch. Joe kept punching down on him, and Godoy would come up and throw a punch and go back down, and Joe said to me, 'Goddamn, I ain't gettin' to this guy, but I got it figured out though. I'm gonna count each time he comes up, and on the third time he comes up I'm gonna nail him.' And Godoy would punch and punch when he'd come up, and Joe would jab him. When he'd come up, he'd have to open up. You can't punch in a Crouch. Joe waited for two, and then the third time when he started up, that's all she wrote. Joe sat him right on his ass. It took him eight rounds, though.

"One of the reasons Joe was such a shrewd fighter was because he was vain. There was not a mark on him; no cauliflower ears. He got a cyst on his shoulder once, had it removed, then plastic surgery to remove the scar. He didn't want any kind of a mark on him.

"The public loved him because he was not a braggart. If you asked him about most fighters, he'd say something like, 'Oh, he was tough.' He never said anything like, 'Oh, he was nothin'. I knew I was gonna punch him.' If you asked him to predict the outcome of a fight, he'd say, 'I don't know. I'm gonna try.'"

"'What round do you think you'll knock him out in?'"

"'Well, I might get him in the third or fourth round if he's careless.'"

"All the time I spent with Joe, I didn't mind walking in his shadow; instead, it was all those hundreds of thousands of miles in planes.

"In January 1949, we were flying from Minneapolis to an exhibition in Chicago in a little puddle jumper, a C54. We were coming in to land when a side wind hit us and I don't think the wing came more than ten feet from hitting the edge of a house. You could just see it. Bouncing a foot in the air, my hat flew off, and I just knew that was the end of us. The stewardess started to tell us to fasten our seat belts, but before she could even finish, the plane did a dipsy doodle and she fell on top of me. Both of us flew up in the air, and I screamed to Joe, 'This is it!'"

" He said, 'This can't be it. We have to go to Manila.'"

"We got on another flight and went to Manila where we did the act, and coming back the plane had a stopover in Honolulu. We sat out on the runway for 25, 30, 35 minutes and I knew something was wrong. We're just sitting there. Finally the Captain came on the p.a, and said, 'There's been a delay due to bad weather, but now we're going to take off.'

"Flying, I always watched that little light that says to keep your seat belt fastened. When that's on, it isn't too cool. I kept my eyes on it when we took off from Honolulu, and it never went off. Suddenly, after about a half-hour in the air, the plane started lurching about and, truly, lightning seemed to be shooting down the aisle, and water started coming in. Everybody was screaming and hollering; one newspaperman had a fifth of something tilted up to his mouth trying to get as drunk as he can get. I jumped up out of my seat. Joe, however, just sat there reading a magazine as cool as you please as if nothing was happening. Finally, he turned a page, looked up at me, and said, 'There ain't nothin' gonna happen, Leonard. Sit down.' About to pee in my pants, and he says there ain't nothin' gonna happen!

"When we landed in Los Angeles, the baggage and just about everything else were wet. I said to Joe, 'This is where we separate. I'm not going on another plane. This is it.'"

"Marshall Myles, Joe's manager, was standing at the gate and said to me, 'Here, Bearcat, here's the tickets. Your plane takes off in a half-hour and you're going to New York and then you go from New York to . . . .'"

"I interrupted him. 'Not going, Marshall. You give those tickets to Joe.'"

"Just then, Joe came up behind me, saw what was going on, grabbed me by the neck, and said, 'We're going,' and just dragged me right into the waiting room and stood guard over me."

"'Joe, I am *not* going on this plane!' He saw to it otherwise. I got on the plane, which was headed for Chicago.

"Two close calls in less than a week, and we'd not been off the ground an hour before the pilot comes on the p.a. and announces number three coming my way. 'Ladies and gentlemen this is your Captain. We are encountering some bad weather ahead and we are going to *try* to land in Omaha, Nebraska.'"

"'Joe, I told you, goddamnit, I didn't want to get on this friggin' plane!'"

"'Ain't nothin' gonna happen.'"

"Then he went back to the conversation he was having with Tony Martin and Cyd Charisse seated behind us. John Garfield was across the aisle with Manny Seamon, Joe's trainer. I don't know how the other two movie stars were taking the announcement about trying to land in Omaha, but Garfield—this big movie tough guy—is reading his newspaper upside down, scared to death. Joe saw this, started laughing."

"And then the captain comes back on. 'We are unable to land in Omaha, Nebraska. We are going to give it a try in Kansas City.'"

"So, we fly around for about another hour, and he comes back on and says, 'Everything looks great for landing in Kansas City, so fasten your seat belts.'"

"We landed. In the waiting area, Tony Martin and Cyd Charisse and Joe are standing there talking, and I just walked right on past them. Outside, there was a cab. I ran, jumped in, and told the driver to take me to the local train depot, Union Station. Looking back, the last thing I saw was Joe standing there, waving his arms and screaming. This was in the afternoon."

"The next train out of there for Chicago was not until the Super Chief coming from Los Angeles late that night. So, I laid over in Kansas City for a few hours. Many of my old friends from high school and my early show business days were there, and I gave them a call. Meanwhile, Joe and the rest had waited an hour-and-a-half at the airport, and by the time I caught the Super Chief they were already in Chicago. Getting into town the next morning at eight o'clock and checking into the hotel, I called Joe's room and at first he wouldn't speak to me."

"When he finally did talk, though, he laughed and told everybody what a coward I was. 'How do you like Bearcat? Took fourteen hours on the train and we got here in an hour-and-a-half.'"

"I flew a lot after that because he insisted. Once, we were doing some army dates with our act, traveling in a B-29, and Joe was up in the cockpit. Looking up, there was the pilot was walking back through the plane, and saying hello to everybody."

"Fearing the worst, I asked, 'Where's Joe?'"

"'Oh, he's flying the plane,' he said.

"'You've got to be kidding!'"

231

"I went up to the front and he was sitting alone behind the controls. The pilot had it on cruise control, but I didn't see that right off.

"Having to fly practically all over the globe was somewhat compensated by meeting people like Edith Piaf in Paris, when Joe and I worked there in 1948 at the Colony Club, owned by our good friend Jo Longmans.

"Some other experiences were not so great—like New Orleans. They would not let me ride in the limo with Joe, wouldn't even let me ride in a cab with me, and refused to let me check into his hotel. As far as they were concerned, he was Black and I was White.

"Joe wasn't educated, but he was not stupid. He was very smart, with a wonderful sense of humor and a strong ability for thinking things out in advance. Take the way he changed while he spoke. When we first began touring and traveling, if he was ready to leave for someplace he'd say, 'I'm ready *for* to go.'"

"Never coming back to him with 'Don't say that!,' instead, I'd answer, 'If you're ready to go, let's go.'

"Eventually he started saying, 'I'm ready to go.' He'd announce to me, 'I ain't gonna do this.'"

"And I'd reply, 'I'm not going to do it either.'"

"It wasn't too long before I had him saying, 'I'm not going to tell you' instead of 'I ain't going to tell you.' We once put a bit in the act about 'To be or not to be.' Joe said that when he died and went to heaven he'd 'axe' Shakespeare whether he actually wrote those lines. I'd say, 'Okay, then you *ask* him. However what if he isn't in heaven?' Joe would say, 'Okay, then you axe him.' It took a while, but eventually, he began to say ask instead of axe."

By the mid-1940s, in baseball, a modicum of interracial decency had begun in sports with the signing in 1947 of Jackie Robinson to play for the Brooklyn Dodgers. Still, for a number of years after that, when it came to both amateur and pro golf—to invoke the title of the well-known book about the Negro baseball league—*Only the Ball Was White*. There was, for

232

example, only one White country club in Chicago, the Tam O' Shanter, that allowed Blacks to use their course, and then only on off-hours when it was closed. Otherwise, then as now, most private courses were closed to Black golfers, who had to make do almost exclusively with public links. The game being such a part of an old (White) boys' network, the struggle to become an adept player was, then as now, seriously hindered by the color of one's skin. The exception to these off-putting playing conditions in the 1940s were a handful of Black-owned private courses.

There were many areas in the south in the 1940s and 1950s, when Joe Louis and Leonard Reed's golfing mania was at its peak, where Blacks had no access to private or public links. Obviously, the freedom and power that came along with being the Heavyweight Boxing Champ made it a good deal easier for Reed and Louis, than for the average weekend Black golfer, to practice and excel at the sport, but still it was difficult.

Public courses that were open to Blacks (at least in the North) found a mild form of racial harmony prevailing with "separate but equal" parties of players sharing the courses. When Black pro and am tournaments were held, these integrated courses were roped off and only Blacks were allowed to play. The number of major yearly Black tournaments amounted to approximately seventeen when Louis and Reed where at the peak of their form, including one tourney that bore Louis' name. These events, which came into being because of the PGA (Professional Golfers' Association) and its ban against Black membership, were held in July and August and followed a route.

Reed recalled, "From Chicago to Detroit to Toledo to Cleveland to Columbus to Dayton to Pittsburgh to Cincinnati to St. Louis to Kansas City . . . and so on. Some of them were fifty-four-hole tournaments. Some of them were thirty-six-hole. Fifty-four holes was not much of a tournament that's three days. But the others were four days. That meant you got into a town two days before the tournament, had a practice round, and played four days. The big national tournament was known simply as the Black National Tournament. It was a four-day event. You came there on a Monday, you played a practice round, and Tuesdays and Wednesdays were the qualifying days. The national tournament had amateurs and professionals. They moved it around. One year, it was held at Rackham in Detroit right after Joe's own tournament there. The next in Pittsburgh. I suppose there were about 125 amateurs and professionals that followed the circuit with more amateurs than professionals. In Joe's tournaments, we usually had twenty or thirty foursomes, eighty or ninety players."

Joe Louis and Dinah Washington snapped by Leonard

In 1947, Reed scored 69 and 70 in two rounds to capture the Ohio amateur championship of the Forest City Golf Association, and as the decade wore on, he came to be regarded as one of the top amateur Black golfers in the country. And while estimates of Louis' ability on the links tend to vary, most everyone with an opinion on the subject concur that Louis was a very good player, although not in the same league as a golfer as he was as a boxer. What many also agree upon is that the wagering aspect of the game was just as fascinating to him as was the athletic challenge of sport. Marva Louis Spaulding, the boxer's first wife, insists, "Golf contributed to his [Louis] downfall. In one summer, he lost $90,000 gambling on the course. Players would raise their handicaps with him and bet for high stakes." Part of the "problem," however, had to do with Louis' largesse rather than ineptitude on the links. A game played at Chicago's Wayside Golf Course between Louis and Alvin James, the owner of a small dry cleaning operation, resulted in James winning $10,000 from the champ, who the next day offered to play James again, this time for double or nothing. Louis ended the day $17,000 ahead and accepted from James a check for $10,000 and an IOU for the rest with his cleaning establishment as collateral.

However when Reed wanted to inspect Louis' "new business," the boxer asked to see the IOU, then tore it up, telling Reed, "How's the man going to live if you take his pressing shop?"

Says Reed, "I know Alvin James would've collected from Joe had he won, but Joe said, 'Give him his pressing shop,' and left it at that with Alvin owing him $7,000."

Names of top Black golfers Reed recalls from this period include Pat Ball, Calvin Sills from New Orleans, Charlie Sifford, Ted Rhodes, "who was probably the best Black golfer of that era," Howard Wheeler, and Tup Holmes and Zeke Hodgefield, both from Atlanta. And the one thing they had in common, says Reed, was that "all of them yearned to play in the White tournaments, period."

In golf, "Joe probably was the greatest single factor in destroying the color line—merely by the force of his skill and his personality," contends *Washington Post* sports writer Shirley Povich. However, there came a time when the boxer laid more than just his personal charisma on the line in the fight against discrimination on the golf links. The occasion was the 1952 PGA (Professional Golfers' Association) tournament at San Diego's Chula Vista golf course. Louis and several other Black golfers, including Ted Rhodes, Charlie Sifford, and Bill Spiller, had been led to believe that they would be allowed to play in the $10,000 tourney, but at the last minute they were uninvited because of the PGA's non-Caucasian clause. (Reed had already registered to play with no problem because he was presumed to be White.) Most of the rejected golfers had converged on San Diego, and Louis and Reed were on the road en route when the word came down. Deciding to show up at Chula Vista anyway, Louis arrived in San Diego and told reporters that he didn't expect they'd allow him to play but that he "wanted them to tell me personally. I want to bring this thing out into the light so people can know what the PGA is." Like father like son. In more recent times, Louis' son, Joe Louis Barrow, Jr., has become a major "player" in the world of golfing and also contributed material to the book, *Uneven Lives: The Heroic Story of African-Americans in Golf*, which features a photo of Leonard and Joe (along with Bill Spiller and Ted Rhodes) on its cover.

Leonard and Joe (far left and far right) with Bill Spiller and Ted Rhodes in the middle.

236

CHAPTER TWENTY-NINE
Joe . . . Down for the Count

"Arriving in Sam Diego, Joe thought that he might be able to negotiate something, and finally they did agree to let him play by himself. He wanted no part of that. He told me, 'Call Walter Winchell.'"

"I got on the phone. This was on a Saturday. By Sunday, Winchell had it on the air. He said on national radio, 'I thought they shot birdies not skunks on the golf course.'"

"When the local sponsors of the tournament got wind of this, they called an emergency meeting for the following day, which was a Monday; the tournament was to start Thursday. Joe and I were there, along with Sam Snead, Jimmy DeMerritt, and Jackie Burke—three of the top golfers of the day. So was Horton Smith, the president of the PGA, who was responsible for most of the trouble in the first place."

"Snead said, 'What's the meeting about? I gotta go hit some balls.'"

"Smith said, 'We gotta see if we're going to let these colored boys play.'"

"Snead said, 'Let 'em go ahead and play. They gotta beat me.'" And he walked out. I always liked him after that."

"Jackie Burke, a friend of Ted Rhodes from when Ted had caddied for him in Nashville said, 'These are my friends, let 'em hit it.'"

"So they had to let us play. This was big news in the papers, and before it was even resolved, Joe got telegrams from Dallas, Tucson, and Phoenix inviting him and his entourage to play on their courses in tournaments, which previously had been Whites only. After San Diego, we were in the Arizona Open, but when we got there the members wouldn't let us come into the clubhouse; we had to change our shoes in the cars. There was still a ways to go. Charlie Sifford was one of the few Black golfers to keep forcing the issues. It took nearly another ten years for the PGA to adopt across-the-board non-discrimination policies.

"From the time that Joe came out of the army in 1946 on through '52, we were on the golf course together five days a week, and sometimes six. About the only time we weren't out playing was when we were between cities. He was such a fanatic. I remember one Easter we were in New York and it was snowing like hell, and Joe said, 'isn't this a shame. Damn, call Washington and see how the weather is down there.'"

"So, I called a guy in D.C. who reported, 'It's raining and pouring down here.' Joe then told me to phone this fellow in Cleveland we knew by the name of Corn Dogger, who told us the weather was 'Fine, beautiful. We're getting ready to go to the golf course right now.'"

"Joe jumped up and said, 'Call the airport!'"

"Two-and-a-half hours later, we were in Cleveland, where, by the time we were at the fifth hole, it was snowing like all get out. We just kept on playing right on through the snow till we got to the ninth hole. That's how crazy we were.

"Because of Joe, I became a golf bum through most of the late 1940s and early '50s. With the exception of my appearances with Joe, show business was pretty much on hold for me during most of this period. Traveling all over the place, just playing in tournaments, I participated in the Black Six City Tournament in 1951, which I won. The first year I was on the PGA—1952—I played the Dayton Open . . . also won that.

"Although most Black golfers were still experiencing problems, Joe and I by now had it pretty easy. Then again, there were people like Ben Hogan, one of the great golfers of all time, but just *nothing* when it came to being a human being.

"Somewhere around the end of '52, Joe and I were playing on the Tam o' Shanter in Chicago, which was desegregated. Hogan had just finished 18 and Joe was in the foursome behind him when I overheard some guy from a newspaper say to Hogan, 'Ben, can you wait a minute. I want to take a picture of you and Joe Louis together?'"

"Hogan said, 'I don't want my picture taken with no nigger.'"

"Telling Joe what I'd heard, he just shrugged his shoulders and said, 'It don' t make me no difference.'"

"Joe was a good golfer. It is said that he wasn't, because he lost a lot of money. But he also won a lot. They never talk or write about the money he *won;* always about what he *lost.* There was a guy named Judson Grant, who followed him around the country wanting to play with him, and Judson nearly always lost. He carried around hundreds of travelers checks to pay Joe off with. One time, though, there *were* no more traveler's checks. I stood there and when Grant finished paying me off for the matches that Joe had won, he had nothing left."

"Joe asked him, 'How you gonna get home?'"

"'I don't know. I' m broke,' Judson said."

"Joe ordered me to 'Give him $500 to get home.'"

"'$500! It doesn't cost any $500 to get anywhere in the country.'"

"'Yeah, I know,' Joe said, 'but give him $500.'"

Once, Bill Spiller beat Joe out of $1,400 one day, and Joe said to him, 'We'll be here tomorrow.' The next day Spiller showed up, and Joe said, 'I'll play you for $500.'"

"'I don't have that kind of money,' Spiller replied. 'However, you just beat me out of $1,400 yesterday! I'll play you for a hundred dollars.'"

"'Forget it,' Joe said. 'You'll never get another bet with me as long as you live.'"

"And he never bet Spiller again.

"There was a golfer named Ed Fergal with a withered arm. He was a good player and he used to give Joe one-up, two-up, and three-up for x amount of dollars. Joe always won the one-up, but he always beat Joe two-up and three-up. So, Joe would always win one bet. It was $1,000 every time.

"Joe also played people like Harry Ritz of the Ritz Brothers and Tony Martin in Vegas a lot, and he practically made a living off of them. Then there was Ted Rhodes, the Black golfer, who Joe was sponsoring. Once, I reminded Joe, "Don't forget to have me give Ted the $200."

"'For what?'"

"'His rent.'"

"Joe came back with, 'I'll tell you what. Tell him I'll play him double or nothing.'"

"'You can't beat him!,' I said."

"'I *might* beat him. However if I don't, he'll have $200 extra.'"

"One day, he finally beat Ted, who cried and hollered and cried."

"Joe laughed and laughed and said, 'Give him $500. That'll stop him from crying.'"

"Joe would usually nickel-and-dime me over lousy-ass dollar bets when we played together, but in general he just gave away a lot of money.

"After the Rhumboogie, he became involved in all kinds of business ventures: Joe Louis Bourbon, the milk business, bread, soda pop, a restaurant and bar on Edgecombe Avenue in New York. When people say he lost a lot of money with these operations, though, they're way off base. He just let people use his name and had no financial stake. The only real money Joe lost in business was the Chicken Shack and the Rhumboogie (and most of that money was mine).

Other Joe Louis "enterprises": a. Joe Louis Punch, b. Joe Louis Bourbon,
c. Brown Bomber Bread, d. Joe Louis Hair Pomade

"We also came out on the short end in the numbers business [racket] which we went into in Chicago shortly after the Rhumboogie failed. However, we really didn't drop that much. I was against it from the beginning. I didn't know anything about the numbers, and neither did Joe. Because of my mathematical mind, though, he insisted we do it; but they had never had numbers in Chicago before—only what they called 'policy'—and it didn't take off. In six or eight weeks, we lost $10,000. That was nothing. Joe sometimes lost or *won* that much money on the golf course in a single day.

"The final nail in Joe's financial coffin probably wasn't all the unwise investments in numbers, restaurants, and night clubs, but a decision he made in 1948. To understand what happened, you have to go back to January of 1942, when Joe had a match with Buddy Baer in Washington, DC and gave up his entire fee to the Navy Relief Society, a charity for families of war casualties. Then a few months later, he fought Abe Simon, and once again turned over his entire winnings to wartime charity, this time to the Army Relief Fund. The total he contributed to these two groups amounted to many hundreds of thousands of dollars. He was given tribute after tribute for his generosity, after which he went on himself to serve in the armed forces.

"Now comes the '48 Dewey-Truman election. Joe wanted to stump for Dewey, and I begged him not to. If I said do something, he wouldn't do it, and vice versa. He didn't want me to leave him, so he was always trying to drag down my confidence in myself. Against all my advice to keep out of politics, Joe got romanced by a congressman from Chicago, who made extravagant promises to him about what he would do for him in return for Joe's support of Dewey who, he had him thinking, was a shoe-in for the presidency.

"'If Dewey wins I'm gonna be mayor of Chicago if I want. I can do anything I want,' Joe insisted.

"'You want to be the mayor?' I said."

"'Hell, I might be chief of police. Dewey's gonna win.'"

242

"We were in Birmingham, Alabama, when the hammer fell. Joe was sound asleep. I took him the newspaper, woke him, and said, "Well, you're in, old buddy.'"

"'So, Dewey won. By how much?' he asked."

"I showed him the paper [which by now had reversed the initial infamous incorrect "Dewey Defeats Truman" headline].

"Now Truman's people are mad at Joe Louis because of his support for Dewey. Blacks throughout the country generally had three pictures in their home: the President, Jesus, and Joe. It didn't matter that they'd won; they were out to nail him, and they did so primarily by refusing to waive taxes on the money Joe had given to the two war relief agencies in '42. Internal Revenue's attitude was 'It's none of our business what he does with his money.' He could just never get out from under the interest rates after that. No matter how many matches he fought, he never could get even. His wife, Marva, who he divorced in 1945 and then briefly remarried the next year, was also breathing down his neck for money for herself and their two kids.

"Joe was $1,000,000 in debt to the I.R.S., with interest penalties rising into the area of hundreds of thousands of dollars. Finally, they began to let up on him a bit, but even after that when we needed some money, or else when I felt Joe needed a little publicity I'd put an ad in the paper, 'Taxes Are Eating Joe Louis Up and He's Going To Give An Exhibition To Help Pay Them.' It was necessary at the time, but in hindsight I now realize that it contributed to Joe's image as a broken public figure, However, he was anything but that. Through it all he managed to keep his sense of humor.

"One time I especially remember. We were in a bar across from Madison Square Garden and this guy was sitting there with his hat on. You could just tell by looking he was a cracker. Then, he opened his yap and proved it. He called over to us, saying he was from Atlanta, Georgia, real proud-like. Then, he walked over and drunkenly announced, 'Joe Louis! I want you to know you have been my idol for many years, and you are the greatest fighter I have ever seen. I seen the Dempseys and the Firpos, but Joe you are the greatest. Joe, I just wanted you to know, now that I've met you that I'm writing a book. I'm writing the best book that's ever been writed. You ain't never seen a book like this, Joe. It's gonna have everything in the world in it.'"

"'Well,' Joe said, 'if it's got everything in the world in it, it's gotta have a good title.'"

"'Oh,' the guy answered, 'I got a great title.'"

"'What's the title?' Joe asked."

"'*Niggers I Have Known.*'"

"Well you had to pick Joe up off the floor where he'd fallen, rolling and laughing. That peckerwood was serious. Dead serious! He really was planning on writing a book called *Niggers I Have Known!*"

"And so always after that, I'd say to Joe, 'I'm going to write me a book.'"

"He'd say, 'Yeah, I know. *Niggers You've Known.* And you've known plenty!'"

CHAPTER THIRTY
Mid-Career Limbo

"If it was a career rut from '46 through the early 1950s, devoting my energies almost exclusively to Joe, it was undeniably a velvet-lined rut. I read one time what a non-pro wrote about how exciting it was to walk into a bar or restaurant at the side of Louis Armstrong who couldn't even walk out the door without causing commotion. It was the same with Joe. I remember overhearing a conversation in Memphis where Joe had gone to referee a match. One afternoon there, we ducked in and saw a cowboy movie, the kind that Joe loved, and as we came out of the theater there were two Black guys standing in front of the place.

"One of them, spotting Joe, pointed in our direction as we were walking away, and said, 'There Joe Louis!'"

"'Where?'"

"'Right there.'"

"By now we were getting into our car.

"'Where, man?'"

"'Yon he be . . . yon he . . . in the car.'"

"It was the 'yon' part that got me. And as I looked back while we sped off, I could tell that the second fellow never did see us. Probably, to this day, he thinks his friend was imagining things.

"Joe was a happy guy. With him on the road, he never let up with the practical jokes. Once, we were in Paris doing the act. Both with dates one Sunday night and dressed in tuxedos, we went to see the show at the Lido. I'd learned enough French to get by: *vous etes tres jolie; comment-allez vous?;* and, of course, if all went well: *voulez vous couchez vous avec moi ce soir?* That was all written on notes in my lap. *'Voulez-vous dancez avec moi?'* I asked my date, and as we got up to dance, I put the notes in my seat. When we finished, we came back to the table, and Joe had torn up all my cue cards. I ended up that night with a hooker.

"We did two big tours with our act in the early '50s. One you've already been told a little bit about, *The Big Rhythm and Blues Show*. That's when Ruth Brown got me thrown out of the hotel in Texas. One other incident stands out in from what I recall mostly as a blur otherwise. Jazz great Lester Young was one of the stars; he had a spot with a quintet. He carried gin in a little satchel that he had with him at all times, and was tippling from it constantly. However, he was a pro, and he never failed to show up on time—except once in Oklahoma City. This was where he had done most of his growing up and achieved his musical maturity, and the call of his old stomping grounds was just too much for him to resist. 'Prez' got so hung up with seeing old friends, partying, and talking over old times that when it was time to take off, he didn't show up at the bus. Somebody—I can't recall who— volunteered to stay behind to look for him while the rest of the cast and crew continued on to the next stop. Lester was finally located, and was brought all the way in a cab from Oklahoma City to the next date in Muskogee, where he actually managed to make the show that night.

"The next year—1954—found Joe and me doing another tour of our comedy act. Before that, in '53, he did a ninety-day stint in Canada with Daley Brothers Circus, a big outfit. He was getting $1,000 a day just for riding a Palomino horse with a big saddle covered in silver dollars: he didn't even have to open his mouth. I went with him, and didn't want to just stand around watching him ride for ninety days. I said, 'Hell, get me a horse and let me ride too.' After the matinee we'd play golf wherever we could find a course.

"Right after finishing up with Joe in Canada, I went to California to take care of some business matters in Los Angeles and a guy who'd sung in my Lincoln Theater shows in the mid-'40s, Bill Day, told me about Barbara DaCosta, a young singer from Guatemala, '. . . this gorgeous gal, who sings her ass off.'"

Leonard's wife-to-be, Barbara DaCosta.

"'Really? Why don't you let me meet her?'"

"The idea was that I going to catch her act, make some suggestions, and if she was as good looking as Bill said she was . . . .'"

"Bill was working at this club at Broadway and 43rd, and a day or two later he informed me, 'I called her. She's coming down to the club tonight.'"

"'What time?' I asked."

"'Around ten o'clock.'"

"Ten o'clock for night owls like me is a joke, so taking my time, I got there about 11:00-11:30 just as she was getting ready to leave. Seeing her, I couldn't believe my eyes. I still didn't know whether she could sing or not, but Bill was right on the money about the gorgeous part. She was really angry, though, because she thought she had been stood up. Maybe charm might work. 'If I'd known you were going to look like that, I'd have been here at eight o'clock.'"

"That made her just hate me all the more! She stood up, and started walking toward the exit. However, I ran after her and somehow convinced her to stay. Right then and there I resolved never to try any more of my 'smooth lines' on her; honesty was obviously the best policy.

"Bill did his show, and when the club cleared out, I asked her to let me see her perform. With me accompanying her on piano she sang—operatic style—'All of Me.'

"Afterward, we went out for coffee and I didn't pull any punches. Her style was way too 'legit' for nightclubs, and I told her the truth. 'You're going to have to change. I'm going to have to make a different singer out of you.' Maybe it was because of my brand new Cadillac compared with her '48 Chevrolet that she figured maybe I knew what I was doing. She didn't take offense and agreed to let me select her songs and coach her. Then I told her to take my car because hers was barely running (besides I wanted to make sure to see her again).

"Driving her old beat up Chevy home, the next day didn't hear from her, nor the next, and I thought, *What the hell?* It began to look like I had been ripped off. The third day she finally phoned and we made a date. Taking her out to King's restaurant, a fabulous place on LaBrea Avenue, I asked her, 'What are you going to have to drink?'"

"'I don't drink, but you can,' she said."

"'I don't drink either,' I informed her."

"Later on, Barbara told me she thought I was lying that night, but as time went on she found out it was the truth, and that made a 'thing' between us. What made us stick together, though, was the fact that I *wanted* us to stick. Having been married three times, Barbara was the pretty, talented girl I'd been looking for all my life.

"For the first year of our marriage, we were apart most of the time. She'd work in clubs around the country, while I was with Joe. We'd meet up three or four times a year. The most time we ever spent together during that period was about a month when she was one of the performers on the second big tour that Joe and I did. [This show also featured the Nicholas Brothers, tenor saxist Hal "Cornbread" Singer, and a chorus line known as The Dyerettes.] This time we played the circuit with what was called a 'presentation show,' which meant that we were booked into theaters and backed by various bands in different cities.

"After my getting together with Barbara, it started to become apparent to Joe that I had an eye cocked on settling down somewhere and keeping off the road. This became obvious to him when he offered me a job to work in Las Vegas with him at a Black hotel, the Moulin Rouge, on an extended basis, and got turned down because the money wasn't enough for a man with a new wife and plans for a family. So, then, Joe ups and also gets married–not too much longer after Barbara and I wed! Christmas 1955, he married Bose Morgan, a woman who ran a large beautician's business in Harlem. It was a copycat thing. The only reason he got hitched—I'd bet on it—was because of my having done the same thing. There was no way he could survive on the road without me. I was setting down . . . he was setting down. Not too long after my marriage to Barbara, I found exactly the kind of settled 'family man' job I was looking for. The timing, the city, and the place . . . none of it could have been better.

PART THREE
Retire to *What*?

CHAPTER THIRTY-ONE

Showtime at the Apollo

"BILLIE HOLIDAY WAS HEADLINING A 1954 BENEFIT AT THE APOLLO, and the emcee was a dee-jay I'd heard of but never met before, Tommy Smalls, otherwise known as 'Dr. Jive.' Assuming Smalls knew me, after he finished introducing one of the acts, I went backstage to see him. Walking up and saying hello, I told him I'd like to be a part of the show ... thinking he'd be thrilled because Joe Louis and I were one of the most popular acts on the circuit.

"'Okay, Okay,' he said, but kept introducing more and more acts, and it didn't take too long to figure out he thought I was some kind of joker. Not only was he one of the few people in Harlem who didn't know who I was, Smalls had no intention of letting me go on stage; he thought I was White.

"I was still standing in the wings when Billie finished her set. When she saw me, her face lit up. We went back together to my club days in Detroit.

"'Hey, Baby,' I said, 'let's take a bow,' and swept right out on stage with a smiling Lady Day on my arm."

"Just then, Smalls was coming on the stage from the other side and, grabbing the microphone before he could get it, I said, 'Ladies and Gentlemen, let's hear it once again for Billie Holiday.' By now Smalls was slightly panicked. I said to him, 'Thank you very much, sir. Now I'm going to take over.'"

"And, Wham . . . I started doing my act. Not really having any jokes; I just danced and clowned around, but the audience loved it. After playing out my string, I shouted out to Smalls standing in the wings, 'Who's on next?' He could not believe my nerve. Introducing whoever it was, they came on, and I walked off the stage.

"The Apollo owner's son, Jack Schiffman, was there. Smalls probably thought Schiffman was going to dress me down. Instead, he said, 'How'd you like a job?'"

"Before leaving that evening, it was all set for me to work the Apollo on a recurring basis emceeing various presentation shows (those packages that weren't overseen by dee-jays like Tommy Smalls) and, also, the Wednesday Amateur Night, which I would do on a rotating basis with one other emcee. And who should that turn out to be but my old partner, Willie Bryant.

"For some reason, Frank Schiffman and Ralph Cooper, the original emcee in 1934, didn't get along too well, and Willie Bryant took over the Amateur Hour sometime in 1936. Willie had his own band and would lead it and emcee the show, giving Frank Schiffman two for the price of one. Willie did it on a fairly regular basis until I came to the Apollo in '54. We alternated Amateur Night for a while, but finally, one day Willie said to me, 'I don't want to do this thing anymore. You keep doing it.' [See appendix II for a rundown of a typical Wednesday Night Apollo Amateur Hour.] And I did, until a short time after that, when Jack

Schiffman came to me one day and said, 'I'm retiring, and Dad's going to need an assistant. How'd you like to be manager?' I thought he was kidding, but saw where they'd gotten the idea; during the year, I'd also come in and rehearsed the regular shows for them.

"Accepting the Apollo's offer, after I took over I continued overseeing rehearsals and, in addition to which, I now had to be at the theater three or four days a week when Frank Schiffman wasn't there. On those days, I'd arrive at 9:30, 10 o'clock, open up the theater, put the girl into the cage, give her the tickets, and so on.

"Much of the rest of my time was spent around town, dealing with talent. Also, I started producing shows of my own, Apollo shows with a line of girls called the Leonard Reed Dancers. After we'd played the Apollo, I took the shows on the road to places like Washington and Baltimore. The last one of these I did was in the summer of '54 with Sarah Vaughan (the theater was traditionally closed from the second week of August till the first week of September). As far as I'm concerned, it the last good show we had at the Apollo for, *then*, came Rock and Roll.

"I'd just returned from the tour with Sarah when a Washington, D.C. theater owner by the name of Frank Gerber rang up Schiffman. 'I've got a show here you won't believe!' Gerber said."

"'What kind of a show is it?' Schiffman asked."

"Frank replied, 'I don't have a comedian on the show, I don't have a dancer on the show, I don't have a girl on the show. I got Big Maybelle and Bo Diddley. And people are lined up around the corner at 7th and T Street trying to get in.'"

"When Mr. Schiffman got off the phone, he turned to me and said, 'C'mon, I want you to go to Washington with me.'"

"We went to Washington and, just like Gerber had said, we couldn't get through the crowd. Neither of us had ever seen anything like it. We always figured you had to have a singer, you had to have a dancer, this kind of act, that kind of act. A few weeks later, Mr. Schiffman booked the same show at the Apollo and the response was just like D.C. So, the Apollo started playing all these Rock and Roll and Roll and R and B [Rhythm and Blues] acts, and the response was fantastic every single time. I've been wrong twice in my life. The first was when I said that Cole Porter's 'It's All Right with Me' was a bad song, and the second was when I declared Rock and Roll would never last. Told myself it would soon just fade away, but a few months later, Rock and Rhythm and Blues was still king at the Apollo, and I began to get nervous. One day in his office I asked Frank Schiffman, 'When are we going to stop this and get back to the good shows?'"

"'Leonard,' he said, 'you've been real fine here, but you've got a lot to learn. Come here. I want to show you something.' He walked over to the window and pointed down 125th Street in the direction of St. Nicholas Avenue, where I saw people four abreast for about 150 yards trying to get into the theater. He said, 'When that crowd starts lining up and reaches only to here (he pointed directly below the marquee) and there ain't nobody there—he pointed to the end of the line again—then that's when we'll switch and go back to the other stuff.'"

"The only music that truly rivaled the popularity of Rock and Rhythm and Blues at the Apollo was Gospel. Whenever we played a Gospel show, the house was always packed. One time, there was a gospel show on, and my wife Barbara brought a girlfriend of hers from Canada to the theater. As the two of them began walking down the aisle, this singer up on stage lets out this big Gospel scream and Barbara's friend ran out of the theater like a bat out of hell, scared to death. Even the regulars were sometimes shaken up by the experience. We had nurses on hand, three or four or them, taking care of these people in the audience who'd stand up and holler and then pass out cold and have to be revived. The crowds came in with baskets of food and more or less lived there."

"There were two disc jockeys, Fred Barr and Doc Wheeler, and they played nothing but Gospel and they'd bring in these shows: The

Sir Laurence Olivier at the Apollo. (left to right) docent Leonard Reed, Olivier, Joan Plowright, Victoria Ward, and Alan Bates.

Gospelaires, Mahalia Jackson, Sam Cooke when he was with the Soul Stirrers, and just about every 'name' in the business.

"I had a little problem with one of the Gospel acts. The curtain always had to come down at 11 p.m. sharp. We didn't care who it was. However, this one show just kept on going. 11:20, 11:30, 11:50, and we're paying terrific overtime to the crew. I said, 'We've got to cut this show.'"

"And one of the Gospel people said, 'Mister Reed, you just don't understand. You just don't get the spirit anytime you wanna. You got to wait until the spirit hits you.'"

"And I said, 'Well, I'll tell you what. If the spirit doesn't hit you by eleven tomorrow night, the curtain will. So you better let the spirit hit before eleven o'clock.'"

"At eleven, I went backstage and said, 'Roy, pull the curtain.' After that, every Gospel show they were on, I would remind them, 'The show must come off by eleven o'clock.'"

"And they'd say, 'Wellllll, we'll try, Mister Reed.'"

"And I'd say, 'The curtain will try its best, too.'"

"Modern Jazz never did that well at the Apollo. Even when we had the likes of Miles or Dizzy, in the afternoon we had maybe sixty people, and at night we'd have a 3/4 house. Part of the problem was that you couldn't mix Jazz with anything else; people who liked Jazz didn't want to hear Blues or Rock and Roll. Mixing different kinds of acts became increasingly trickier as the 1950s wore on. When we tried to put Johnny Mathis on the same bill with Bo Diddley, they booed Mathis offstage. We brought Johnny back a few weeks later with Diahann Carroll and they were fabulous together.

"One saw youngsters hitting the scene so fast, from out of nowhere, that they often came into the Apollo without any arrangements, something unthinkable during the days I came up in. I'd have to give the house band their record the day before and they'd transcribe an arrangement from it. Up-and-comers didn't know how to bow, walk on, walk off. I took them down in the basement and showed them how to do it as best I could in the limited amount of time we had. I remember Linda Hopkins and the first show she did at the Apollo. She came out and she had a big record at the time, but she didn't even look like she was dressed fit to go shopping—nothing matched, patent leather shoes, a horrible dress. After the show, Dinah Washington went backstage and talked to her and told her what a wonderful job she did, and then said, 'Please I don't want you to be offended, but I've been in the business a long time, and in my basement I've got trunks full of gowns and jewelry and shoes, as well. You're welcome to take any of it. You're just starting out in the business and you can use some of these.' The truth was if you didn't get on Dinah's bad side, she was a lovely person.

"Ruth Brown, a singer nearly as popular as Dinah Washington, was another Apollo standby. However, once when she was scheduled to do a week's run there, two key acts dropped out almost at the last minute. No performer could do an entire show alone, and we didn't have anything else on the show. Just a headliner . . . Ruth.

"Out of desperation I hired a (then) totally unknown singer by the name of Roy Hamilton, who'd been Third Prize winner on amateur night a few weeks before, to help take up the slack. However, in the period between the time he was called in to help fill the holes and the week of the show, his recording of 'Ebb Tide' had become a major hit not just in Harlem but throughout the country, as well. When Bobby Robinson's record shop across the street from the Apollo found out about Roy coming in, they started playing it out on the street through loudspeakers. By the time his appearance rolled around, 'Ebb Tide' was #1. This was great for Hamilton but not necessarily Ruth.

"Opening night, the band was first, and then Roy came on. Ruth had a road manager and he pulled me aside after the first show. Ruth couldn't get on after Roy because people were standing, hooting and hollering so much. He had to keep coming back and singing 'Ebb Tide' over and over again. The audience wouldn't let him off."

"Ruth's manager growled, 'We've got to get this boy off of the show.'"

"'How you gonna do that?' I asked."

"He handed me $50 and said, 'I don't care how you do it, just do it.'"

"'I can't do that.'"

"'Well, do something.'"

"'Do you want me to put Ruth before him?'"

"'No! Ruth's the star! She's gotta close.'"

"So, the second show went on. Same thing. Third show. Same thing. Over and over. That was the most miserable week in Ruth Brown's life. I moved Roy all over the bill. I put him second. Put him third . . . fifth and, finally, *did* have to put Ruth on before him.

"James Brown was still a teenager when he came rushing up to me one day, begging to be booked on the regular show without an audition. To try and get him off my back, I told him there was no room that night.

Little Willie John was on the regular show that week and James Brown bragged, 'I'm better than him. Put me on. Put me on this week.'"

"'I'd never met up with quite that much nerve in all my years. So I let him go on. Willie John did his act, and when he finished, he got his usual great reception. Then, James Brown comes out with that straw suitcase and starts singing 'Please, Please, Please,' and goes down on his knees and hollering and screaming. You've never seen an audience so ripped apart in your entire life. Whoever was next couldn't get on.

"I had all the amateurs signed up. They had to go with me as manager in case anything happened career-wise. I didn't believe in all these Rock and Rollers, but if they became a hit, I told myself, *I'm gonna get something out of it*. However, nothing happened with James Brown and me. He went away for two or three weeks after that first night and, finally, I forgot all about him. The next thing you know, he got a record deal, but I'd already torn up the contract. The same thing with Roy Hamilton. The same with Frankie Lymon and the Teenagers. Had them signed, but when nothing happened within a week or ten days, like with James Brown, I tore up the contract and let them go. I was in a hurry and couldn't wait around for a month or two.

"Right around the time of signing on at the Apollo, I took part in a project that, at the time, didn't seem to be such a big deal: staging and filming of musical acts. All the hundreds and hundreds of stage and club shows I appeared in or produced are gone with the wind, but these little musical shorts for Studio Films live on. Hardly a day passes but what you don't see one of them crop in a TV documentary or on cable as time fillers. Did them for a fellow by the name of Ben Frye, and they were produced at just the point when Rhythm and Blues was crossing over to the Pop record charts. Willie Bryant emceed, and there's hardly anyone big at the time in Rhythm and Blues or Jazz who didn't appear in them: Dinah Washington, The Clovers, Amos Milburn, Larry Darnell, Joe Turner, Faye Adams, Count Basie, Herb Jeffries, Ruth Brown, Duke Ellington. Initially, we called these little films *Harlem Variety Revue*, but

Reed oversaw these filmed recreations of his Apollo stage shows.

they've since appeared in a number of formats, including two feature versions called *Rhythm and Blues Revue* and *Rock and Roll Revue*. When we packaged them for TV in the mid-1950s, the name I gave them was *Showtime at the Apollo* (a name that has come around again recently [1990] as the name of a TV show that's broadcast from there). Most numbers were about three minutes long, which were then put together into twenty-two-minute two-reelers, each of which also includes a comedy routine: Willie Bryant and I did a couple; Nipsey Russell

261

appeared in a few; so did Mantan Moreland. Even dancers Honi Coles and Cholly Atkins took part in a skit that also featured them tapping. Coles and Atkins went about as far as Blacks could go on Broadway in *Gentlemen Prefer Blondes* in 1948. Then suddenly, they went all the way back to long spells between engagements. I tried to book them at the Apollo as much as possible could during this dry spell and also used Cholly as my assistant from time to time.

"These featurettes presented the work of a number of entertainers. We used 'live' sound, which wasn't true of most movie shorts then, so what you're seeing really is a true performance, but if someone had told me then that these would still be shown—much less exist—more than forty years after we filmed them, I'd have thought they were crazy."

There was hardly a single Black act exemplifying the new teen sound that didn't play the Apollo during the formative years of Rock music along with many great ones, as well, including Buddy Holly, Bobby Darin, and Jerry Lee Lewis. In the film *The Buddy Holly Story*, the notion is advanced that Holly and the Chirpin' Crickets were booked at the theater under the mistaken notion that they were Black. Reed, however, insists, "Frank Schiffman never booked anyone without knowing who they were." Little Richard was a special favorite of Reed's at the Apollo after the change in music fashions set in. Still, he couldn't get behind the new sound. He even got his own Rhythm and Blues group, The Regals. "However," he laughed, "they didn't have any rhythm, and couldn't dance worth a damn." He also managed one other Rhythm and Blues act, Ruth McFadden, who scored a minor hit with "You Can't Come in the Door."

When Joe Louis and Reed played the Apollo with their act—a few months after Leonard went to work there—the rumor circulated around Harlem that on the closing night of the show, the boxer wasn't just going to pretend to knock out his partner out but was actually going to punch him out cold for real. Author Ted Fox recalls, "Everybody in the theater knew it including Reed, but Reed never said a word. This comedy dance bit, which usually lasted two minutes, stretched to eighteen minutes because Leonard was afraid to get too close to him. Louis wasn't a great monologist, and all the talk emanated from Reed and his fear that Louis was going to pop him. However, the bit couldn't end until he got close enough for this to happen, and Leonard is trying to figure out how the hell to end this bit. Finally he got too close and Louis (really) hit him. Instead of doing the flip ending up on his head, he just sank right to the ground. It was like he was cold cocked."

Reed, though dazed, was revived by one of the longest and loudest volleys of laughter that had ever reverberated off the walls of the venerable showplace.

The Apollo was a combination city hall-town square-outsized rec room for the most important Black community in America, and its audiences possessed the power to make or break careers of entertainers who played there. Winning the approval of a crowd on Amateur Night or any night could take you far. Ella Fitzgerald, Sarah Vaughan, Dionne Warwick, and Frankie Lymon are just a few who, at the Apollo's Wednesday night version of the Roman Circus, got their first big break in show business. Conversely, those performers who gave less than their all, or who were highhanded in their attitude, could seriously damage their careers. Apollo word of mouth traveled fast.

Singer Nina Simone once offended an Apollo audience with a verbal tirade and they walked out en masse. Yet, a few months later, she dared to play there again. The problem from the earlier appearance was a failure to sing her big hit, "I Loves You, Porgy." The crowd clamored for it. Now she was back. It was the Friday afternoon show, her first of the week. There weren't too many people there. Maybe it was because of the incident a few months earlier, but Friday afternoons were almost always slow. This time, Simone wasn't taking any chances. She opened with "I Loves You, Porgy." However, it was too late. Three women stood up in the back of the house, sashayed down the aisle, threw some pennies on the stage, and walked out. Those that remained behind laughed throughout the rest of Simone's set. An offended Apollo audience seldom forgave or forgot.

CHAPTER THIRTY-TWO

California, Here I Come . . . Again!

"It was now 1959, and I was into my sixth year at the Apollo. After half a lifetime of never remaining with the same job or being in the same city for more than a few weeks at a time, I was now into a pleasant groove. Adding to my satisfaction was the fact that Barbara and I were now practically an old married couple. We had adopted a little girl and were settled into the suburbs. The only problem was the locale; because of physical problems stemming from the '37 car wreck, the cold climate was really beginning to take its toll on me.

"Then, one day walking down the street in New York, carrying my young daughter, I slipped and fell on the ice. Barbara had been wanting to return home to California anyway. Now, I told her, 'Fine, let's go. This isn't worth it.' In August, turning in my resignation at the Apollo, I headed for Mexico City, where Barbara was performing at the Club Del Prado."

"Couldn't believe it when Frank Schiffman followed me all the way there trying to get me to reconsider. He told me he just *happened* to be there on vacation at the same time. He said, 'Don't make a mistake. You've got a good thing. I've practically turned over the Apollo over to you.'"

"I wouldn't budge and tried to convince him to hire Honi Coles as my replacement. I'd known Honi since the 1930s—he'd been around— and was certain he could do as good a job backstage as onstage. Schiffman took my advice; Barbara and I headed off for California.

"Arriving there and phoning up Willie Bryant, who'd moved to L.A. in '58 to work for radio station KDAY, he got me a dee-jay job. Barbara's career was still going strong, though, and since I managed her and wrote her material, I left KDAY after a year to concentrate on her. Then one night in '63 while she was playing the Cocoanut Grove in Hollywood, I overheard her in her dressing room say to a reporter for the *L.A. Times* that she was 'retiring from the business.' As close as we were, that was the first I'd heard of it. I was hurt.

"Later that night, we talked about what I'd heard her say to the *Times* guy. Was really serious? After we'd come this far, was she really going to throw in the towel just as she was beginning to make it really big? She was. After being on the road for nearly twenty years, she said she was tired of it.

"Taking stock of our finances the next day, it was clear to me that there wasn't enough in the bank to keep us going. A few months earlier, Joe had asked me about reviving the act. Then, my answer was no. Now, it was yes. So we went to Honolulu where for six weeks we played a club called the Forbidden City. It would turn out to be the last time we ever worked on stage together.

"When we got back to L.A, Joe sold his house and moved to Vegas, and it looked like the Reeds might have to pull up stakes, as well.

However, unlike Joe, I had no choice in the matter. Waiting for me when I got back from Hawaii was a letter from the county assessor telling me that the very house in El Monte that I was sitting in was 'going to be sold at auction for $800 worth of taxes.' How had I managed to slip up? Going to Joe, I told him I needed $800 desperately, and he gave it to me.

"Then calling Frank Schiffman's son, Bobby, in New York, who was now back in the business booking shows around the country, I told him about my needing work. Could he get me some weeks? He said, 'I can get you two here, two in Washington, two in Baltimore. Will that help you?' It would.

"$750 a week they paid me. Meanwhile, I booked Chicago on my own for two weeks. That gave me eight weeks at $750. While on the road, I sent Barbara $500 and kept $250 for myself. Instead of the two weeks, I just kept playing these emcee dates steadily for a couple of years until we were out of the woods. Coming off the road permanently in 1966, I got an offer from Ben Frye (he was the producer who had released those *Harlem Variety Revue* shorts I'd done in the mid-1950s) to do my own local TV talk show. It was a show a lot like Johnny Carson's, but right from the beginning there were problems.

"Ben Frye kept saying, 'Look into the camera!' My background was stage, and I wasn't used to cameras. Trying to get laughs, I kept turning to my guests. Too cocky for my own good, I told him, 'I'm doing this goddamn show! You just take care of your end of things, and I'll take care of mine.'"

"About the sixth week during a camera run-through, Frye handed me my paycheck. 'We're not doing the show anymore with you.' To the best of my recollection it was the first time in my life that I'd ever been fired from a job. I deserved it.

"By now, Barbara was working in a day job as a secretary, so we could survive. However, even though now nearing the big 60, my attitude was much like George Burns' when he said, 'Retire to what?'"

"I sat around for a few weeks feeling sorry for myself. Then one day, an agent called me about a club date out in Pomona. Frankly, I'd never even heard of Pomona, and the club wasn't exactly the Cotton Club or the Grand Terrace. Instead, it was a strip joint that needed a comic, Looking back, you might say I'd hit rock bottom, but I didn't think that way. Found my way to Pomona and the club, but the strippers there were just so awful that there was no way I was going to get onto the stage with either of them. They had big boobs, and they were young, but could barely walk. I'd seen better strippers in the '20s.

"One of them, Teri Starr, was better than the others. She told me that what she really wanted to do was learn to play guitar. I knew enough chords to teach her, and she was pretty enough for me to want to teach. She came over to the house the next day, and one thing led to another, but it's not what you think. I started teaching her how to move, how to dance, how to take off her jacket and her pants and her drawers.

"After a few weeks, the other stripper at the club began asking Teri, 'Gee where are you learning all this new stuff'?' Teri told her, 'I got myself a choreographer.'"

"The next thing you knew, I had *two* strippers, Teri, and now this other girl, Leah, paying me to teach them how to strip. I rehearsed them in my den in El Monte. Then one day, Teri said to me, 'You ought to open a studio. How much would it take?' It was just like the Chicken Shack all over again. She let me have the money to open up a school for strippers at 1610 Argyle Avenue in Hollywood. Before long, I branched out into booking them, and was making as much money—maybe even more—than in previous, more 'respectable' areas of the business. All because of not being too proud to drag myself out to a job in what they call in the business, a 'toilet.'"

"I was good at what I did, because the same rules apply whether you're trying to put over a song, tell a joke, or striptease. The trick is simplicity. Neighbors or my friends always asked me, 'How can you teach a stripper? What do you teach a stripper to do?' The answer was simple. 'How to take off their drawers, their stockings, and their pants.'

Reed in his Hollywood Boulevard studio – 1990

"Booking them all through the Midwest, starting them out with $750 as my minimum, I got my girls up as high as $1,500, $2,000 a week. There were eight or nine girls that I booked. I kept them working all the time, packing them in. Sending Teri on the road, $400 a night was not unusual. Before sending them out, I usually went in advance to book the club to see if it was all right and to bring in the photos and publicity. There were schoolteachers, housewives, and college students making $200 a night. I made strippers out of everybody who wanted to make money.

"Opening up my studio on Argyle, I never advertised. Just one girl told another. Or, seeing a girl in the street, if she was pretty, I'd give her a card and ask her if she wanted to be a dancer. If she came up, I'd ask, 'What's your name? How old are you? Are you married? Do you have

269

any children? Can you travel? Have you danced before? You know this is for nude stripping?'"

"'Yes, I know.'"

"'Fine. My minimum salary is $500 a week. I won't send you on any job for less than $500, and I can get you as much as you can make if you get good. Do you think you'd like to try it?'"

"'Oh, yes.'"

"My office had two rooms. 'Go in the other room. Take off your clothes, and call me so I can come in and take a look at your body.'"

"'Okay.'"

"They'd go in the other room, take off their clothes, and in a couple of minutes I'd hear, 'I'm ready, Mister Reed.' I'd walk in, ask her to turn around so I could check for stretch marks and see if she looked good.

"'Let me see you move . . . dance . . . give me some floor work . . . whatever you can do . . . fine. Get dressed and come in the room.'"

"Some housewives were sent out on day jobs. Mostly they were the ones who didn't want their husbands to know anything about it. I'd ask them, 'How many hours a day do you want to work?' If they said, 'Three hours,' that meant at $60 a day, 5 days a week, they were making $300 a week, which was probably more than most of their husbands made.

"A couple of girls told their husbands what they were doing. The men came to see me and said, 'What else is going on?'"

"'I don't understand what you mean by, 'What else is going on?'"

"They said, 'Well, do they have to go to bed with anybody?'"

"I said, 'Look, they're out there dancing. They don't have to go to bed with anybody. They're making money.'"

"Or they *were* until the bottom fell out around 1970. The thing that killed the golden goose was total nudity. Then, the salaries started failing to $15 an hour, then they went to $12. As long as the girls hid *it*, as long as the audience could just barely see *that thing*, they loved it. However, a man doesn't want to just sit there and look right up into a girl's crotch. If he sees through a little blind or a shade, or he almost can, and the girls are hiding and turning, it's interesting to him. However, when the man sees that thing over and over and over, it's no longer a novelty. Here's a nude gal shaking her rump, up there absolutely naked, and he's sitting and talking to his friend about his new car. If he's got to peep, he can't talk to his friend.

"The girls ruined the business themselves. They figured they'd make more money if they took off everything. However, they were wrong. Not only did the salaries start dropping, but the police would come in and close up the places and the girls would get busted. Nudity. That's what killed the business. To give you an idea of how raunchy it got, they had a strip club here in L.A. called the Bat Cave. It cost you $2.00 to get in, and $1.00 to rent a flashlight.

"There was a Burlesque club called The Hat near my house in El Monte. One night in 1968, going in there to catch the show, the comic was so bad that I asked one of the waitresses, 'Who's the owner here?'" She told me his name, Ray Dagnaught, and said, 'That's him sitting down at the end of the bar.' I asked him, 'How often do you change comedians?'"

"'Why?'"

"'Because,' I said, 'I'm your next comic.'"

"'Well, the show's over. Let me see you.'"

"'No, I don't do auditions. My name's Leonard Reed and I'm a comic. If you want to hire me for a week, if you don't like me the first night, you fire me.'"

"So, he said, 'Okay. You come in two weeks.'"

"Then it dawned on me, *I'm going to work in a burlesque house, and don't have any off-color material!* So, I start buying *Playboy* and other magazines looking for dirty jokes. I only put in three or four of the ones I found, but I had enough clever material. And I danced! That's something this other comic couldn't do.

"Two weeks later, I went on, and Ray's wife fell in love with my act. She just thought I was great . . . a better emcee than anybody they'd ever had. Worked there for five years! Naturally, I ended up booking most of my girls at The Hat.

"Walking into The Hat the first time, it wasn't because I wanted or needed a job. However, there was something about that bad comic that got on my nerves."

In 1970, Joe Louis also found himself a new line of work. He took a job as what is usually described as a greeter at Las Vegas' Caesars Palace Hotel. The resort's management set Louis and his wife Martha up in a large house with a swimming pool. Little more was required of Louis other than that he more or less shill by betting with house money whenever action at a table slowed down, sign autographs, and play golf with V.I.P.s. Louis' installation at the Caesar's Palace casino came upon the heels of his detention in a Colorado mental hospital where he was taken because of increasingly erratic behavior and decreasing mental faculties.

Prior to being put the facility, Louis successfully stalled deputies long enough for him to try and place a call to the President protesting his pending incarceration. It was also time enough for the press to get wind of what was happening and to surround the house with photographers and reporters.

In Colorado, it was determined that Louis' mental deterioration had nothing to do with—as had at first had been suspected—blows to the head in the ring, but instead with addiction to cocaine and other drugs. Reed, however, had been increasingly aware of Louis' substance abuse problem for some time before it became a matter of public knowledge.

Leonard and Joe!

CHAPTER THIRTY-THREE
Spiraling Down . . . .

"PLAYING GOLF WITH JOE ONE DAY IN VEGAS AT THE HILTON COUNTRY Club in 1968, around the third hole he lit up a cigarette and I grabbed it away from him just the way he used to do to me when I smoked. He would say, 'Don't you ever that again. I'll knock you out.'"

"He smoked the cigarette. Later on, about the fifth or sixth hole, he reached in the bag and got out a bottle of Courvoisier and started drinking. I said to myself, *What's going on here?*

"A short while after his drinking and smoking on the golf course, he came to L.A. I picked him up at the airport and we were driving down Sunset, and when we reached Hughes Market, he said, 'Pull around the corner. Pull around the corner.' He got out, peeped around the corner, then came back to the car and said, 'I guess they got lost.' Next, he swore someone was after us. Paranoid. Turns out, I learned later, he was on cocaine! Some hooker got him started on it.

"Caesars paid Joe something in the neighborhood of $35,000 a year. I visited him there often. He'd go to a cage and say, 'Give me a thousand.' Then he'd go and sit at the blackjack table and play, and people would follow him to get his autograph or shake his hand, and then *they'd* start playing. He was allowed to keep his winnings, and the hotel ate his losses . . . he was notoriously unlucky at gambling. If there were winnings, he'd usually hand them to me to cash them in. Often, I'd come home from Vegas with $400 or $500 without even gambling.

Joe at Caesar's was a *performance*. People were constantly coming up to him and asking how he thought he'd fare against Muhammad Ali in the ring. In his usual modest way Joe said, 'It would be a tough fight.' Privately, though, Joe thought he could 'take' him, somewhere around the fourth or fifth round when Ali had started to wear himself down from all the dancing around he did in the ring.

"From the beginning, he never could really cope with Vegas. You take a person like Joe out of his old surroundings and put him with (what were to him) different strange types, intellectuals, gangsters, social figures, and so forth, and it was like the movie *2001* to him. The vernacular of the sports world was what he was accustomed to. When his wife, Martha, tried to put him together with attorneys and lawyers and owners of casinos who talked about things he didn't know anything about, he'd just sit there and listen. They'd take a drink, and eventually he started taking a drink.

"The Vegas people now had a say-so in his life and he wasn't used to that. When Joe was single and by himself he pulled all the strings, 'Leonard, get over there!' 'Freddie, get this!' Now it was the Caesars people saying, 'Joe, we want you here.' Or his wife Martha, 'C'mon, Joe, we're going home.'"

"Worst of all, friends he'd known all of his life were suddenly kept from him. Harry Mills of The Mills Brothers went to his house one time to pick Joe up to play golf. Martha opened the door. 'I'm Harry Mills.'"

"'Yes, I know. What can I do for you?'"

"'Joe asked me . . . .' Harry began."

"'Yes, I know. He ain't goin' . . . .' and closed the door in his face."

"When Joe had heart surgery in 1977, I drove from L.A. to Houston twice to be with him. Staying ten days the first time, when Martha saw me she said, 'What are *you* doing here?'"

"'I came to see my friend.'"

"She didn't want me around because she thought his old pals were a bad influence. The person who damaged Joe the most, though, was Martha. She put televisions in every room in the house including the walk-in closet, so that everywhere he went there was television to keep him kind of hypnotized. She was basically a good person, but she knew about his womanizing and figured all of his old friends were going to get girls for him. She made a terrible mistake when she gave an interview about his using dope to a reporter when she had him put in the hospital in Colorado.

"Eventually, Marv realized that I was good for Joe and she stopped minding my coming around. So, after his surgery, he was confined to a wheel chair, and I went to Vegas nearly every week or ten days to see him. Back in '37 when I was on crutches, he'd say to me, 'Get off the crutches.' So, I did the same while wheeling him around. 'You better get out of this chair.'"

"And he just grunted."

"'If you don't, I'm going to push you out in the middle of traffic.'"

"'If you do,' he said, 'I'll get up and kick the shit out you.'"

"That's what he said. That's the kind of humor he had. However, he didn't get out of the chair. After a while, he'd say—a little depressed, 'Drive me back home.'"

"The last time I saw Joe was on April 11, 1981. Afterward, on the way out of Vegas the next day, Barbara and I stopped for a bite to eat at a coffee shop when a news bulletin came on the radio: Joe had just died of a massive heart attack. I just stared at my wife for the longest time, then began to smile about remembering something called 'Joe Louis Punch.' Back in the '40s, we were in St. Louis promoting the stuff and the champ was on the radio with an interviewer, who asked him what his favorite drink was, and Joe answered coolly, 'Coca Cola.' That's how honest he was; that's how funny he was; that how much his own man he was.

"I'm sad about some of the things that happened to Joe later in life, but commentators and writers made him out to be some kind of tragic figure then, and that just never was the case . . . not even at the very end. Even when he was crippled and could barely talk or recognize old friends any longer, the Joe who had the nerve to answer 'Coca Cola' was still locked in there somewhere. You could see it in his eyes that last day in Vegas as he sat there smiling while I played him tapes of our act together."

CHAPTER THIRTY-FOUR
Tricks of the Trade

"Like I said, coaching strippers was just like teaching anything else. It was just a variation on something that I'd done a lot of in the '50s and '60s coaching singers. One of my biggest clients was Motown Records. We passed like ships in the night at the Apollo; just as I was phasing out my activities there, Motown was coming in. We finally made contact a few years later, when I went back on the road because of my financial problems. Most of the theaters I emceed at around the country were featuring Motown artists, and during the day I ended up doing a lot of coaching work for acts, such as The Supremes and The Contours. The tricks of the trade that I shared with them were pretty much what I'd shown Dinah Washington twenty years earlier; and what I'd taught my strippers; i.e. how to get on and get off, how to move, bow, and be able to do little things like fake exits, i.e., you know you're coming back on one more time after your big finish, but you don't want to the audience to know that you know. There's a fine art even to that.

"One Motown act that I went a bit further with was Marvin Gaye. When he first came to Motown, he didn't really want to be a rocker; he had plans to become a singer like the two he idolized most, Frank Sinatra and Nat Cole. So, Berry Gordy came to me shortly after Marvin was signed with Motown and asked to put together an act for him that was class all the way. This was before any record of his had hit the charts. We sat down to go over material; some of the ideas were his and some were mine. Songs like 'The Best Things in Life Are Free,' 'The More I See You,' 'All or Nothing At All,' and about a dozen more. I don't remember who picked what in every instance, but do know that 'Nobody's Chasing Me' (a Cole Porter song), and a tune called 'Rolling Along' (which went back to the teens) were definitely my choices. Writing arrangements and patter for him, and picking out wardrobe for him, we hit the road. However, we'd only done a couple of the dates at very swank clubs, when Motown pulled the plug on us and canceled the remainder of the tour. The problem was 'Hitch Hike,' Marvin's second or third single. It had shot all the way up to the top of the charts and they wanted him to strike while the iron was hot with TV shows, and Rock concerts.

"With me standing there holding the bag, still we remained friends, and at a show I was emceeing in Hollywood in 1984, he got up out of the audience, came on stage, and sang his hit 'Sexual Healing' acapella—the entire number—with the audience keeping time clapping. This was only a short time before he died.

"When stripping began to get really raunchy in the late '70s, I went back to coaching singers. Clients included Chelsea Brown from *Laugh-In*, and Mel Carter, a singer who'd had several hit records. His manager brought Mel to me to write an act for him. I also traveled and conducted for him, and he's still [1990] using the basic act I created for him twenty years ago.

280

"Also began to teach tap. Not so much for the money, but to pass along some of the tricks of the trade that might otherwise be lost. A number of the new, young, hot dancers still come to me on a regular basis trying to learn what I know. And I'm glad to help them, but have come to the conclusion that a lot of people in this town are stealing.

"I had a young woman come to me for a tap lesson. We sat there for half an hour asking and answering questions, then I said, 'How long have you been taking lessons?'"

"'Two years.'"

"'Wonderful,' I said. 'You should be good. Put on your tap shoes.'"

"And I wish you could have seen her. She couldn't lift her feet, let alone tap!

My wife Barbara also let me down when she up and quit the business in the early '60s. She was the best singer I'd ever seen. She played the big clubs, television shows, top echelon stuff, and then just said . . . 'I'm through.' That's surely why I absolutely refused to give up on my star pupil, Angela Teek, until her name was up in lights on Broadway. Somehow I knew that she was capable of going the distance."

From the New York Times, August 8, 1990:

"WHO'S KA Y? SHE'S KAY, OK ? O. K.

"Anyone who ever tried out for a Broadway show knows that a simple thank you and, less frequently 'We'll be in touch,' are the standard comments when an audition is finished.

So it was pretty obvious that when Angela Teek auditioned last week for *Oh, Kay!* and twice tasted applause from David Merrick, the producer, that she was a shoo-in. And, in fact he announced on the spot, 'She's Kay.' (The musical, which began rehearsals this week, was without a title character so long that insiders began calling it, 'No Kay.')

The George and Ira Gershwin musical with an all-Black cast begins Sept. 29 at the Richard Rodgers Theater."

It was the kind of break that Reed and his protégé had been looking for since they had begun working together in 1981 when Teek was a teenager. The daughter of Reed's then-client, singer Spanky Wilson, Teek was participating at a workshop in Hollywood, when, as a favor to Wilson, he agreed to watch the girl perform there. He was unimpressed with what he saw, but Barbara Reed thought that she had seen something and he reluctantly accepted her as a pupil. It took Reed nearly ten years to—in his words—"create Angela Teek."

The day after the appearance of the article in the *New York Times*, Reed phoned everybody he knew to tell them that "my girl is starring on Broadway." However, shortly before *Oh, Kay!* was set to open with Teek in the lead, a postponement was announced—and then another, and another. Soon, all three daily newspapers in the city were running daily blow-by-blow accounts of what really was going on behind official announcements about scenery that didn't "fly."

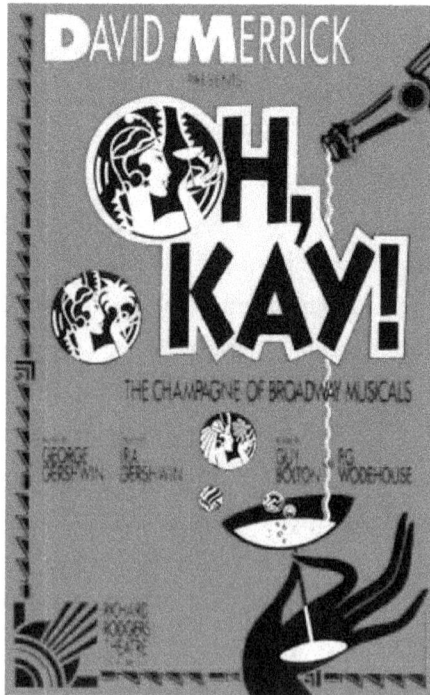

Leonard Reed back on Broadway . . . in a way.

CHAPTER THIRTY-FIVE
Back on Broadway

"There's only one man in show business who really knew what Blacks were like and that was Lew Leslie. [Leslie was the Broadway producer of the various *Blackbirds* revues (1926, 1930, 1933, and 1939) that featured an all-Black cast.] Lew lived Black and he understood them. He moved in with them, listened to them, talked to them, had their mannerisms. He knew more about the Blacks than the Blacks did themselves. The only person who came close to running second was the Apollo's Frank Schiffman. In my opinion, *Oh, Kay!* could have been very good if it had been a little more—and I hate to say these things—a little more Black than it was. You can't make a Black man a White man just by adopting his dialogue and his mannerisms. The choreographer tried to make the dancing too balletic. There was always turmoil in rehearsals; every day, something wrong. Trying to keep Angela's spirits up, I said things to her on the phone like, 'You've made it! You've done something that most performers will never accomplish. You made it to Broadway. You made it all the way from [L.A.'s] Rosco's Chicken and Waffle Shack to Broadway.'

"However all this was costing a fortune phoning me up every night, Angela telling me what went down in rehearsals. Finally she was about to lose the job. There was no choice; I had to go to New York. Arriving, I coached Angela every night after rehearsals. She'd had very little acting experience before this, and that threw the director. He didn't know what to tell her, he didn't know *how* to tell her . . . and all those notions he had about Black mannerisms and delivery!

"Opening night party at Sardi's—the show finally premiered exactly one month and a day after it was supposed to—and everybody was friendly. Still, after it opened, rehearsals were called every day and changes made. Finally, even though she *was* 'Kay,' eventually Angela didn't have a song of her own until the end of the first act.

"Even though there was only one really negative review of the thirty-some that finally came out, it was a doozy and a killer. It was from Frank Rich in the *New York Times* and he didn't have a kind word to say about Angie or anything else. At the time, I was unaware of how make-or-break the Frank Rich review was. Angie was devastated by Rich's attack, but it rolled right off my back; I'd gotten cruel write-ups like that before. The time in 1930, for instance, emceeing a revue at a theater in Chicago's Loop and the guy came out and wrote the next day, 'Leonard Reed, a good-looking mulatto, is too ambitious for his own good.' Good reviews or bad, I could always get work, but show business has changed since my day. Angela felt that her whole career was riding on this one single show, and she was nearly right. She was good in *Oh, Kay!*, but there's no question that this one review killed the show."

In many ways, the real show was taking place off stage of the Richard Rodgers theater where *Oh, Kay!* managed to limp along despite Rich's scabrous negative review, a notice that made David Merrick see red and led to his running an advertisement in the theatrical section of the *New York Times* the Monday after *Oh, Kay!* had opened. It led off with a banner that read "AT LAST PEOPLE ARE HOLDING HANDS IN THE THEATRE AGAIN." Just beneath this was a large heart outlining two of the worst non-money quotes contained in Rich's pan, to wit, "Things are not as okay at David Merrick's *Oh, Kay!*," etc. And just below the heart was the inscription "To Frank and Alex—all My Love, David Merrick," an inside reference to Rich's romantic involvement with *Times* theatrical columnist Alex Witchel. This was a situation which many in the theatre community at the time felt to be untenable, with the take on the Rich/Witchel liaison being that it could likely result in productions receiving not just one, but two critical pokes in the eye with a sharp stick for the price of one. Only the first edition of that day's *Times* ran the ad, however, with its disappearing from subsequent runs. Copies of it flew fast and furiously over faxes, though, and (false) rumors began circulating that Rich had resigned from the paper. Several other salvos were fired in both directions before the situation finally reached the level where Merrick was running an ad for his show featuring rave *Times* quotes for *Oh, Kay!* culled from the paper's Nov. 9, 1926 reviews for the original production. Thus, proving that whatever else the producer might have suffered in the way of diminished capacities due to illness, his fabled ability to wage warfare on the critics was undimmed.

"It's the biggest laugh of the year on Broadway," said the *New York Post*, referring to the contretemps, and reverberations were felt all the way to the west coast where the *Los Angeles Times* noted that affair was "giving theatergoers more theatrics off stage than on." Finally, however, the lobbed volleys from both sides began to abate.

Oh, Kay! managed to run for nearly two months despite extremely poor attendance (leading many to speculate on the sheer stubbornness of Merrick), then closed, then was set to open again. The new show would be, his spokespersons said, virtually the same as the old one, with most of the original cast intact, but with one exception. Film actress Rae

Dawn Chong, a non-singer and a stage neophyte, would be replacing Angela Teek.

Oh, Kay! was now taking on the dimensions of a legendary theatrical mess, with opening night of the retooled show proving to be the icing on the fatal cake. Chong received such an irreverent reception from first nighters (presumably because of an inept performance) that she was barely able to make her way through to the finale. The cost of Merrick's breathing life back into *Oh, Kay!*, a move possibly born either of hubris or desperation, was certainly costly. Finally, though, all he got for the additional expenditure was a secure place in the annals of theatrical fiasco somewhere alongside the likes of *Moose Murders*, a 1982 comedy of legendary awfulness. A closing notice was posted opening night of the new version of the Gershwin classic.

Several days after *Oh, Kay!* shuttered, a cryptic news item appeared in the *New York Times* noting that Merrick had been stopped at airport customs on his way to Europe packing several hundred thousands of dollars in currency and . . . a gun.

Frank Rich, remained at the *Times* until 2011, but, eventually, not in the position of drama critic. Merrick died in 2000 after producing, in 1996, one more show after *Oh, Kay!*

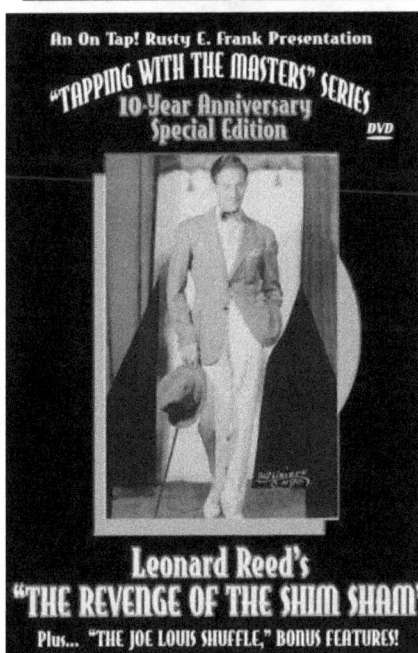

Reed's tap dance instruction video on VHS (1994) and DVD (2002.)

AFTERWORD

As for Reed and Teek, they would come up smelling like the proverbial rose. Just a year later, she appeared in a production of Cole Porter's *You Never Know* at California's Pasadena Playhouse and received the best notices of her career, quotable and laudatory enough to undo even the personal and professional damage wreaked by the Busby Berkeley movie from hell that she had recently lived through in real life.

After *Oh, Kay!*, it was back to business as usual. Leonard returned to Los Angeles and continued working out of the same office as before: more teaching, and more wheeling-dealing. There was even a short-term revival of his old revue, *Sweet and Hot*, featuring mostly his students (I even had a walk-on!)

As to all men it must *not* necessarily come, alas; however, before his death in 2004 at age 97, Reed began to finally receive some much overdue recognition. Perhaps the initial trigger was the rise in popularity of tap dancing in the 1990s. As a result, dance historians began popping out of the woodwork all over the place and didn't have to look very long or hard to figure out that—among other his other almost century-long activities—Leonard Reed had been a major contributor to the Jazz tap art form. Slow but surely, awards started coming thicker and faster: a Doctor of Performing Arts here; a Leonard Reed Day there (including Los Angeles). There were also numerous TV, radio, and newspaper interviews, and even a set of (still available) Shim Sham Shimmy instruction videos.

Clearly Joe Louis, along with Reed, played a major role in the erasure of the lines between Black and White golf. When Reed finally met venerated African-American golfer Tiger Woods in December 2001 in San Diego at one of the latter's clinics, Woods went on the record praising Reed for his major contributions against segregation in golf.

To jump just a few years forward—2004—the content of the obituaries that followed in the wake of his death will give you an idea of how Reed's celebrity status (that had once fallen so far beneath both White and Black below radar) had risen so dramatically in the final decade of his life. To wit (and just for starters):

• IN MEMORIAM; One Step Ahead; When Leonard Reed choreographed a new routine, it was like Moses descending from Mt. Sinai with an additional tablet of commandments. –*Los Angeles Times*

• Leonard Reed, tap dancer extraordinary, died on April 5th, aged 97. –*The Economist*

• . . . one of the greatest tap dancers of the 20th century. –*London Telegraph*

• "World Renowned Nowata Dancer's Life Left Huge Legacy." – *Nowata Star* (Reed's hometown newspaper)

And *all of this* without a press rep within a country mile!

Leonard understood that the dozens upon dozens of hours of oral history I conducted with him were for a potential biography, one that somehow had just never managed to make it to publication . . . until now. My last phone conversation with Leonard was one in 2000, when he informed me that he'd made a deal with an unspecified university press to write his memoirs. That was fifteen years ago, but inasmuch as nothing of the sort had to pass in the decade and a half since then, I decided—not so long ago in late 2014—that it was about time to excavate those quarter-century-old interviews and get back to work. My unbounded thanks to BearManor for their immediate 2014 enthusiasm regarding publication of *Brains as Well as Feet*.

APPENDIX I

For nearly twenty years, Joe Louis and Leonard Reed performed a stage/nightclub act hundreds of times at locales in North, Central, South America, Europe, and Asia. The routine that Reed wrote in 1946 varied slightly over the years, but basically, the two adhered to the following formula:

They came on dressed in suits and began to banter back and forth as to who, exactly, is going to manage whose "comeback." After a bit of repartee, it became clear that Joe Louis had never heard of Leonard . . . the boxer.

Joe: "Well, what was your fighting name?"

Leonard: "Bearcat Reed, the Horizontal Kid."

A bit more ribbing followed, along the lines of:

Joe: "Were you a club fighter?"

Leonard: "Yes, I fought with clubs, bricks, sticks, knives, rocks, anything."

Next, they arranged to engage in a match for "The Heavyweight Championship of the World—The Bearcat Versus the Brown Bomber."

Leonard went off-stage and came back in an enormous pair of oversized trunks and wearing boxing gloves. He also brought on and enormously well-built beautiful woman.

Next, the two men engaged in a mock fight. After Joe knocked Leonard down several times, the woman finally picked him up, and her chest jutted out.

Leonard (to her): "You don't have to point; I know where he is."

Joe (walking over to Leonard): "Get up."

Leonard: "Hell, you didn't get up when Marciano knocked you down."

Then, they started all over again. Leonard ducked. Joe threw a left hook over his partner's head.

Leonard: "You missed me!"

Joe hit his glove. Leonard lay flat on his ass, and Joe began to count: "One, two, three . . . ."

Leonard: "Count to 300. I ain't getting up."

Then, Joe grabbed Leonard by the foot and dragged him off. After the laughter and applause died down, they came back on. Joe sang, "Baby, Baby, Baby" and the two of them duet on the Shim Sham. The End.

The act lasted from 10-12 minutes [you can usually see a version of it on YouTube today] depending on the degree of audience response. Usually, there was a lot of that going on . . . wherever in the world they performed. The crowd loved Joe Louis!

APPENDIX II

A TYPICAL WEDNESDAY NIGHT AT THE APOLLO IN 1954 WITH REED AS emcee was captured on record for the 1955 Vanguard Records release, *A Night at the Apollo*. Here's a rundown: The last professional show of the evening is over ... the week's attractions include Count Basie, comedians "Moms'" Mabley and George Kirby, and the great dance team of Honi Coles and Cholly Atkins, but it's doubtful that anyone stirred from their seat after the presentation. Some probably didn't even bother with the high-paid talent, arriving late for the non-pro part of the evening. If so, they probably ended up standing in the aisles.

The house band starts things off by playing the Apollo's unofficial theme song, "I May Be Wrong But (I Think You're Wonderful)." Then Reed comes on asking the crowd if they've had a good time so far. Their lusty response demonstrates how accurate Langston Hughes was, in his liner notes for the recording, in likening the Apollo experience to a bullfight. If you listen carefully enough, you can almost detect the taste for blood in the crowd's response.

Finally, things simmer down enough for Reed to continue with his intro. He then brings on the night's first contestant, and the crowd cranks itself up to a mega-decibel level of yelling and hooting before the girl has even reached center stage. Leonard implores them to simmer down. Eventually they comply. He asks the girl's name, and she mumbles something inaudible.

He says, "I didn't get the name, dear."

She says, "Pearl Jones." Her reply to his next query as to her locale of origin—"From Georgia, but I'm from Brooklyn now"—has the audience in stitches.

He asks, "What are you going to do on the show? Are you going to sing or dance?"

She answers, "I'm going to sing . . . this time!"

More audience hilarity ensues.

"Have you been on the show before?" he queries.

"I think so."

Additional crowd merriment. And so it goes for a few more questions culminating in Reed's mistaking the song she's going to sing as a love ballad. "He went wrong and you got in and went on?"

"NO! Jesus went on it!"

Pearl now sings her song . . . not terribly well. However, the crowd doesn't seem to mind too much. Some of them even join in clapping their hands in time to the rhythm. When it is over, about half the crowd can be heard applauding.

There's more laughter and hooting when the next contestant comes out, because he won't touch the good luck tree for luck; he compounds the insult by calling it a "stump." [Actually, this was not the original tree, but a stand-in. No one seems to recall the fate of the original.]

"You've never been on our show before have you?" says Leonard.

He tells Reed he hasn't.

The hopeful now goes hog wild and begins climbing all over the tree. The crowd loves it.

Reed brings him back down to earth. "I didn't mean for you to fall in love with it . . . just touch it!"

His name, we learn, is Danny Rogers, and he's from Goldsboro, North Carolina.

Reed repeats the name of the town.

Danny takes a little bow.

Reed then chides him, "Danny, don 't bow until you're finished! I just want to say one thing to this man from Goldsboro, North Carolina . . . I want to welcome you to the United States." A bit more repartee follows before Reed asks, "What are you going to sing for us, Danny?"

"I want to sing 'I Believe.'"

Reed says, "Good tune. Go right ahead. And good luck."

Danny proceeds to launch into the song before the band even has a chance to play the first note. He sings wildly off-key at the top of his lungs.

Reed interrupts him. "I believe, too, Danny, but give us a chance. Wait a minute. I think the first thing that you should do is let the conductor give you an arpeggio, and then you start. Okay?"

Reed's impromptu coaching goes unneeded. Danny starts right in again with an almost unworldly scream.

By now, the crowd is ready for the kill, and Danny is given the hook, an Apollo holdover from the early days of Vaudeville. However that doesn't work; the orchestra starts up again, then—another Apollo tradition—blanks are fired from a gun while a bullhorn goes off. Now the microphone begins to be lowered into the floor, and finally when all else fails, two stagehands come out and drag the hopeful youth from Goldsboro, North Carolina, off the stage.

Next, a young woman comes on and does a passable Ruth Brown-inspired version of the Brown hit, "24 Hours of the Day."

Then another male singer comes on almost as bad as the *non pareil* Danny. This would-be Billy Eckstine only gets in a couple of bars of "Don't Worry 'Bout Me" before he loses his way, with his voice wobbling all over the place. The crowd turns on him in a hot Harlem minute. Again . . . the hook. However this one isn't giving up without a fight, either. He keeps right on singing, following the microphone as it goes down into the stage! It's turning into a Christians vs. Lion's bout, but still the singer won't give up. He's finally driven off stage by the sheer force of the audience's opprobrium. End of recording.

Reed later recalled, "It was quite a sight. After that, we ended things by bringing out the winner of the previous week. It was a close harmony acapella group called The Heartbreakers. They sang in the style of Frankie Lymon and the Teenagers, and they were every bit as good. The crowd knew it, too, because they just loved them. And that's pretty much the way it went for me, every Wednesday night for a full year in the 1950s."

APPENDIX III

Shortly after I began work on this book, Reed phoned me up anxiously and asked me take down the following information; the names of every comic he could ever recall working with, either on the T.O.B.A. circuit, or later when he was producing shows at various popular nightclubs around the country. All were African-American. He loved showing off his remarkable memory in doing this.

THE COMICS LIST:

<u>John Mason</u>: Well-known, and one of the biggest comics in the Black idiom. Situation comic.

<u>Dusty Fletcher</u>: Fletcher was even more well-known than Mason because of the popular song, "Open the Door Richard." A lawsuit was finally settled in court. Dusty finally got some credit and royalties. A faller.

<u>Ashes and Bilo</u>: One of the best two-man acts. Did a lot of stock around in Philadelphia. Eventually worked the Lincoln in L.A.

<u>Detroit Red</u>: Circa early 1930s; worked Cleveland, Detroit. Song and dance; verbal comedy. One of the dirty comedians, like Hattie Noel.

<u>Willy Too Sweet</u>: Was with The Whitman Sisters most of his career, and before that, carnivals. As long as they ran, he ran. Parody and situation comic.

<u>Boots Hope</u>: Parody man; monologist. Eastern seaboard. Lincoln Theater, New York; the Royal in Baltimore: the Standard, Philadelphia. A rival of Travis Tucker's in the parody field. Travis would write a parody of a song, and Boots would try to top him. People tended to side with one or the other as to who was the best, particularly people in show business.

<u>Maceo Ellis</u> (the Cut-Out Kid): My partner for a few years; he invented the dance of the same name. Born in Holyoke, Pennsylvania around the turn of the century. Became paralyzed and passed around 1936 or '37.

<u>Baby Seals</u>: From Birmingham? He invaded New York in the mid-1930s. Situation comic. Worked with Pigmeat Markham in the '60s.

<u>Allen Drew</u>: One of the first monologists (standup) comedians I ever saw. No situation or parody, which was rare for the times Blue material. People would cringe. Dirty jokes.

<u>Pigmeat Markham</u>: Came to New York with a show called *Sugar Cane* produced by the Hardy Brothers; did a bit called "Truckin'." Used to go down to the Eltinge Theater and take down all the jokes and then go back up to Harlem and do them. It's a fact Blacks didn't do much original material but tended to steal from one another and change around. "Ghost" bits and "Here Comes the Judge . . . The judge is evil this morning . . . Everybody's going to do time today . . . I'm going to give 'em from now on, this morning."

<u>Rastus Brown</u>: I did a routine with him once called "20 Minutes in Hell." As opposed to King Rastus Brown, the dancer.

<u>Eddie Hunter</u>: A very fine, witty comic. Wrote a lot of good material.

"God gracious let me get out of here" was his trademark when he did a ghost bit.

Daybreak Nelson: Monologue and song and dance. East coast. Eventually he became part of the act Day, Dusk, and Dawn, who did very funny parodies, especially of operas.

Tim Moore: Was in *Blackbirds*, intelligent, one of the best. Worked the Apollo a lot. Was on TV in *Amos and Andy*.

Harris and Holly: ("You pull, my end will follow"); Bud Harris worked with several people after Holly died.

Moss and Frye: I worked with Moss and Frye when Cutout and I did stock with Joe Bright in Philadelphia. "How high is up?" "Up Where?" "Up anywhere!" And "If you go to a railroad station to buy a ticket, where you going?" "How do I know where I'm going?" "Then what'd you buy the ticket for?"

Dancing Dotson: Did a wench (i.e. female impersonation) act. Out of my home town. Played the big-time.

Dinah Scott: Another wench comic who wore a bustle; pants so tight you wondered how he got in 'em.

Glenn and Jenkins: They did a famous street cleaning routine with brooms. I worked with them at the Howard Theatre. Jenkins was a good pool player. Bill Robinson went crazy trying to beat him.

The Jones Brothers: A routine in a boxcar; a pin spot on them. One wore a large alarm clock on his arm.

Lillian Fitzgerald: Red-headed girl. One of the first female comedians I remember. She was in the era of Moms Mabley. I worked Cleveland, Columbus, Dayton, Detroit, the Midwest with her. She was a little more sophisticated than Moms. She didn't do colored material.

Joyce and Rookie: Female blackface comedy team. They played maids and did a cleanup act. Joyce Robinson and Rookie (?) With teams, you seldom knew full names.

Mushmouth: A singing, dancing comic. Worked with him in nightclubs in St. Louis and Tulsa.

Doe Doe Green: An eastern comic, a little like Dusty Fletcher.

Johnny Hudgins: A blackface comic, who did pantomime; never said a word. If it was cold outside, he threw confetti up in the air and skated on it.

Hattie Noel: One of the first Black dirty comedians. She was very, very raw. She came to the west coast from back east and created quite a sensation. My first job with her was at the Kratinka Club on 55th Street in Chicago back in 1933.

Radcliff and Rogers: Frank Radcliff was a comic who played the trumpet.

Miller and Lyles: They were very clever comedians. Their specialty was something called "indefinite talk."

Wilton Crawley: Comic dancer, who played clarinet and did back bends and flips. He worked in blackface.

Marshall "Garbage" Rogers: A local Chicago comic. He went to New York and did a couple of things. but he wasn't as funny in New York as he was in Chicago.

Billy McClain: I worked with Billy McClain in Kansas City when he had a tent on 18th and Tracy . . . 18th and Floral, no it wasn't that far down . . . 18th and Lydia? He didn't work in the shows at the time: he was producing the shows.

Happy D'Nover: There was a controversy going over who was the best "buzzer." The Buzz was a dance step. He did jokes and did a dance, unlike the comedians today, who only stand and do jokes.

Jazzlips Richardson: A blackface contortionist, who did the Chinese split [legs straight out to either side] for his big finish.

Ed Lee and Lincoln Perry: Perry became Stepin Fetchit. He took the name after the show *Step 'n' Fetch It* broke up. I have no idea what happened to Ed Lee.

Joyner and Foster: Did army material. One of them, Joyner, dressed in an army uniform; Foster was the straight man.

Sam Theard (Spodie Odie): A comedian, singer, songwriter; he wrote "I'll Be Glad When You're Dead You Rascal You." He worked in my show *Rhythm Bound* with John Oscar. Sam worked with me all over the country.

John Oscar: (see Sam Theard)

Rastus Murray: He came on the scene with Eddie Lemons. His claim to fame was a scene called "Ten Minutes in Hell." It was sensational.

Emmett Anthony: His biggest claim to fame was *Blackbirds*. A good singer; a high tenor. Blackface; stretched his eyes and opened up his mouth wide like all those who blacked up.

Butterbeans and Susie: I don't think I ever knew their real names, but I worked with them off and on for years. Like Dinah Scott, Butterbeans wore the tightest pants imaginable. I don't know who got the idea first. Little bitty hat on his head, and a coat.

Stringbeans and Bessie: A man and wife putdown act. They worked for me in stock in Indianapolis.

Gulfport and Brown: Both first names were Billy. Came from Birmingham, Alabama. I worked on the Toby circuit with them.

Mantan Moreland: a very agile comedian. His claim to fame was the Alligator Crawl . . . you get on your back and you crawl backwards. That was his finish. He worked with Nipsey Bussell in one of my shows; he also worked with Flournoy Miller for a while.

And Miller and Lee (Johnny Lee after Lyles died), Harris and Holly, George Williams and Bessie Brown, Joe Byrd and Billie Higgins, Sparkplug George, Rufus Brown, Billy (Big Foot) Mitchell, Billy (Big Mouth) Mitchell, Sparky Anderson, Eddie "Rochester'" Anderson.

APPENDIX IV

THE FOLLOWING IS A TYPICAL THE FOLLOWING IS A TYPICAL T.O.B.A. (BLACK THEATER CIRCUIT) tour of a show as recalled by Reed to me one afternoon.

"When you left St. Louis, you were on Toby Time. You started out in Chicago (the Grand Theatre), from there to St. Louis (the Globe), to Kansas City (the Lincoln), then on to Tulsa (and Zell Roan's Princess), to Oklahoma City (the Bro), to Muskogee (the Star), then Dallas, Houston (the Ella B. Moore), and Galveston. Leaving Texas, you'd head for Shreveport (the Star), New Orleans (the Lyric), the Flame Theatre in Gadsden, Alabama. Then, the 81 Theatre in Atlanta, the Frolic in Birmingham, the Star Theatre in Savannah. Other cities along the way might include Biloxi, Jackson, Pensacola, Winston-Salem, Jacksboro, Raleigh.

There were enough theaters to supply a number of the companies with the desired forty-eight weeks of work a year. (There were several other smaller circuits of Black theaters, one called "'Round the World" consisting of New York, Newark, Philadelphia, Baltimore, Washington,

Richmond, Winston-Salem. They didn't own theaters; they booked. Tutt and Whitney were in on it. And there was another group in the Midwest including Detroit, Cleveland, Columbus (Pythian), Pittsburgh (Center), and Chicago that had nothing to do with T.O.B.A.

Leonard!

INDEX

Numbers in bold indicate photographs.